First World War
and Army of Occupation
War Diary
France, Belgium and Germany

7 DIVISION
Divisional Troops
Manchester Regiment
24th Battalion
1 June 1916 - 30 November 1917

WO95/1646/2

The Naval & Military Press Ltd
www.nmarchive.com
Published in association with The National Archives

Published by

The Naval & Military Press Ltd

Unit 10 Ridgewood Industrial Park,

Uckfield, East Sussex,

TN22 5QE England

Tel: +44 (0) 1825 749494

www.naval-military-press.com

www.nmarchive.com

This diary has been reprinted in facsimile from the original. Any imperfections are inevitably reproduced and the quality may fall short of modern type and cartographic standards.

© Crown Copyright
Images reproduced by permission of The National Archives, London, England, 2015.

Contents

Document type	Place/Title	Date From	Date To
Heading	WO95/1646/2-7 Division 24 Battalion Manchester Regiment (Pioneers) Jun 1916-Nov 1917		
Heading	BEF 7 Divisional Troops 24 Bn Manchester Regt (Pioneers) 1916 June-1917 Nov From 22 Bde 7 Division To Italy Sane Division		
Heading	War Diary Of 24th Bn Manchester Regt 1st June To 30th June		
War Diary	Billets	01/06/1916	01/06/1916
War Diary	Bois des Tailles (Sheet Albert Squars K.)	01/06/1916	02/06/1916
War Diary	Bois Des Tailles	03/06/1916	30/06/1916
Operation(al) Order(s)	24th Battalion The Manchester Regiment. Instructions For Forthcoming Operations No. 1	16/06/1916	16/06/1916
Operation(al) Order(s)	24th Battalion The Manchester Regiment. Instructions For Forthcoming Operations No. 2	17/06/1916	17/06/1916
Operation(al) Order(s)	24th Battalion The Manchester Regiment. Instructions For Forthcoming Operations No. 3		
Operation(al) Order(s)	24th Battalion The Manchester Regiment. Instructions For Forthcoming Operations No. 5	20/06/1916	20/06/1916
Operation(al) Order(s)	24th Battalion The Manchester Regiment. Instructions For Forthcoming Operations No. 4	19/06/1916	19/06/1916
Operation(al) Order(s)	24th Battalion The Manchester Regiment. Operation Order No. 15	22/06/1916	22/06/1916
Operation(al) Order(s)	24th Battalion The Manchester Regiment. Instructions For Forthcoming Operations No. 6	22/06/1916	22/06/1916
Map	Sketch Of Roads & Tracks on 7th Divn Front In Connection With Operations		
Operation(al) Order(s)	24th Battalion The Manchester Regiment. Instructions For Forthcoming Operations No. 7	23/06/1916	23/06/1916
Operation(al) Order(s)	24th Battalion The Manchester Regiment. Instructions For Forthcoming Operations No. 8	24/06/1916	24/06/1916
Operation(al) Order(s)	24th Battalion The Manchester Regiment. Operation Order No. 16	27/06/1916	27/06/1916
Operation(al) Order(s)	24th Battalion The Manchester Regiment. Operation Order No. 17	29/06/1916	29/06/1916
Heading	Pioneers. 7th Div. War Diary 24th Battn. The Manchester Regiment. July 1916		
War Diary	Grovetown L I d 8 4 (Albert Sheet 1	30/06/1916	01/07/1916
War Diary	Grovetown	01/07/1916	04/07/1916
War Diary	Mericourt	05/07/1916	06/07/1916
War Diary	Mericourt (Somme)	07/07/1916	08/07/1916
War Diary	Mericourt	09/07/1916	10/07/1916
War Diary	Wellington Redoubt	11/07/1916	16/07/1916
War Diary	Wellington Redoubt (F 17 C)	17/07/1916	17/07/1916
War Diary	Wellington Redoubt	18/07/1916	19/07/1916
War Diary	Bivouacs at E 12 C 2 2 Albert 1/40000	20/07/1916	20/07/1916
War Diary	E. 12 b. 2 2 and E 13 C 10 10	21/07/1916	22/07/1916
War Diary	St. Vast, Enchaussee (Amiens Sheet 17)	22/07/1916	22/07/1916
War Diary	St Vast Enchavssee	23/07/1916	25/07/1916
War Diary	St Vast	26/07/1916	31/07/1916
Heading	Appendices 1, 2, 3, 4 & 5.		

Type	Description	Start	End
Operation(al) Order(s)	24th Battalion The Manchester Regiment. Operation Order No. 17 Appendix 1		
Operation(al) Order(s)	24th Battalion The Manchester Regiment. Operation Order No. 18 Appendix 2	13/07/1916	13/07/1916
Operation(al) Order(s)	24th Battalion The Manchester Regiment Operation Order No. 19 Appendix 3	18/07/1916	18/07/1916
Operation(al) Order(s)	24th Battalion The Manchester Regiment. Operation Order No. 20 Appendix 4	18/07/1916	18/07/1916
Operation(al) Order(s)	24th Manchester Rgt Operation Order No. 21 Appendix 5	19/07/1916	19/07/1916
Heading	7th Divisional Troops. 1/24th Battalion Manchester Regiment (Pioneers) August 1916		
War Diary	St Vast Enchaussee	01/08/1916	04/08/1916
War Diary	St Vast	04/08/1916	11/08/1916
War Diary	Ribemont	12/08/1916	16/08/1916
War Diary	H Q Ribemont 4 Companies Becordel E 12 C 9 7	17/08/1916	18/08/1916
War Diary	H Q at Ribemont 4 Companies at E 12 C 9 7	19/08/1916	25/08/1916
War Diary	Fricourt Wood (Ref Map Montauban)	26/08/1916	27/08/1916
War Diary	Fricourt	28/08/1916	31/08/1916
Operation(al) Order(s)	24th Battalion The Manchester Regiment Operation Order No. 22	04/08/1916	04/08/1916
Operation(al) Order(s)	24th Battalion The Manchester Regiment Operation Order No. 23	11/08/1916	11/08/1916
Operation(al) Order(s)	24th Battalion The Manchester Regiment Operation Order No. 24	15/08/1916	15/08/1916
Operation(al) Order(s)	24th Battalion The Manchester Regiment Operation Order No. 25	25/08/1916	25/08/1916
Operation(al) Order(s)	24th Battalion The Manchester Regiment Operation Order No. 26	29/08/1916	29/08/1916
Operation(al) Order(s)	24th Battalion The Manchester Regiment Operation Order No. 27	31/08/1916	31/08/1916
Heading	War Diary Of 24th Manchester Rgt Volume XI Sept 1916		
War Diary	Fricourt Wood Ref Map Albert. Combined Sheet and Montauban 1/20000	01/09/1916	11/09/1916
War Diary	Fricourt Wood Albert Oisement Hallencourt	12/09/1916	12/09/1916
War Diary	Hallencourt (Somme)	13/09/1916	13/09/1916
War Diary	Hallencourt	14/09/1916	17/09/1916
War Diary	Hallencourt-Longpre-Bailleul-Meteren-Rouge-Croix.	18/09/1916	19/09/1916
War Diary	Rouge-Croix	20/09/1916	20/09/1916
War Diary	Rouge-Croix to Oosthove Farm	21/09/1916	21/09/1916
War Diary	Oosthove Farm Sheet 36 NW B.11.d.	22/09/1916	24/09/1916
War Diary	Oosthove Farm	25/09/1916	30/09/1916
Operation(al) Order(s)	24th Battalion The Manchester Regiment. Operation Order No. 27 Appendix I	31/08/1916	31/08/1916
Operation(al) Order(s)	24th Battalion The Manchester Regiment. Operation Order No. 28 Appendix II	02/09/1916	02/09/1916
Miscellaneous	After Battalion Orders By Lieut Colonel J.B. Batten Commanding 24th Battalion Manchester Regiment Appendix III	07/09/1916	07/09/1916
Miscellaneous	24th Battalion The Manchester Regiment. Operation Order No. 29 Appendix IV	11/09/1916	11/09/1916
Operation(al) Order(s)	24th Battalion The Manchester Regiment Operation Order No. 29 Appendix IV	11/09/1916	11/09/1916
Operation(al) Order(s)	24th Battalion The Manchester Regiment. Operation Order No. 30 Appendix V	16/09/1916	16/09/1916

Type	Description	Start	End
Operation(al) Order(s)	24th Battalion The Manchester Regiment. Operation Order No. 31 Appendix VI	16/09/1916	16/09/1916
Operation(al) Order(s)	24th Battalion The Manchester Regiment. Operation Order No. 32 Appendix VII	19/09/1916	19/09/1916
Operation(al) Order(s)	24th Battalion The Manchester Regiment. Operation Order No. 33 Appendix VIII	20/09/1916	20/09/1916
War Diary	Oosthove Farm B 11 d Sheet 36 NW	01/10/1916	12/10/1916
War Diary	Oosthove Farm (B 11 c Sheet 36 Nw)	13/10/1916	21/10/1916
War Diary	Pt W. 30 C 5 3 (Sheet 570)	22/10/1916	23/10/1916
War Diary	Tara Hill W. 30 c 5 3 Sheets 57 D	24/10/1916	30/10/1916
War Diary	X. II a Sheet Albert Combined Sheet	31/10/1916	31/10/1916
Miscellaneous	24th Battalion The Manchester Regiment Preliminary Move Orders Appendix I	19/10/1916	19/10/1916
Operation(al) Order(s)	Operation Order No. 1 By Major J. H. Chadwick Commdg. 24th Battalion Manchester Regt. Appendix 2	19/10/1916	19/10/1916
Operation(al) Order(s)	24th Battalion The Manchester Regiment. Operation Order No. 2 Appendix 3	30/10/1916	30/10/1916
Operation(al) Order(s)	24th Battalion The Manchester Regiment (Pioneers) Supplementary To Operation Order No. 2	30/10/1916	30/10/1916
Operation(al) Order(s)	24th Battalion The Manchester Regiment. Operation Order No. 3 Appendix 4	31/10/1916	31/10/1916
War Diary	X II a Map Albert Combined Sheet	01/11/1916	02/11/1916
War Diary	X II a	03/11/1916	16/11/1916
War Diary	Thiepval Wood.	17/11/1916	22/11/1916
War Diary	Mailly Wood W. P. 17 B.	23/11/1916	28/11/1916
War Diary	Mailly Wood W.	29/11/1916	30/11/1916
Operation(al) Order(s)	Operation Order No. 4 By Major J. H. Chadwich Commanding 24th Battalion The Manchester Regt. Appendix 1	03/11/1916	03/11/1916
Operation(al) Order(s)	Operation Order No. 5 By Major J. H. Chadwick Commanding 24th Battalion The Manchester Regiment Appendix 5	06/11/1916	06/11/1916
Operation(al) Order(s)	Operation Order No. 6 By Major J. N. Chadwick Commanding 24th Battalion Manchester Regiment. Appendix 3	07/11/1916	07/11/1916
Operation(al) Order(s)	Operation Order No. 6A. By Major J. H. Chadwick Commanding 24th Battalion The Manchester Regiment. Appendix 4	14/11/1916	14/11/1916
Operation(al) Order(s)	Operation Order No. 7 By Major J. H. Chadwick Commanding 24th Battalion The Manchester Regt. Appendix 5	16/11/1916	16/11/1916
Operation(al) Order(s)	Operation Order No. 8 By Major J.H Chadwick Commanding 24th Battalion The Manchester Regt. Appendix 6	17/11/1916	17/11/1916
Operation(al) Order(s)	Operation Order No. 9 By Major J. H. Chadwick Commanding 24th Battalion The Manchester Regt. Appendix 8	21/11/1916	21/11/1916
Operation(al) Order(s)	Headquarters, 4th Canadian Division.	23/11/1916	23/11/1916
War Diary	Mailly Wood West P. 23 b. 5 7 Sheet 57 D Se.	01/12/1916	31/12/1916
Miscellaneous	4th. Canadian Division. A. 42-71 24th. Bn. The Manchester Regt. (7th. Divisional Pioneers). Appendix 1	11/12/1916	11/12/1916
War Diary	Mailly Wood. W P. 23 b. 5 7 (Sheet 57D S E)	01/01/1917	31/01/1917
Operation(al) Order(s)	Operation Order No. 10 By Lieut Colonel J.H. Chadwick Commdg. 24th Battalion The Manchester Regt. Appendix 1	10/01/1917	10/01/1917

Type	Description	Date From	Date To
War Diary	Mailly Wood West P. 23 b. 5 7 Sheet 57D S.E	01/02/1917	05/02/1917
War Diary	Beauquesne	06/02/1917	21/02/1917
War Diary	Mailly-Maillet	22/02/1917	28/02/1917
Operation(al) Order(s)	Operation Orders By Lieut Colonel J. H. Chadwick Commanding 24th Battalion Manchester Regiment. App I	04/02/1917	04/02/1917
Miscellaneous	24th Battalion The Manchester Regiment. (Pioneers) Instructions For Forthcoming Review	16/02/1917	16/02/1917
Operation(al) Order(s)	Operation Orders No. 12 By Lieut Colonel J. H. Chadwick Commanding 24th Battalion Manchester Regiment. App III	21/02/1917	21/02/1917
Miscellaneous	Appendix IV. 24th. Battalion The Manchester Regiment. Appendix IV	22/02/1917	22/02/1917
War Diary	Mailly Maillet.	01/03/1917	18/03/1917
War Diary	Puisieux. L. 20 a. 3 8 Maps 57 D N.E. 57C N.W.	19/03/1917	26/03/1917
War Diary	Ablainzeville F. 28 b 6 8 Sheets 57D N.E. & 57 C N.W.	27/03/1917	31/03/1917
Operation(al) Order(s)	Operation Order No. 14 By Lieut Colonel J. H. Chadwick Commanding 24th Battalion Manchester Regiment. App 1	17/03/1917	17/03/1917
Operation(al) Order(s)	Operation Order No. 13 By Lieut Colonel J. H. Chadwick Commanding 24th Battalion Manchester Regiment. App 2	12/03/1917	12/03/1917
Operation(al) Order(s)	24th (Pioneer) Battalion The Manchester Regiment. Administrative Instructions For Operations In Accordance With Operations Order No. 13, Dated 12-3-17	12/03/1917	12/03/1917
War Diary	Ablainzeville F. 28 b. 6 8 Map Sheet 57 D N.E 57C N.W.	01/04/1917	01/04/1917
War Diary	HQ 91 Coy. 3 Coys at Courcelles Halte A. 16 B. 4 8	02/04/1917	11/04/1917
War Diary	Courcelles Halte A. 16 b. 4 8 Sheets 57C N.W. 51B S.W.	12/04/1917	30/04/1917
Operation(al) Order(s)	Operation Orders No. 16 By Lieut Colonel J. H. Chadwick Commanding 24th Battalion Manchester Regiment.	14/04/1917	14/04/1917
War Diary	A. 16 b. 4 8 Courcelles Halte. Maps 57C N.W. 51B S.W	01/05/1917	02/05/1917
War Diary	B. 17 C. O. 3	03/05/1917	15/05/1917
War Diary	Maps. 57C N.W. 57D. N.E.	16/05/1917	25/05/1917
War Diary	Map 57C N.W. and Ecoust-St-Mien 10000	26/05/1917	31/05/1917
Operation(al) Order(s)	24th Battalion The Manchester Regiment Preliminary Instructions For Operations No. 1	11/05/1917	11/05/1917
War Diary	Maps 57C. N.W. Ecoust-St-Mein 1/10000 (Bullecourt Map)	01/06/1917	30/06/1917
Miscellaneous	Headquarters, 7th. Division.	08/06/1917	08/06/1917
Miscellaneous	24th Bn. Manchester Regt. (Div. Pioneers). App B	09/06/1917	09/06/1917
Miscellaneous	O.C. 24th Bn. Manchester Regt. App C	07/06/1917	07/06/1917
Miscellaneous	Officer Commanding 24th. Manchesters. App D	30/06/1917	30/06/1917
War Diary	Mory B 15 C O 3 Maps 57C N.W. Ecoust-St Mein 1/10000 (Bullecourt Map)	01/07/1917	31/07/1917
War Diary	Mory	01/08/1917	01/08/1917
War Diary	W.T.S	02/08/1917	09/08/1917
War Diary	Maps. 51C and 57D. New. Camp 51C. R 27 d. 8 3	10/08/1917	29/08/1917
War Diary	Map. Belgium & France Sheet 27 1/40000 Edition 2	30/08/1917	30/08/1917
War Diary	Map. Belgium. Sheet 28 N.W. Eon 6A. 1/20000	31/08/1917	31/08/1917

Operation(al) Order(s)	24th Battalion The Manchester Regt. (Pioneers). Operation Order No. 16	28/08/1917	28/08/1917
War Diary	Ypres Maps-Belgium Sheet 28 N.W. Edition 6A 1/20000	01/09/1917	02/09/1917
War Diary	Map Belgium Hazebrouck 5A Can 2 1/100,000	03/09/1917	14/09/1917
War Diary	Map. Sheet 36 D. N.E 1/20000	15/09/1917	21/09/1917
War Diary	Map Belgium and France Sheet 28 Edition 3	22/09/1917	30/09/1917
War Diary	Map. Gd 1st Belgium France Sheet 2 B	01/10/1917	31/10/1917
Operation(al) Order(s)	24th Bn. The Manchester Regt. (7th Divl. Pioneers) Operation Orders No. 1	03/10/1917	03/10/1917
War Diary		01/11/1917	05/11/1917
War Diary	Belgium, France Sheet 2B 1/40000	06/11/1917	30/11/1917
Miscellaneous	24th. Battalion The Manchester Regiment. (Pioneers) Move Order.	10/11/1917	10/11/1917
Operation(al) Order(s)	24th. Battalion The Manchester Regt. (Pioneers). Order No. 1	17/11/1917	17/11/1917
Operation(al) Order(s)	24th Battalion The Manchester Regiment. (Pioneers). Order No. 2	27/11/1917	27/11/1917
Operation(al) Order(s)	24th Battalion The Manchester Regiment. (Pioneers). Order No. 3	29/11/1917	29/11/1917

WO 95/1646/2-7 Division

(2) 24 Battalion Manchester Regiment (Pioneers)

Jun 1916 – Nov 1917.

BEF

7 DIVISIONAL TROOPS

24 BN MANCHESTER REGT (PIONEERS)

1916 JUNE — 1917 NOV

FROM 22 BDE   7 DIVISION

TO ITALY   SAME DIVISION

BOX 1646

SECRET

WAR DIARY

OF

24TH BN MANCHESTER REGT

1st JUNE TO 30th JUNE

WAR DIARY or INTELLIGENCE SUMMARY

Army Form C. 2118.

24/month. R. (P)

Place	Date	Hour	Summary of Events and Information	Remarks and references to Appendices
BILLETS BOIS des TAILLES (Sheet ALBERT Square) K.	1st June	10 pm	VOLUME VIII Weather – Fine and warm. Wind light N.NE. Working Parties A Coy { 37 OR digging communication trench II a Subsector. 6 hours { 29 -- cutting firesteps, levelling parapet. 6 hours { 43 -- 40 yds wiring 6 feet deep; Parapets covered with sods – work on mined dug out. B Coy 150 OR digging communication trench. 6 hours C Coy { 30 OR night work 8 hours making horses and putting in dug outs in CEMETERY ST. (C2 subsector) { 40 OR working on T.M. emplacement in C1 subsector 6 hours { 50 OR cleaning communication trench and laying trench boards.	GBR
	2nd	10 pm	Weather Much cooler, wind varying W to N. Situation Enemy shelled the MORLANCOURT – BRAY Railway near BOIS des TAILLES for a few minutes – no damage done. Working Parties As on the 1st June	GBR

Army Form C. 2118.

WAR DIARY
or
INTELLIGENCE SUMMARY
(Erase heading not required.)

Place	Date	Hour	Summary of Events and Information	Remarks and references to Appendices
BOIS des TAILLES	3rd	11 pm	**Weather** Fine: rather cooler wind N.W. light.	
			Working Parties	
			A Coy { (a) Work on LUCKNOW AVENUE 80 yds deepened. 30 yds probat cut 35 OR for 6 hours	
			(b) 28 OR Covering parapet with sods and carrying for R.E. 6 hours	
			(c) 48 OR Relieved a party 6 hours	
			(d) 43 OR making traverse in and widening STAFFORD AVENUE.	
			B Coy { 150 OR working on MANCHESTER AVENUE and widening, deepening and laying trench boards. This party worked in relief of 6 hours.	
			C Coy { Party of 30 OR putting in traverse in CEMETERY ST. (C.2 subsectn) 25 OR at work on mines dug out in CEMETERY ST " 45 OR T.M emplacement in C1 & C2 Sub Sectors	
			Party of 1 officer and 10 OR assisted by transport from 7th D.A.C at 7th The N.S.C. Train repairing roads about the BOIS des TAILLES	Y35
"	4 12 pm		**Weather** Changed & cool and wet, Wind westerly. Hot wind, Rain at intervals with heavy hail shower in morning.	
			Situation Heavy gun fire heard & flashes seen in neighbourhood of ALBERT	

WAR DIARY
or
INTELLIGENCE SUMMARY

(Erase heading not required.)

Army Form C. 2118.

Place	Date	Hour	Summary of Events and Information	Remarks and references to Appendices
—	(Continued)		Working Parties / work was carried on as on the 3rd June	905
BOIS de TAILLES	5th	6pm	Weather. Much cooler and wet. Heavy rain in morning and throughout night 5th-6th. Wind strong with heavy bombardment again in direction of ALBERT. Situation. Very heavy bombardment starting about 11pm and lasting until 12.30am. Working Parties. As on the 3rd June.	905
—	6th	10pm	Weather. hot, kind N.W. much cooler with continual heavy rain during 24 hours. Working Parties. A Company went to rest at MARRET WOOD, TREUX (ref. map ALBERT combined sheet). D Company took over A Company work.	

WAR DIARY or INTELLIGENCE SUMMARY

Army Form C. 2118.

(Erase heading not required.)

Place	Date	Hour	Summary of Events and Information	Remarks and references to Appendices
			D Company — (One platoon in have mining dug outs in FORT OLDHAM (B Sector)) 20 OR. Carrying party for R.E. 6 hours. 29 OR Constructing concrete slabs 6 hours. One platoon making traverse LUCKNOW AVENUE 6 hours	Yes
			C Company — Deepening and widening communication trenches 6 hours	
			B Company — " " 150 OR Working on roads in vicinity of BOIS DESTAILLES 8 hours	Yes
	7	10pm	Weather. Wet and cold. wind along N.W.	
			Working Party. Account as entry.	
	8	10pm	Weather. hot - Still cold. Increase in temperature during night. 2Lts A. S. & Walsh Jones. St Clarke auts. 2 Lt W. Soward 11th (S) Bn. E. Surreys joined for duty	Yes
			Working Parties. as entry. Joined for duty	

Army Form C. 2118.

WAR DIARY
or
INTELLIGENCE SUMMARY

(Erase heading not required.)

Place	Date	Hour	Summary of Events and Information	Remarks and references to Appendices
BOIS des TAILLES	9th	10 pm	Weather. Cold and wet. Wind gusty N.N.W. Rain at intervals during day and night.	
			Working Parties. A Company rested at MARETT WOOD, TREUX (ALBERT MAP). B Company 1 platoon working in Medical aid post - BLENHEIM AVENUE B Sector 6 hours. " " " " MANCHESTER ST 6 hours. " " " deepening and improving trenches in B Sector 6 hours. " " " Strengthening dug outs in B Sector 6 hours. " " " Straightening dug outs at RAT HOLE and HIGH ST 6 hours. C Company worked in relief, straightening dug-outs, building traverses and improving trenches in C1 and C2 subsection. Shift 6 hours each. D Company Revetting in WELLINGTON REDOUBT (B Sector). Constructing dug outs B Sector. Carrying material for R.E. in MAPLE REDOUBT (C1 subsector). Extending LUCKNOW AVENUE (B sector). Working on T.M. emplacements.	yes yes
—	10th	10 pm	Weather. Cold. Rain at intervals. Wind still N.N.W. Dead.	
			Working Parties. En route 9k.	yes

WAR DIARY
or
INTELLIGENCE SUMMARY

(Erase heading not required.)

Army Form C. 2118.

Place	Date	Hour	Summary of Events and Information	Remarks and references to Appendices
BOIS des TAILLES	11th	11pm	Weather Fine during day after 8am. Warmer wind Westerly light.	
			Working Parties There were no working parties.	
			Church Parade Church Parade was held in the morning.	
			Movement of Spoke — A Company held company sports in MARETT WOOD, TREUX. In the afternoon they moved up to the BOIS des TAILLES taking over the work from D Coy who then supplied working parties for the 95th Coy RE	G/5.
"	12th	10pm	Weather Wet during greater part of day. Cold. Wind N.N.W.	
			Working Parties A Company Digging communication trench from LUCKNOW AVENUE to LITTLE BEAR WOOD. 29 men 6 hours. Deepening ESSEX AVENUE and revetting hurdles. 31 OR 6 hours. Digging and finishing latrine ('IS') in BOLD ST & LORD ST. 35 OR 6 hours.	
			D Company Provided carrying parties and parties for cleaning trenches in B Sector. Small parties detached for work in R.E. shop making concrete slabs etc.	

WAR DIARY or INTELLIGENCE SUMMARY

Army Form C. 2118.

Place	Date	Hour	Summary of Events and Information	Remarks and references to Appendices
BOIS des TAILLES	12th		D Company One platoon making T.M emplacements near UNION ST. in relief of the above. One platoon making T.M emplacements near HAVANNAH ST	YBS
	13th	10pm	Weather Heavy rain during day and night of 12th-13th. Wind N.W.	
			Situation Heavy bombardment from 11.40pm for 1½ hours in neighbourhood of A Coy.	
			Working Parties A Company On in the 12th	
			B Company Clearing trenches in B Sector / 6 hours. Carrying parties for R.E.	
			C Company Work in C Sector. Traverses in CEMETERY ST Dugouts at bottom of B4 of trench in UNION ST C1 Sector	
			D Company Trench mortar emplacements in UNION ST & HAVANNAH ST B Sector	YBS

Army Form C. 2118.

WAR DIARY
or
INTELLIGENCE SUMMARY
(Erase heading not required.)

Instructions regarding War Diaries and Intelligence Summaries are contained in F. S. Regs., Part II. and the Staff Manual respectively. Title Pages will be prepared in manuscript.

Place	Date	Hour	Summary of Events and Information	Remarks and references to Appendices
	14th	10 p	Weather. Fine but cold, wind N.E. freak.	
			Working Parties. B Sector { A Coy. Routing and filling traverses. Deepening trenches and making M.G. position. Latrine in DUKE ST. 6 ST widened and deepened and howevered Trench cut from LUCKNOW AVENUE to WATERLOO J.	
			B Coy. Revetting Grenade Store; Brigade Battle HQrs. b hours 6 hrs. Cairo; Gas Post FRANCIS AVENUE and LONDON RD all in B Sector 157 men b hrs.	YES
			C Coy. Constructing emplacement for gas cylinders. C Sector 16 men 6 hrs.	
			D Coy. Ramps made 180 men 6 hrs B Sector.	
	15th	11 am	Weather. Fine warm. wind E.N.E. freak.	
			Working Parties. As on the 14th	YES

2449 Wt. W14957/Mgo 750,000 1/16 J.B.C. & A. Forms/C.2118/12.

Army Form C. 2118.

WAR DIARY
or
INTELLIGENCE SUMMARY

(Erase heading not required.)

Instructions regarding War Diaries and Intelligence Summaries are contained in F. S. Regs., Part II. and the Staff Manual respectively. Title Pages will be prepared in manuscript.

Place	Date	Hour	Summary of Events and Information	Remarks and references to Appendices
Bois de TAILLES	16th	10pm	Weather Working Parties	

Warm and fine. Wind light E.N.E.

A Company One Platoon deepened and widened track running from LUCKNOW AVENUE to K WATERLOO JUNCTION. 35 O.R. 6 hrs. trestreat (B sector) deepened and widened 40 OR 6 hrs. Two other platoons working parties relief to about

B Company 6 hrs work on AID POST FRANCIS AVENUE
10 O.R.   BATTLE CENTER   MIDDLESEX POST
12   GRENADE STORE
20   CARRYING PARTY
20

C Company Firing gas cylinders in C sector. 169 or 6 hrs.

D Company Completing T.M. emplacements in HAVANNAH ST and BRITISH ST. 100 or 6 hrs. Gas near

The enemy shelled junction of BRAY–CORBIE R⁴ & MORLANCOURT R⁴ K square MAP ALBERT that evening.

Appendix 1

2449 Wt. W14957/M90 750,000 1/16 J.B.C. & A. Forms/C.2118/12.

WAR DIARY
or
INTELLIGENCE SUMMARY

Army Form C. 2118.

Place	Date	Hour	Summary of Events and Information	Remarks and references to Appendices

BOIS des TAILLES	16th 17th	11 pm	Weather
			Working
			Parties
			Fine and warm. Wind N.E. fell
			A Company as on the 16th
			B Company 12 O.R. working 6 hours on A.11 Post FRANCIS AVENUE
			  " " 12 " " " " " Battle Creche B Section
			  " " 16 " " " " " Trench Store MINDEN POST.
			  " " 20 " Carrying stores for 1/3 R.E. (Durham Co)
			  " " Relief to the above.
			C Company Fixing Gas Cylinders C section. 1 night work 4 hours
			  " " Deepening & widening CEMETERY ST - C 2 Sub section.
			D Company 1 platoon 6 hours improving SOUTH AVENUE
			  " " 1 platoon " " " Constructing trench between
			  " " 1 platoon E71 N. 71 S
			  " " 1 platoon " " Carrying party E71 N. 71 S -
			                                    from CITADEL to UNION ST C1 sub section
			                                    BRAY-CORBIE and MORLANCOURT
			The enemy 13 cm gun fired on the junction of
			roads from 4 pm. No damage was done.
				Gas

"	18th	10 pm	Weather Fine but dull. Wind changed to N. by N.W. light. Working A Company Completed with relief in SUSSEX AVENUE (B Section) 36 O.R. 6 hours Parties " " " " " DUKE ST & LORD ST 36 " "	Appendix 2

Army Form C. 2118.

WAR DIARY
or
INTELLIGENCE SUMMARY
(Erase heading not required.)

Place	Date	Hour	Summary of Events and Information	Remarks and references to Appendices
BOIS des TAILLES	18th	10 pm	**A Company** Traverse in ANKLE WALK and deepend 68&P 2 g.o.r. 6 hours. Extra steps finished in BOLD ST.; cleaning 70A ST. 31 O.R. 6 hours	
			B Company Rested and went back to BRAY.	
			C Company Constructing shrapnel stellis, mine dug out in CEMETERY ST. 6 hrs 15 O.R.	Y.B.A.
			D Company Improving trenches and dug outs and Forward Battn. Area B Section 50 O.R 6 hours and Ammunition Store 44 O.R 6 hours Hut AID POSTS at FRANCIS AVENUE and LONDON RD WEST 5D O.R 6 hours Carrying Party for 1/3 Durham R.E. Co. 20 O.R 6 hours	
			Enemy again shelled BRAY-CORBIE Rd at 5·30 pm. Party of shell back measured 13cm circumference.	
	19th	11 pm	**Weather** Fine but cold. Very slight shower in afternoon wind N/NS	G.S
			Working Parties as on the 18th	Appendix 3 Appendix 4

Army Form C. 2118.

WAR DIARY
or
INTELLIGENCE SUMMARY
(Erase heading not required.)

Place	Date	Hour	Summary of Events and Information	Remarks and references to Appendices
BOIS DES TAILLES	20th	10pm	Weather. Fine. Wind N. light.	
			Working Parties: A Coy { 4th OR making dug outs at No. R. Earthworks (BRAY-MAMETZ RD) 6 hours 34 " " 36 " " 3rd " relief of above	
			B Coy { Resting. The company practised rapid wiring and laying out staking parties.	
			C Coy { 4OR or Working on T.M. Emplacement / C Sector 6 hours 2 " " New dug out " 20 " " CEMETERY ST. R.E.	
			D Coy { 50 OR Carrying party 37th Co. R.E. 4 " Kindle and dug out at Brigade Battle H.Qrs. 5D " " Stokes Gun Ammunition store 15 " " Aid Post FRANCIS AVENUE. 1/3 Coy R.E (Durham) RE workshop	GAS Appendix 5 GAS
	21st	10pm	Weather. Much warmer. Wind N.E. fresh.	
			Working Parties. As for the 20th.	

Army Form C. 2118.

WAR DIARY
or
INTELLIGENCE SUMMARY

(Erase heading not required.)

Instructions regarding War Diaries and Intelligence Summaries are contained in F. S. Regs., Part II and the Staff Manual respectively. Title Pages will be prepared in manuscript.

Place	Date	Hour	Summary of Events and Information	Remarks and references to Appendices
BOIS de TAILLES	22nd		Weather — Fine and bright wind N.N.W. light	
			Working Parties — B Coy resting	
			A Coy resting except 1 platoon making Company HQ dug out at WORK 2. VAUXHALL B Sector. (BRAY-MAMETZ Rd.) 6 hour shift 3 shifts	
			C Coy supplied 108 OR carrying party for R.E. 6 hours	
			D Coy A relief } 20 OR constructing AID POST LONDON Rd WEST B Sector. GRENADE STORES at DURHAM TRENCH	See Appendix 6
			B relief } 10 "	
			10 OR digging trench, CARNOY 6 hours	
— "—	23rd	10 pm	Weather Hot and close. Heavy rain from 4 - 4:30 pm & 9 to 11 pm. Thunder storm at 4 pm.	Appendix 7
			Working Parties A Coy. { 9 OR unloading at BRAY DUMP	
			{ 9 OR GROVETOWN } 6 hours	
			{ 38 working on C.R.E. dug out GROVETOWN	
			(27" on dug out WORK 2 B Sector	
			B Coy Resting except one platoon working on Bn HQ battle dug out at GROVETOWN Camp.	
			C Coy Carrying parties as before. One lewis gun were attached to 10 Lancs Fusiliers in B Sector	GBW Appendices 8 & 9
			D Coy As in 22nd	

WAR DIARY
or
INTELLIGENCE SUMMARY

Army Form C. 2118.

Place	Date	Hour	Summary of Events and Information	Remarks and references to Appendices
BOIS de TAILLES	19th		Weather	Dull and Sultry, wind S.W. Rain in afternoon.	
	24th	10pm	Situation	"U" Day bombardment and preliminary gas attack on enemy trenches as per attached Orders.	
			Work	A Coy } Resting B Coy } C. Carrying party from BECORDEL cross roads to C section 20 men 4 hours D Coy Section parties constructing AID POST LONDON Road & BSecln BRIGADE S/5150 110 OR 6 hours	(Gas) Appendix 10
—	25th	11pm	Weather	Fine and bright until late afternoon when there were heavy showers. Wind fresh W.N.W.	
			Situation	"V" day	
			Working Parties	A, B and D Companies resting C Coy provided 27 men for 6 hours work on Shrapnel wood shelter in C. Secln. D. Coy. 1 NCO of 8 men for Night Listening Patrol HQ to out GROVETOWN VALLEY.	Gas

Army Form C. 2118.

WAR DIARY
or
INTELLIGENCE SUMMARY

(Erase heading not required.)

Instructions regarding War Diaries and Intelligence Summaries are contained in F.S. Regs., Part II. and the Staff Manual respectively. Title Pages will be prepared in manuscript.

Place	Date	Hour	Summary of Events and Information	Remarks and references to Appendices
BOIS des TAILLES	26th	10pm	Weather Bright in morning. Wind fresh N.N.W. Rain in afternoon. Situation "W" day, a unconcentrated bombardment from 9 – 10:20 am. Working Parties Company {A – resting, B – 1 platoon working on HQ Battle dug out GROVETOWN - 2 shifts, C – resting, D – resting}	Copy Appendix
-1-	27th		Weather Wet and dull Wind NNW. Rain at intervals. Working Parties Two companies went up to front line during night to repair front line trenches damaged by enemy fire. Could be done. Situation X day. Concentrated bombardment from 4.30am to 5.50am enemy's wire levelled. A Company went up and occupied work 2. Companies rested. J.W. B Seeker	Copy Appendix II

WAR DIARY or INTELLIGENCE SUMMARY

Army Form C. 2118.

Place	Date	Hour	Summary of Events and Information	Remarks and references to Appendices
BOIS des TAILLES	28th	10pm	**Weather** Wind N.N.E. Fine: almost continuous rain upto 3pm. **Situation** Y day - Concentrated bombardment from 6am to 7.30am later in afternoon message was received that all operations were to be postponed 48 hours. The 29th is therefore now as "W" day. Concentrated bombardment 4-5.30pm Smoke attack 5.10pm The Companies rested. One Lewis Gun section returned. **Work**	G98
"	29th	10pm	**Weather** Dull. Wind Shing N.N.W. **Situation** Y1 day. Concentrated bombardment from 4 to 5.30pm Smoke attack 5.10pm **Work** All Companies rested except C Coy who supplied a working party at midnight. D 120 O.R.	G98 Appendix 12

Army Form C. 2118.

WAR DIARY
or
INTELLIGENCE SUMMARY
(Erase heading not required.)

Place	Date	Hour	Summary of Events and Information	Remarks and references to Appendices
BOIS du TAILLES	30th	10 pm	Weather - Wind gusty N.N.W. Dull inclined to rain. Situation - 1/2 day. Concentrated bombardment 6 - 9.20 am with 1/2 day smoke attack 9.10 am. The battalion was split up as follows :- PRE- A Coy with 95th Field Co. R.E. B " " 1/3 Durham Field Co. R.E. C " in reserve at GROVETOWN D " 1/2 coy in reserve. The other half proceeded to form line system with the 1/2 companies in reserve moved to Headquarters with the 1/2 companies in reserve moved to GROVETOWN at 11.15 pm.	
	30/6/16			

J.B.Baker. Lieut Colonel
Comm'dg 24 Manchester Regt

SECRET   Copy No. 5

24th Battalion The Manchester Regiment.
INSTRUCTIONS FOR FORTHCOMING OPERATIONS NO. 1.

INTENTION I. (a) In conjunction with the remainder of the 4th Army and the French, the 7th Division will assume the offensive on "Z" day and will establish an objective, a line from track at S.25 b 58.32 to WILLOW AVENUE at X.29 b 5.6.

(b) The 18th Division will be on the right, the 21st on the left.

(c) Boundaries on the right will be, F.12 c 39 — F.6 a 62.11 (leaving the junction of BEETLE ALLEY and DANZIG ALLEY to 18th Division and Gun position at F.6 a 6.1 to 7th Division) — track at F.6 a 8.9. along the track to junction of tracks at S.25 b 45.00 — S.25 b 37.91 leaving the trench running N.W. to S.E. to 18th Division.

Boundaries on the left will be WILLOW AVENUE STREAM.

(d) The main attack is to be carried out by the 91st and 20th Infantry Brigades.

(e) The attack of the 91st Brigade will be divided into 3 phases.

1st OBJECTIVE BUCKET TRENCH, BULGAR ALLEY to DANZIG ALLEY, DANZIG ALLEY to Northern and North Eastern edge of MAMETZ.

2nd OBJECTIVE FRITZ TRENCH, VALLEY TRENCH and BUNNY ALLEY.

3rd OBJECTIVE Final objective allotted to 7th Division.

2. The 20th Brigade will form a defensive flank facing North Westward to cover the advance of the 91st Brigade and will seize the North Eastern outskirts of MAMETZ, ORCHARD ALLEY to its junction with APPLE ALLEY, APPLE ALLEY to our front trenches.

3. The 22nd Brigade will clear the German trenches North of BOIS FRANCAIS.

DISTRIBUTION II. "A" Company will be attached to the 95th Coy. R.E. and "B" Company to the 1/3rd Durham R.E. to assist in consolidating captured position under instructions of O.C's, R.E. Companies.

"D" Company, less 2 platoons are detailed for special work in opening up communication trenches.

"C" Company and two platoons "D" Company remain at Battalion H.Q. in reserve.

Lewis Guns will be detailed for special work in the offensive.

DRESS III. All Officers will carry rifles and wear similar equipment to the men.

(a) 1. Rifle and equipment less pack (120 rounds S.A.A)
2. Haversack on back containing two tins of meat, eight hard biscuits and canteen filled with grocery ration.
3. Waterproof sheet with jersey rolled inside fixed on back of waistbelt by supporting straps of pack.
4. Sandbags as ordered by R.E.
5. Two Mills Grenades, one in each lower jacket pocket.
6. Two smoke helmets.
7. Tools as directed by O.C. R.E. Companies.

(b) Grenadiers will wear ordinary equipment and carry rifles and if required for bombing will collect grenades from men of their platoon.

Appendix 1

2.

(c) The following badges will be worn:—

I.	Men carrying wire cutters	White band 2" wide on right forearm.
II	Carriers	Red patch 2" deep on right shoulder strap.
III	Bombers	White Grenade 2½" in length on right sleeve just below shoulder.
IV	Runners	Yellow badge 2" square on each forearm.
V	All Ranks	Square patch of pink flannel sewn on flap of haversack. Top edge level with the seam marking the turnover of flap.

IV   It is to be distinctly understood by all ranks that pioneers are not to take part in the offensive but only act on the defensive if ordered by an Officer or the senior N.C.O. on the spot. Their work is the most important, i.e. Consolidation of captured positions.

V   Greatcoats, caps and spare kit will be packed in pack, and will be stored. Packs will be clearly marked with the number, name and Regiment of owner. Personal property must not be put in the pockets of greatcoats as it may be necessary to reissue these.

VI   During march to trenches water in waterbottles is NOT TO BE DRUNK under ANY circumstances.

Water can be obtained at the following points if men require a drink on the way up.

K.6 c 2.0	North of BOIS DES TAILLES
L.8 a 50.95	On road EAST of GROVETOWN
L.4 a 8.9	Opposite GROVETOWN Infantry Dug-outs.
F.21 b 5.2.	CITADEL at point where metre gauge railway crosses road.

VII   Battalion Headquarters will be at GROVETOWN.

VIII   Transport will remain parked at BOIS DES TAILLES, East of H. area.

IX   No Officers kits exceeding 39 lbs. will be accepted by the Quartermaster for packing on waggons. Arrangements will be made if possible to store surplus kits but no responsibility will be taken for the loss of these.

X   These orders will be added to from time to time.

Copy No. 1.   O.C. "A" Company
         2.   O.C. "B" "
         3.   O.C. "C" "
         4.   O.C. "D" "
        5.   War Diary
        6.   War Diary

O.E.DEMPSEY Lieut. & Adjutant.
16-6-16   24th Battalion Manchester Regiment.

NOTE   The date of assault is referred to as "Z" day, proceeding days will take the letters in reversed order e.g., "Y", "X", "V", etc., i.e. if a Thursday is "Z", Wednesday will be referred to as "Y", Tuesday "X", etc.

SECRET   Copy No. 5

24th Battalion The Manchester Regiment
INSTRUCTIONS FOR FORTHCOMING OPERATIONS NO. 2

17-6-16.

CONSOLIDATION OF POSITIONS CAPTURED

1. Establishments of strong points and supporting points.
   In addition to the ordinary consolidation to be carried out by Infantry as each objective is captured, the following strong points will be established:-

   (a) In the line of the final objective of the Division at:-
       X. 30. A. 5.0
       X. 29. d. 9.9
       X. 29. b. 6.5 (The northern end of the trench running to this point)

   (b) The line of FRITZ Trench:-
       At some point in FRITZ Trench between points 5410 and 4482 whence a good field of fire is obtained in a north-easterly direction.
       At point 4482.
       At the end of gully X.29. d. 3.5

   (c) The North-eastern and eastern faces of MAMETZ village will be prepared for defence.
       BUNNY WOOD.

   (d) When FRICOURT WOOD and WILLOW AVENUE are clear of the enemy, ORCHARD Trench North will be consolidated by the 20th Infantry Brigade and the ORCHARD prepared as a strong point.

   (e) The following are the positions of strong points to be prepared by Divisions on our flanks:-

On our Left	On our right
X. 29. b. 0.5	S. 25. b. 45.00
Eastern corner of FRICOURT WOOD	F. 6. c. 85.45
F. 4. a. 8.5	F. 6. a. 76.15
WILLOW TRENCH	F. 6. c. 86.75
	F. 6. c. 68.07
	A. 1. b. 50.20

2. ACTION OF R.E. AND DIVISIONAL PIONEERS.

   (a) For the consolidation of the strong points enumerated in sub-para (a) and (b) para 1, the 1/3rd Durham Field Coy. R.E. and "B" Company are allotted. These troops will assemble at MINDEN POST and will move forward under orders of G.O.C., 91st Infantry Brigade.

   (b) To place MAMETZ village in a state of defence and prepare BUNNY WOOD as a strong point, the 95th Field Coy. R.E., less one section, and "A" Company are allotted. These will assemble in No. 2 work Intermediate Line, and will move forward under orders from Divisional Headquarters.

   The O.C. 95th Field Company R.E. will arrange for two Orderlies to be at the signal test station at GRANTOWN (the present Infantry Brigade Headquarters)

   (c) The duty of opening up communication tunnels running from our trenches to BULGAR POINT and MAMETZ Trench is allotted to "D" Company, less two platoons, who will assemble in GEORGE AVENUE. The O.C. Company is responsible for opening up the tunnels at the earliest opportunity. On completion of this duty this party will be used to open up

Sheet 2

a communication trench from BULGAR POINT through FERDINAND ALLEY, MAMETZ, and BRIGHT ALLEY to FRITZ Trench and from the head of the left of these communication tunnels to the HALT, thence via DANZIG ALLEY to MAMETZ.

(d) The O.C. 174th and 183rd Tunnelling Companies will arrange for completion of shallow tunnels and the management of traffic passing through.

3. The 54th Coy. R.E. and "C" Company and two platoons of "D" Company will form part of the Divisional reserve assembling at GROVETOWN.

                    G.B.DEMPSEY.   Lieut. and Adjutant.
                24th Battalion Manchester Regiment.

Copy No. 1.   O.C. "A" Company
        2.   O.C. "B"   "
        3.   O.C. "C"   "
        4.   O.C. "D"   "
        5.   War Diary
        6.   War Diary.

SECRET

Copy No. 7

24th Battalion The Manchester Regiment.
INSTRUCTIONS FOR FORTHCOMING OPERATIONS NO. 3.

1. **DIVISION OF 1st LINE TRANSPORT**

"A" Echelon will consist of :- Pack animals, S.A.A., Grenade and Machine Gun Limbers.

"B" Echelon will consist of : Tool carts, Cookers, Water carts and Maltese Carts.

Each Echelon will be grouped by Brigades, and each Group will be under an Officer whose name will be reported to Divisional Headquarters.
Transport of R.E. Companies will be attached to Brigade Groups as follows:-
   With 20th Brigade Group, 95th Company R.E.
   With 22nd Brigade Group, 54th Company R.E.
   With 91st Brigade Group, 1/3rd Durham Field Company R.E.

"A" Echelon will be under Brigade control and will be in the following places at the commencement of the attack:-
   20th Infantry Brigade, near Durham Field Coy. billets L. 3. c.
   22nd Infantry Brigade, GROVETOWN Valley about L. 1. d. 9.0
   91st Infantry Brigade, GRANTOWN
   Pioneer Battalion with 22nd Infantry Brigade.

"B" Echelon will be located in the BOIS DES TAILLES in Brigade Areas which will be allotted, 20th Brigade on the North, 91st Brigade in the Centre and 22nd Brigade with Pioneer Battalion on the South.

Each Brigade Group and the Pioneer Battalion will send 1 Mounted Orderly to Divisional Headquarters "Q" Office at GROVETOWN by 6 a.m. on the day of the assault.

There will be a telephone exchange at K. 12. a. 6.7. and each Brigade Group of "B" Echelon transport will also keep one Orderly at this exchange.

There will be a second telephone exchange at ORCHARD CAMP connected with Divisional Headquarters and should Brigades wish to keep an Orderly from their "A" Echelon at this exchange they can communicate with him through Divisional Headquarters.

II. **SUPPLY OF FOOD AND WATER**

On the night before the assault rations for consumption on the following day will be issued to the men to be carried by them in addition to the Iron Ration. It must be clearly impressed on all ranks that the Iron Ration is not to be eaten except on the order of a C.O. If any Iron Rations are consumed the fact must be reported to Divisional Headquarters immediately.

Each man will also be given a sandwich to be eaten shortly before the assault, for which purpose ¼lb. bread per man will be issued in adition to the normal ration.

On the night following the assault, as soon after dark as movements of troops and guns will allow, Cook's vehicles and water carts, will be sent up in Brigade groups by the following route:- No "B" Echelon transport will move except on receipt of an order from Divisional Headquarters.

   Red Road to L. 9. a. 3.2.
   By track to L. 4. c. 6.5.
   By MAMETZ Road to F. 22. d. 5.9.
   By track to F. 23. a. 7.4.

   MANSEL COPSE
   HALT.

Sheet 2.

Each unit will send guides to the BRAY-MAMETZ Road at the Western Point of the great Bear to be there by 10-30 p.m. and await arrival of Transport, which wilml then be conducted as far forward as circumstances permit, where ration parties must be arranged. The petrol tins allotted to Brigades should if possible, be made available to take water from the water cart.

The number of vehicles per Battalion to be taken up to units must not in any case exceed five, including 2 water carts. If desired, and if circumstances permit 2 Cookers per Battalion,(included in the above 5 vehicles) with water and tea may remain up in the neighbourhood of the HALT during the following day, but the horses must return with the remainder of the transport and the vehicles must be clear of the PERONNE-FRICOURT Road.

Should the above arrangements not be suited to the circumstances in which any unit is placed, special orders will be issued for that unit, but unless this is done, these orders will apply to the 3 Infantry Brigades, Pioneer Battalion, and the 3 Field Companies R. E.

After delivering to units, transports will return by the same route and park close to the BRAY-CITADEL Road in L.3.d. and there await orders.

Lorries of the Mobile Water Column will arrive during the night on the BRAY-CITADEL Road at L.3.d. and all water carts must be refilled from these lorries as soon as possible after returning from units. The 40 additional water carts will be retained in Divisional reserve. Horses will be watered at troughs at L. 9. a. 8.5.

III. BAGGAGE WAGONS

All baggage wagons will be sent to units on the morning of "Y" day and must be returned to the train loaded not later than 9 p.m. that evening.

IV. REFILLING POINT

Refilling point on "Z" day will be as at present, on the MERICOURT-TREUX Road at 7 a.m. Supply wagons of the train will deliver supplies tpo 1st Line Transport in the BOIS DES TAILLES.

V. DRAFTS

All drafts will be sent to "B" Echelon 1st Line transport. Brigades will be informed of the numbers that have arrived for their Battalion, but they will not be sent up to units until Brigadiers repprt that they can be absprbed.

VI. OFFICERS

The following Officers will accompany the Battalion intp action:-
"A" Company 1 Major or Capt. and 4 Subalterns *The remainder, including the 2nd in Command, will be left with "B" Echelon 1st Line Transport. When any of these Reserve Officers are required to rejoin their units, Divisional Headquarters should be informed.*
"B" Company 1 Captain and 4 Subalterns.
"C" Company 1 Captain and 4 Subalterns.
"D" Company 1 Captain and 4 Subalterns

VII. REPLACEMENT OF ORDNANCE.

The quick replacement of lost or damaged Ordnance Stores is of great impprtance , especially in the case of Lewis or Vickers Guns. The D.A.D.O.S. has been authorised to accept telegraphic indents and these should be submitted with as little delay as possible, and repeated to Divisional Headquarters.

VIII. STORAGE OF PACKS

Reference Instructions for Forthcoming Operations No. 1 packs will be stored under Brigade arrangements in MORLANCOURT as follpws :-

Sheet 3.

  20th. Infantry Brigade   No. 7 Rue de Chateau
  91st. Infantry Brigade   No. 9 Rue de Chateau
  22nd. Infantry Brigade & Pioneer Battn. No.4 Rue de Calvaire

  2 men per Brigade will be left in charge under the orders of the Town Major who will arrange to provide them with rations by drawing from the Reserve Store at the Crucifix K.8.d. These 6 men will be provided under Divisional arrangements from "unfits" and will be handed over to the Town Major by "Y" day.

IX. SUPPLY COLUMN.

  The Supply Column will resume drawing rations at Railhead commencing on "Y" day.

X. VETERINARY.

  A Veterinary collecting station will be established at the Northern end of the BOIS DES TAILLES at K.12.a.2.8.
  The Mobile Veterinary Section will remain in MERICOURT.

XI. STRAGGLERS.

  A line of straggler posts will be formed connecting with Divisions on the right and left from a point on the BRAY-MAMETZ Road about L.4.c.3.3. via ORCHARD CAMP to the FILIFORME TREE.

  These posts will pass all men walking back, to the Central post at ORCHARD CAMP, where the wounded will be Medically dealt with, and any stragglers sent under escort to the "B" Echelon of their units Transport where they will be handed over to the Officer in charge, re-equipped, fed, and returned to their units at night.

  These posts will move further forward as opportunity occurs.

XII. SALVAGE.

  Preliminary Salvage operations will be commenced by the Divisional Salvage Company as soon as possible, on receipt of orders from Divisional Headquarters.

  The detailed scheme issued under 7th. Division No. Q/764/6 will not come into operation until progress of operations can be ascertained, when orders will be issued by Divisional Headquarters for the scheme to be put into operations.

XIII. PRISIONERS.

  A Divisional Prisoner Collecting Station will be established at a point 200x S. of ORCHARD CAMP. Any prisoners made by units will be sent there under escorts to be found from units. These escorts after getting a receipt for their prisoners from Officer in Charge Collecting Station will return to their units.

  As a rule 5% of the number of prisoners will be a sufficient escort.

  Officer prisoners should be kept seperate from the men.

  Care should be taken that documents in possession of prisoners are not thrown away on their way back.

Copy No. 1. O. C. "A" Coy.	Copy No. 5. Quartermaster.
Copy No. 2 O.C. "B" Coy.	Copy No. 6. Transport Officer.
Copy No. 3. O.C. "C" Coy.	Copy No. 7. War Diary.
Copy No. 4 O.C. "D" Coy.	Copy No. 8. War Diary.

      G. B. DEMPSEY, LIEUT. &. ADJUTANT,
       24th. Battalion The Manchester Regt.

XIV. OFFICERS' KITS.

Any surplus kit over 38 lbs., 1 mess basket per Coy., and Mens' surplus kits will be stacked behind Headquarters Mess kitchen at 10-0 a.m. on the 19th. instant. These kits will be stored at MERICOURT by D.A.D.O.S.

SECRET   Copy No. 5

24th Battalion, The Manchester Regiment.
INSTRUCTIONS FOR FORTHCOMING OPERATIONS No. 5.
                                                 20-6-16.

I. **SIGNAL COMMUNICATIONS**
   Contact Aeroplanes and Kite Balloons
   Brigade and Battalion Headquarters only, will communicate with these. Urgent messages which cannot be sent by any other method should be sent through the nearest of these Headquarters, in preference by Brigade.

II. **MEDICAL**
   The two Advanced Dressing Stations are situated at MINDEN POST, and the CITADEL, and the Divisional Collecting Station is on the BRAY-ALBERT Road, South of ORCHARD CAMP.
   Routes from advanced dressing stations to collecting stations are:-
   From MINDEN POST.   By wheeled stretcher down NORFOLK AVENUE to VAUXHALL thence by Motor Ambulance.

   From CITADEL.   By trench tramway via ORCHARD CAMP.
   The Main Dressing Station will be at MORLANCOURT.

III.   Map references in connection with forthcoming operations are to the following:-
   1/20,000 - Sheets   57. D. S.E.   57. C. S.W.
                       62. D. N.E.   62. C. N.W.

   1/100,000 Sheets   11 and 17.

IV. **TOOLS**   "A" and "B" Companies will make arrangements with the O.C., R.E. Company to which they are attached as to the tools to be carried.
   "C" and "D" Companies will take all their picks and shovels and arrange a method of slinging them on mens backs; men not carrying picks and shovels should take crowbars.

V. **BOMBS**   On parties arriving at their positions for work, bombs should be collected in sandbags and stacked, at any points they are likely to be wanted, in charge of Grenadiers.
   During work Bombing sentries should be posted in any position not covered by Infantry where there is danger of attack by hostile bombing parties. It must be borne in mind that there is always danger of attack from parties of the enemy behind our new lines, who may have escaped our Infantry by hiding in dug-outs and cellars.

   Copy No. 1   O.C. "A" Coy.
        2   O.C. "B" "
        3   O.C. "C" "
        4   O.C. "D" "
        5   War Diary
        6   War Diary

                              G. B. DEMPSEY. Lieut. and Adjutant.

S.E.C.R.E.T.   Copy No. 5

24th Battalion The Manchester Regiment
INSTRUCTIONS FOR FORTHCOMING OPERATIONS NO. 4

June 19th 1916.

I. **COMMUNICATIONS**

(a) In addition to telegraph and telephone communication by visual signalling, by signalling to contact aeroplanes and Kite balloons, by pigeons and by wireless will be established.

(b) **VISUAL SIGNALLING**

Stations will be established as far as possible as shown below:-

Receiving Station	Sending Station
91ST. INFANTRY BRIGADE	For two right Battns
F. 23. b. 8.9. Brigade (H.Q)	(1) F. 11. b. 8.4.
	(2) F. 6. c. 05.40
	For two left Battns.
	(3) F. 11. b. 2.3.
	(4) F. 11. a. 6.9.

When communication is established between 2 and 4, 1 and 3 will be closed.

20th INFANTRY BRIGADE	
F. 23. b. 8.9.	For right Battalion
	(1) F. 5. c. 25.05
	For left Battalion
F. 11. d. 7.7.	(2) F. 10. d. 5.9.
22nd INFANTRY BRIGADE	
(1) F. 9. d. 05.70.	(1) F. 9. d. 05.70.
(2) F. 8. d. 1.3.	(2) F. 9. b. 6.1.
Brigade Headquarters	(3) F. 9. b. 7.4.

(c) **CONTACT AEROPLANES AND KITE BALLOONS**
Instructions issued later.

(D) **PIGEONS**
Instructions issued later.

(e) **WIRELESS**
It is hoped to establish a Trench Wireless set at the South-Western corner of MAMETZ. The position will be marked by a blue and white flag.

II. **ADMINISTRATIVE SIGNAL SERVICE**

(a) Telegrams may be handed in at the following offices for transmission:-

Divisional Headquarters.
All Infantry Brigade Headquarters.
35th Brigade R.F.A. Headquarters (Trench 12 Intermediate line)
A.D.M.S's Office, MORLANCOURT.
17th Divisional Headquarters, TREUX.

(b) **EMPLOYMENT OF TELEPHONES**

(1) Conversation will be between Officers only.
(2) Conversation will be on official matters only and will be as brief as possible.
(3) No telegraph messages will be sent through on telephone lines. Arrangements must be made to hand in all telegrams to the nearest telegraph office.

Sheet 2.

III. CAPTURED GUNS

(a) Three teams will be kept in readiness at GIBRALTAR for the removal of captured guns if required. Application for their services will be made to Divisional Headquarters.

(b) Captured guns should be at once rendered useless. The best methods of doing this are either to punch a hole in the buffer case which is underneath the gun itself and which can be pierced by a bullet or entrenching tool, or by burring the breach screw with a bullet, heavy stone, or other implement.

IV. HEADQUARTERS

Headquarters will be established at the following points on "Y" day:-

Divisional Headquarters at GROVETOWN at L. 1. d. 80.35.

20th Infantry Brigade at F. 16. d. 1.9., Junction of ESSEX AVENUE and WELLINGTON AVENUE.

22nd INFANTRY Brigade F. 8. d. 1.3., in MILES AVENUE near BPNTE REDOUBT.

91st Infantry Brigade, F. 23. b. 8.9., DURHAM TRENCH 50 yards East of its junction with NORFOLK AVENUE.

Divisional Headquarters will be established at 4 p.m.

V. The Commanding Officer delegates the power of ordering the consumption of the emergency ration to O.C. Companies should they be detached from Battalion Headquarters and unable to communicate with it, should it be necessary to do so. It must be borne in mind however that an emergency ration is only to be used as a last resort and when men are actually on the point of starvation. Only one tin of beef should be opened for every four men at a time. Divisional and Battalion Headquarters should be informed as soon as communication can be established as to how many rations have been used.

```
Copy No. 1.    O.C. "A" Coy.
         2     O.C. "B"  "
         3     O.C. "C"  "
         4     O.C. "D"  "
         5     War Diary
         6     War Diary.
```

G. B. DEMPSEY. Lieut. and Adjutant.

S E C R E T   Copy No. 5

24th Battalion The Manchester Regiment
OPERATION ORDER NO. 15

Reference — 1/20,000 MONTAUBAN, 57D N.E., 57D S.E., 57D S.E. 57C N.W., 57C S.W.
1/100,000 AMIENS and LENS Sheets.

NO ORDERS OF MAPS LIKELY TO BE OF USE TO THE ENEMY WILL BE TAKEN INTO THE FIELD

22nd June, 1916.

I. **INFORMATION**

(a) **The Enemy**

The enemy's defences on our front consist of two well defined systems of trenches, and a third partially completed.

The front system from a point 600 yards south-east of MAMETZ runs in a westerly direction towards FRICOURT in the form of a salient into our line, and the ground in rear is covered by cross fire from our Artillery.

The second system runs from LONGUEVAL between the BAZENTIN and MAMETZ WOODS and passes East of POZIERES.

The third system from south and south-west of FLERS runs to LE SARS.

The 12th Division, VIth Corps, is holding the trenches from the SOMME to the south of FRICOURT, with the 23rd Regiment immediately in our front, the 62nd and 63rd Regiments between it and the SOMME in the order named.

To the north of the 12th Division the 28th Reserve Division, XIVth Reserve Corps were in position with the 111th Regiment occupying FRICOURT until lately, but it is believed that a relief has taken place. It is possible that the 12th Division may also be shortly relieved.

(b) **Our own troops**

The 18th Division, XIIIth Corps, is on our right. On our left is the 21st Division of our own Corps; the 17th Division is in Corps Reserve.

One Infantry Brigade, 17th Division, is attached to and will be on the right flank of the 21st Division.

II. **INTENTION** (vide I.F.O. No.1 Section 1)

The following additional information is published:-

(a) The Third, First, and Second Armies are undertaking offensive operations in conformity with the attack of the Fourth Army.

(b) After the capture and consolidation of the objectives for which orders have already been issued preparations will be immediately undertaken to take part in a further advance to capture BAZENTIN-le-GRAND and the enemy's defences between that village and MONTAUBAN. This operation will be undertaken by the XV Corps connecting with the XIIIth Corps at MONTAUBAN and the III Corps who will capture BAZENTIN-le-PETIT.

It is impressed on all Commanders that the success of the operations as a whole depend largely on the consolidation of the definite objectives allotted.

No serious advance is to be made beyond these objectives until preparations have been completed for entering on the next phase of the operations

The additional Sections of this Operation Order have already been issued as follows:-

Sheet 2

		L. F. O. No.	Section
III	Distribution	1	2
IV	Dress	1	3
V	Consolidation of Captured positions	2	1
VI	Action of R.E. & Divisional Pioneers	2	2
VII	Battalion reserve	2	3
VIII	Division of 1st Line Transport	3	1
IX	Supply of food and water	3	2
X	Baggage wagons	3	3
XI	Refilling point	3	4
XII	Drafts	3	5
XIII	Officers	3	6
XIV	Replacement of Ordnance	3	7
XV	Storage of packs	3	8
XVI	Supply Column	3	9
XVII	Veterinary	3	10
XVIII	Stragglers	3	11
XIX	Salvage	3	12
XX	Prisoners	3	13
XXI	Communications	4	1
XXII	Administrative Signal Service	4	2
XXIII	Captured Guns	4	3
XXIV	Headquarters	4	4
XXV	Emergency ration	4	5
XXVI	Signal Communications	5	1
XXVII	Medical	5	2
XXVIII	Map reference	5	3
XXIX	Tools	5	4
XXX	Bombs	5	5
XXXI	Mines – Shallow galleries	6	1
XXXII	Regulation of Traffic in Communication trenches	6	2
XXXIII	Lewis Guns	6	3

```
Copy No. 1.    O.C. "A" Coy.
        2.     O.C. "B"  "
        3.     O.C. "C"  "
        4.     O.C. "D"  "
        5      War Diary
        6      War Diary.
```

G. B. DEMPSEY. Lieut. and Adjutant
24th Battalion Manchester Regiment.

SECRET   Copy No. 5

24th Battalion The Manchester Regiment.
INSTRUCTIONS FOR FORTHCOMING OPERATIONS NO. 6.

22-6-16.

I. **MINES -- SHALLOW GALLERIES**

The mines at the head of communication galleries running from Point MX F. 11. d. 5.8. to BULGAR POINT and F. 11. d. 1.7. to MAMETZ TRENCH will be blown at Zero hour on "Z" day.

II. **REGULATION OF TRAFFIC IN COMMUNICATION TRENCHES**

The traffic in communication tunnels will be limited to the following:-

UP TRAFFIC   Runners (with badge)
              Men carrying written messages.
              Officers, N.C.Os and men of Signal service.
              Linesmen of R.A.
              Ammunition carriers
              Staff Officers
              Forward O. O., R.A.

DOWN TRAFFIC Runners (with badge)
              Men carrying written messages.
              Staff Officers.
              Forward Observing Officers.

III. **LEWIS GUNS**

The Battalion Lewis Guns will be attached to the 20th Brigade.

Copy No. 1.   O.C. "A" Coy.
         2.   O.C. "B" "
         3.   O.C. "C" "
         4.   O.C. "D" "
         5.   War Diary
         6.   War Diary.

G. D. DEMPSEY. Lieut. and Adjutant.
24th Battalion Manchester Regiment.

SECRET

Sketch of Roads & Tracks
on 7th Divn Front

In connection with Operations

FRICOURT — MAMETZ

Scale 1/24,000

Bridge for lorries L
  "   " Horses H
Existing Roads ———
Marked Tracks -----
Proposed Roads -·-·-

Appendix 8

S.E.C.R.E.T.   Copy No. 7
            24th Battalion The Manchester Regiment
          INSTRUCTIONS FOR FORTHCOMING OPERATIONS NO. 7.
                                           23rd June, 1916.

Reference to I. F. O. No. 3.

PARA I   Areas allotted to "B" Echelon Transport in BOIS DES
           TAILLES can be seen by those concerned on map in Orderly
           Room. This transport must be in correct position by 9 p.m.
           "Y" day.

PARA II.   1st Line Transport returning from HALT to the BRAY-CITADEL
           Rpad in L. 3. d. will use the road via F. 4. e. 5.3. the
           cemetary cross rpads in F. 9. a. 5.7., 7(North and the
           Citadel, and not the same route as that used for going
           forward. Sketches showing roads already bridged to our
           front line are issued to those concerned.

PARA IX.   Cancelled. Special orders will be issued when the
           supply column is to commence drawing from Railhead.
               All empty wagons returning from the front must carry
           wounded if required to by Medical Authorities but must not
           divert from normal route.

Reference to I. F. O. No. 6.

PARA II.   REGULATION OF TRAFFIC IN COMMUNICATION TRENCHES

                        Should read

           REGULATION OF TRAFFIC IN COMMUNICATION TUNNELS.

            Copy No. 1.   O.C. "A" Coy.
                 2.   O.C. "B" "
                 3.   O.C. "C" "
                 4.   O.C. "D" "
                 5.   Quartermaster.
                 6.   Transport Officer.
                 7.   War Diary
                 8.   War Diary.

                         G. B. DEMPSEY. Lieut. and Adjutant.
                           24th Battalion Manchester Regiment.

SECRET
                                          Copy No. 5
            24th Battalion The Manchester Regiment.
        INSTRUCTIONS FOR FORTHCOMING OPERATIONS NO. 3.
                                          24-6-16

I. ARTILLERY

        A continuous bombardment will take place from U/V night
    to Y/Z night.
        Concentrated bombardments
        W day 9 a.m. to 10-20 a.m.
        X day 4-30 a.m. to 5-50 a.m.
        Y day 6 a.m. to 7-20 a.m.
        Z day 65 minutes before Zero.

II. GAS

        Gas attacks will take place on night V/W if the wind is
    favourable or W/X or X/Y night and on Z day 15 minutes before
    Zero.

III. SMOKE ATTACKS

        Smoke attacks will take place on:-
        W day at   10-10 a.m.
        X day at   5-40 a.m.
        Y day at   7-10 a.m.
        Z day at Zero on front not being attacked.

IV. INFANTRY

        Rapid fire will be opened just previous to gas attack, and
    on
        T/U night at   1-30 a.m.
        U/V night at   10-15 p.m. and 2 a.m.

        Copy Nos. 1.   O.C. "A" Coy.
                  2.   O.C. "B" "
                  3.   O.C. "C" "
                  4.   O.C. "D" "
                  5.   H.Q. War Diary
                  6.   War Diary.

                    C. B. DEMPSEY. Lieut. and Adjutant.
                        24th Battalion Manchester Regiment.

N.O.T.E. This is only to be made known to anyone concerned,
    such as parties who might be working near the front line trench.

S E C R E T   Copy No. 7

24th Battalion The Manchester Regiment.
OPERATION ORDER NO. 16.

27th June, 1916.

Reference Sheet 1/20,000.

I.   The Battalion will move to their assembly positions on the 27th, 28th, and night of 28/29 June.

II. (a)   "A" Company will move on the 27th under Company arrangements.

(b)   "B" and "D" Companies less two platoons, will move with 1/3rd Durham R. E. from the BOIS DES TAILLES, passing point K. 6. c. 2.0. at 12-35 a.m. 28/29th.

(c)   Headquarters, "C" Company and two platoons "D" Company, will parade on ground South of Camp Area at 11-15 p.m. 28/29th, and move to GROVETOWN via track from the wood at K. 12. b. 2.3. tp road junction L. 7. a. 3.1., thence direct to GROVETOWN.

III.   Companies will move with at least 300 yards between platoons.

IV.   All routes must be carefully reconnoitred.

V.   Lewis Gun Sections will join Battalion Headquarters at GROVETOWN on the night 28/29th.

VI.   All packs to be stacked by sentry box in Company heaps by 7 a.m. 28th.

VII.   Tool carts will be packed by midday 28th.

VIII.   Officers kits and baggage to be ready stacked for loading North of Headquarters kitchen by 5 p.m. 28th.

IX.   Tents and bivouacs will be left standing.

X.   Transport will move up to their position in the BOIS DES TAILLES by 5 p.m.

XI.   "A" Echelon Transport will parade with Battalion Headquarters and move to L. 1. d. 9.0. GROVETOWN when it will come under 22nd Brigade control.

Copy No. 1.	O.C. "A" Coy	Copy No. 2.	O.C. "B" Coy.
3.	O.C. "C" "	4.	O.C. "D" "
5.	Quartermaster	6.	Transport Officer
7.	War Diary	8.	War Diary.

                             G. B. DEMPSEY. Lieut. and Adjutant.
                             24th Bn. The Manchester Regiment.

SECRET   Copy No. 7

24th Battalion The Manchester Regiment
OPERATION ORDER NO. 17.

June 29th 1916.

I.   June 29th will be known as Y1 day.
     June 30th will be known as Y2 day.
     July 1st will be known as Z day.

II. Moves and orders in Operation Order No. 16, June 28th will
     read June 30th, and night of 28/29th will read night of
     30/1st July.

Copy No. 1	O.C. "A" Coy.	Copy No. 2.	O.C. "B" Coy.
3	O.C. "C" "	4.	O.C. "D" "
5	Quartermaster	6.	Transport Officer
7	War Diary	8.	War Diary.

                              G. B. DEMPSEY. Lieut. and Adjutant.
                                 24th Battalion Manchester Regiment.

Appendix 12

Pioneers.
7th Div.

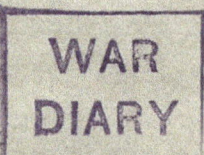

24th BATTN. THE MANCHESTER REGIMENT.

J U L Y

1 9 1 6

Attached:

Appendices 1, 2, 3, 4 & 5.

Army Form C. 2118.

WAR DIARY
or
INTELLIGENCE SUMMARY

(Erase heading not required.)

Vol IX

24th Bn. The Manchester Regt

Place	Date	Hour	Summary of Events and Information	Remarks and references to Appendices
GROVETOWN L/1/d/8.h (ALBERT continued sheet)	July 1st June 30th	12 noon	Weather Fine; wind light N.W. Situation The following moves were made. Bat HQ and C Company with D Coy remained at "WORK 2" GROVETOWN A Coy and C Company with D Coy less two platoons moved to GROVETOWN (F 2g) a Albert continued sheet) B " } moved to MINDEN POST F.n.8.17 d. 6.8 1/2 D Coy } B + D Coy were attached to 1/3 Durham R.E. and Mty. 95 Coy R.E. Artillery fire etc. was carried out as per Operation orders issued (June War Diary)	GAS
-do-	July 1st	12 noon	Weather Fine; wind light. still N.W. Situation The 7th Division attacked the enemy at 7.30 a.m. Artillery barrage and smoke attacks were carried out as per Operation orders in June War Diary. As the attack progressed B and D Coys were employed as follows B Coy moved along roads into N.E. of MAMETZ after it capture from the enemy. 1/2 D Coy two platoons opened up enemy trenches blown in by our bombardment. As the attack was successful these Companies were at once put into clearing roads and removing enemy wire. Troop unable to proceed through MAMETZ over to open ground. A+C Echelon transport parked at GROVETOWN and B Echelon at K 6 a. S. 7 (ALBERT continued sheet)	GAS

2449 Wt. W14957/M90 750,000 1/16 J.B.C. & A. Forms/C.2118/12.

WAR DIARY or INTELLIGENCE SUMMARY

Army Form C. 2118.

Place	Date	Hour	Summary of Events and Information	Remarks and references to Appendices
GROVETOWN			Casualties Our Casualties were Officers nil – O.R. 8 including one who returned to duty.	(over)
"	2nd	11am	Weather Fine and warm wind N.E.	
			Situation The remaining II Coy (2 platoons) moved up to MINDEN POST A, B and II Coy employed clearing roads and building lorry tracks across enemy trenches. C Company worked 8 hours removing enemy wire on MAMETZ – FRICOURT road. Returning to GROVETOWN at night.	YBS
			Casualties Officers nil O.R. 3.	
"	3rd	12pm	Weather Fine and sultry in morning. Wind quarty W.N.W. Heavy thunder storm with much rain at 4 pm.	
			Situation Companies were employed in clearing roads in MAMETZ and repairing cellars.	YBS
			Casualties Nil	

Army Form C. 2118.

WAR DIARY
or
INTELLIGENCE SUMMARY

(Erase heading not required.)

Instructions regarding War Diaries and Intelligence Summaries are contained in F. S. Regs., Part II. and the Staff Manual respectively. Title Pages will be prepared in manuscript.

Place	Date	Hour	Summary of Events and Information	Remarks and references to Appendices
—	4th	11 pm	Weather. Fine, wind fresh N.W. Situation. All companies were employed into cave works of road cleaning and road repairing on the grounds taken from the enemy. Casualties. Officers nil. O.R. 1.	Yes
MERICOURT	5th	12 mn	Weather. Fine and warm. Moonlight n.r. Move. The 7th Division moved out of the firing line, being relieved by the 38th Division. The 24th Manchesters moved to MERICOURT via MORLANCOURT and TREUX. All companies were in billets by 11 pm.	Yes
—	6th	10 pm	Weather. Dull with rain at intervals during the afternoon. Billets. The battalion settled down in billets. Inspections were held and equipment completed. Billets were improved where possible. A regimental Canteen was started.	Yes

2449 Wt. W14957/Mgo 750,000 1/16 J.B.C. & A. Forms/C.2118/12.

Army Form C. 2118.

WAR DIARY
or
INTELLIGENCE SUMMARY
(Erase heading not required.)

Instructions regarding War Diaries and Intelligence Summaries are contained in F.S. Regs., Part II and the Staff Manual respectively. Title Pages will be prepared in manuscript.

Place	Date	Hour	Summary of Events and Information	Remarks and references to Appendices
MERICOURT (SOMME)	19th	10 am	Weather — hot wind W.S.W. quiet. Parades — An inspection parade was held at 10 am, followed by an examination and check of kit. The men spent the remainder of the day in cleaning kit.	
			Transfers & Postings — Major P.H. Magnay left the battalion & command to 9th Bn. Northumberland Fusiliers 17th Division. Major J.H. Chadwick (OC A Coy) took over 2nd in command. Capt J.C.H. Bee from 2nd in command O Coy to command A Coy. Capt H Prendergast transferred from A to D Coy as 2nd in command. Lt E Wood to be 2nd in command C Coy. 2Lt H.S. Browne to be Lewis Gun Officer vice Lt E. Wood.	GOS
	8th	10 pm	Weather — fine, wind N changing to N.H. light. Sports — Regimental Sports were held. Heats were run in the morning and semi-finals & finals in the afternoon. Prizes presented by the C.O.	
			Address — The G.O.C. Division visited the battalion in the afternoon & addressed the officers and men, thanking them for their work in the recent attack.	GOS

2449 Wt. W14957/M90 750,000 1/16 J.B.C. & A. Forms/C.2118/12.

WAR DIARY or INTELLIGENCE SUMMARY

Army Form C. 2118.

Place	Date	Hour	Summary of Events and Information	Remarks and references to Appendices
MERICOURT	9th	10 am	Weather fine - wind light N.W. Parade. Divine Service was held in the morning. The men were free for the remainder of the day	9/3D
"	10th	11 am	Weather fine and bright. Wind fresh N.W. Move. The battalion moved to CITADEL and WELLINGTON REDOUBT. F.K. a and F. 10. d Route MERICOURT — TREUX — VILLE — MORLANCOURT. A Echelon Transport remained at F.15.a.: B Echelon at E.30.e. Operation Orders attached	Ref ALBERT continued sheet. Yes Appendix 1
WELLINGTON REDOUBT	11th	10 pm	Weather fine wind light N.W. Working Parties. 1 N.C.O and 10 men working at R.E. Stores BRAY loading to have 80 O.R. 5 am to 12 noon clearing F.10.a of German material and carrying same to Dump at F.4.c. 70.35. 40 O.R. 9-15 pm — 7 pm building T.M. emplacements at S.20.d.55.65 40 O.R. 8-15 am to 4:30 pm " " " S.19.b	Yes

WAR DIARY
or
INTELLIGENCE SUMMARY

Army Form C. 2118.

Place	Date	Hour	Summary of Events and Information	Remarks and references to Appendices
WELLINGTON REDOUBT	12th	11 p.m.	Weather. Dull, wind fresh W.N.W. Working Parties. Two companies 9 p.m. - 3 a.m. (13th) working on WHITE TRENCH (x 29 d S.8 to S.26 t 3.3 Map MONTAUBAN) converting it into an assembly trench, deepening and widening and making antie steps. Two companies collecting trench tools and material and carrying same to POMMIERS REDOUBT (MONTAUBAN Sheet A.I.S.3) Move. Transport moved to LE CARCAILLOT E 18 a (ALBERT Combined Sheet) Casualties from 10th to 12th inclusive 4 wounded	WHITE TRENCH (MONTAUBAN MAP A.I.S.3) GAS
-"-	13th	10 p.m.	Weather. Dull, inclined to rain. Wind fresh W.N.W. Working Parties. Two companies carrying tools and material as in the 12th. Casualties. One man died (cerebral hemorrhage) 2 wounded slight	GAS, Appendix 2
-"-	14th		Weather. Situation normal. Operation Order no 19 attached	

WAR DIARY or INTELLIGENCE SUMMARY

Army Form C. 2118.

Place	Date	Hour	Summary of Events and Information	Remarks and references to Appendices
WELLINGTON REDOUBT	14th	10pm	Weather fine and bright	Ref map MARTIN-PUICH 1/20.000
			Work & Situation	

A and D Coys were sent out as per Operation Order 15 to follow up the attack on BAZENTIN LE PETIT (map area of MARTIN PUICH). The village had been taken by 7th Division but while the 22nd Manchesters were constructing a keep in the village and putting the CEMETERY into a state of defence, the enemy counter attacked. The C.O. Royal Irish Rgt, 2nd Bn. then took some of our men to help to clear BAZENTIN LE PETIT WOOD and so they asked Red Bn. and went through the wood under 2 Lt W. SOWARD 11th E. Surrey Rgt (attached 24th Manchesters). One platoon of A Coy under Lieut BATEMAN held the CEMETERY against the enemy (who were about 5 a. 5'5") and beat him back by rifle fire. The enemy held the northern end of the village. 2 Lt Soward then reported the wood clear and was then put into a position S.8 & 5.3. He then reported the enemy in the trench S.2 C.8.3. Meanwhile Capt Lee with the remainder of A Coy held the keep at S.8.3.6. under machine gun and shell fire, working as best they could. LIEUT H ANDREW was killed 44 and 2 Lt SOWARD wounded; other ranks killed 5 wounded 47. These two companies remained in position garrisoning the village until evening they were not able to consolidate properly as they took part in the fight. The following officers took part in the defence. Capt W Hall Capt C H Lee Lieut Andrew, Bateman, Roberts 2/Lt Swain, Pickles, Black, Soward, W.C. Collins.

G.A.D.

WAR DIARY or INTELLIGENCE SUMMARY

Army Form C. 2118.

Place	Date	Hour	Summary of Events and Information	Remarks and references to Appendices
WELLINGTON REDOUBT	15th	10 pm	Weather: Fine and warm, large M.N.E.	Map MARTINPUICH 1/20,000
			Work: B Coy 4 Platoons left camp at 6 am and returned 6:30 pm. Work done:- Repaired road from S.14.c.3.5 to road junction at S.14.b.9s.90 making it fit for passage of artillery.	
			C Coy 3 Platoons left camp 11 am returned 7 pm Work done:- Repaired German road from Carnoy X.29.b.5.5 up valley through X.30.a and S.19.a. and S.20.c.	
			One platoon left camp 11 am returned 7:30 pm Work done:- repaired road F.5.d.1.9 to F.5.b.3.7.	
		Casualties	Other ranks wounded 3 "	G.B.S
—	16th	10 pm	Weather: Fine in morning: Rain in afternoon. Wind light M.N.W	Ref map MONTAUBAN
			Work: One company working 8 hours on the roads HALT - SHRINE & MAMETZ CUDA roads filling shell holes. One company on the MAMETZ - BAZENTIN valley road. 8 hours.	
			One company on the Mametz - MANSEL COPSE - LUDGATE CIRCUS (F.17.a 3.1) road filling head trenches and general improvements & hours making a ramp to ammunition loading stage at F.4.c.5.4. Working for 4 hours	
		Casualties	Nil	G.B.S

WAR DIARY or INTELLIGENCE SUMMARY

Army Form C. 2118.

Place	Date	Hour	Summary of Events and Information	Remarks and references to Appendices
WELLINGTON REDOUBT (F 17 c)	17th	10pm	**Weather** Dull and inclined to rain. Wind N.N.W. changing to N.N.E. during night. 17th - 18th.	Ref. map MONTAUBAN 1/20,000
			Work C Company. 1 platoon 39 O.R. 4½ hours cleaning and remaking road from X 5.d.1.9 for distance of 150x. 3 platoons 122 O.R. were compelled by enemy artillery barrage from to retire from work on road North of S 20 a 4.0 to X 5.d.1.9 to work on northern side of the above mentioned platoon. 8 hours	
			Strength D Company. 4 officers 132 O.R. improving HALT - SHRINE - MAMETZ Rd. F 11 d - F 5 c. 6 hours. A Company. 3 officers 128 O.R. 8 hours making and repairing road from LUDGATE CIRCUS (F 17 a 3.1) to MANSEL COPSE (F 11 c 4.5.) B Company. Resting	
			Situation Our artillery commenced bombardment of HIGH WOOD (S 4) Rf MARTINPUICH 1/20 m preparatory to attack on enemy third line. Enemy shelled ground N.E. of MAMETZ wk. tear shells.	YBS
			Casualties Nil	

Army Form C. 2118.

WAR DIARY
or
INTELLIGENCE SUMMARY
(Erase heading not required.)

Instructions regarding War Diaries and Intelligence Summaries are contained in F.S. Regs., Part II and the Staff Manual respectively. Title Pages will be prepared in manuscript.

Place	Date	Hour	Summary of Events and Information	Remarks and references to Appendices
WELLINGTON REDOUBT	18th	10pm	Weather Wind N.N.W light. Dull with rain in the morning	
			Work done Half company working on road F.14.c central to MAMETZ cross roads F.14.c.4.6, F.4.c.2.3 / MONTAUBAN. Other company repairing roads F.14.c.5.3. to F.4.c.5.6.5. MTHT 1/20,000	GPS Appendix 3
			Casualties nil	
-||-	19th	10pm	Weather Fine wind light N.N.E.	Appendix 4
			None The Battalion cleared WELLINGTON REDOUBT by 9am. Headquarters, A & D Coys moved to E.12.b.22. B & C Companies moved to ROSE COTTAGE, FRICOURT with SH & G Ref No 20	Operation Order
			Work B & D Companies worked 4 hours making a horse track from WING CORNER to F.4.c.5.5. and from BECORDEL to WING CORNER (MONTAUBAN map)	Appendix 5
			Situation B and C Companies moved with 20th Infy Bde. as per Operation Order No 21	GPS
Bivouacs at E.12.b.2.2 ALBERT 1/40,000	20th	10pm	Weather Fine and warm; wind fresh wind E.N.E.	
			Work B and C Companies arrived with 20th Infy Bde. 6 men reported at L.15.t.6.8. (Divisional R.E. Store) as loading party. Two companies (8 officers and 356 O.R.) worked 84 hours making a horse track from BECORDEL - F.4.c central track to MAMETZ (Map MONTAUBAN)	

WAR DIARY or INTELLIGENCE SUMMARY

Army Form C. 2118.

Place	Date	Hour	Summary of Events and Information	Remarks and references to Appendices
E.12.d.22. and E.13.c.10.10.	21st	10 p.m.	**Work** Nil. **Weather** Fine and warm wind E.N.E. **Move** The battalion moved at 9.30 a.m. via MEAULTE — E.16.a. 7.3 to BIERNACOURT E.13.c.10.10. when bivouacs were taken over. Ref ALBERT 1/40,000	YPS
	22nd		**Report of Work done by B and C Coys attached 207 Coy** — Order To make a strong point at S.10.d.8.8 (ref MARTINPUICH 1/20,000) with the front and reverse, completely wired and covered by 2 Lewis Guns. After passing CATERPILLAR WOOD a gas shell barrage at S.10.d.8.8 reached at R.S. an (21st) The two companies were heavy shelling. The material was dumped at S.16.a.1.9's. On commencing work the order was received to return to WHITE TRENCH, the headquarters of the half battalion. B Company acted as carrying party. **Work** Nil	
ST. VAST, EN CHAUSSEE (AMIENS SHEET 17)	22nd	11 a.m.	**Weather** Fine and warm wind light E.N.E. **Move** The battalion moved to under to ST VAST A Company By train from MERICOURT to HANGEST (SOMME) thence by road B and HQ " " " " " " " " " to ST VAST via BOURDON, BOIS DU GARD C " " D Companies 11 a.m.	

Army Form C. 2118.

WAR DIARY
or
INTELLIGENCE SUMMARY
(Erase heading not required.)

Instructions regarding War Diaries and Intelligence Summaries are contained in F. S. Regs., Part II. and the Staff Manual respectively. Title Pages will be prepared in manuscript.

Place	Date	Hour	Summary of Events and Information	Remarks and references to Appendices
ST VAAST, EN CHAUSSEE	23rd	10pm	Weather Parade. Dull but fine. Wind N.N.W. light. Roman Catholic Church parade held in morning. Inspection parade & complete Kit. The remainder of the day was spent in improving billets. A regimental canteen was opened in the village.	GBS
—"—	24th	10pm	Weather Parade. Dull. Fine. Wind heat N.N.W. Adjutants parade 7–7.45 am Battalion drill. Company parade 9–12.45 pm Classes in Bombing, Lewis Gun, Joinery, Map Reading, Plumbing from 2–4 pm	GAS
—"—	25th	10pm	Weather Parade. Fine and bright. Breeze light N. Adjutants' parade 7–7.45 am Company Parade 9–12.45 pm Classes in Bombing, Lewis Gun, Joinery, Map Reading, Plumbing 2–4 pm	GBS

2449 Wt. W14957/M90 750,000 1/16 J.B.C. & A. Forms/C.2118/12.

WAR DIARY or INTELLIGENCE SUMMARY

Army Form C. 2118.

Place	Date	Hour	Summary of Events and Information	Remarks and references to Appendices
ST VAAST	26	10pm	Weather. Fine, warm, wind light. N.N.W. Training. There were parades by Companies during the day. Baths. The battalion visited the baths at VAUX & from 8am to 12noon and 1 - 6pm.	G.B.S.
— " —	27	10pm	Weather. Dull in morning. Bright and warm in afternoon. wind light N. Work. The battalion proceeded к Station at POULAINVILLE (650 o.r. proceeded) Time worked 6 hours. No 14017 Sergt (Acting C.S.M.) J. Fisher A Coy. Awarded the 15120 2/Corpl A. E. Clarke A Coy Military Medal for gallantry.	(Ref AMIENS sheet 7)
— " —	28	10pm	Weather. Fine and bright, very warm. Breeze light E.N.E. Training. Company training in morning: Classes in Plumbing, carpentry, tracklaying, saddlemaking in afternoon.	G.B.S.

WAR DIARY
or
INTELLIGENCE SUMMARY

Army Form C. 2118.

(Erase heading not required.)

Place	Date	Hour	Summary of Events and Information	Remarks and references to Appendices
ST VAST	29th	10am	Weather Bright and warm. Breeze light E.N.E. Parade Company training in the morning. Parades cancelled in the afternoon. Football match played A v B Company. C v D Company.	GBS
"	30th	10am	Weather Warm and bright. Breeze light N.E. Parade Buono arrives in morning. Football match Officers v Sergeants in afternoon. A Company used the battalion bath.	GBS
"	31st	10.30am	Weather Warm and bright. Breeze E/N.E. Parade Adjutants parade 7am - 7.45am Company parade 9 - 12.45 pm - Close order drill: physical exercise 2 - 4 pm Lewis Gun: Bombing: Carpentry laying out trenches and strong points. B Company used the battalion bath.	GBS

WBBatler
LIEUT COLONEL
COMMANDING 24TH BATTN MANCHESTER REGT

APPENDICES

1, 2, 3, 4 & 5.

SECRET   Copy No. 9

24th Battalion The Manchester Regiment.
OPERATION ORDER No. 17.

Appendix 1

I.   Battalion will move to-day to WELLINGTON REDOUBT – PERONNE AVENUE.

II. (a)   Parade 2-45 p.m. on Sports Ground.
    (b)   Route:- MERICOURT-TREUX-VILLE-MORLANCOURT-RED ROAD.
    (c)   Order of March:- "A", "B", Band, "C", "D".

III.   Cookers with teas and rations for July 11th will accompany Companies and return after dumping rations to "B" Echelon Transport.

IV.   Transport less above with march in rear of the Battalion as far as TREUX and thence by VILLE and MEAULTE; "A" Echelon to CITADEL, "B" Echelon to E. 30. c.

V. (a)   Packs without Greatcoats to be stacked by Companies on Sports Ground by 12 midday.
   (b)   All Officers kit and baggage to be stacked outside Officers tents and Battalion Headquarters by 2-0 p.m.

VI.   Greatcoats to be worn en banderole across right shoulder

VII.   Tools likely to be required should be packed separately on one wagon and will accompany Companies, returning to E. 30. c. after dumping.

VIII.(a) The Band will accompany Battalion as far as E. 6. d. and then join "B" Echelon Transport.
     (b) All Officers will go with their Companies but only one Captain will go out for work at a time.

IX.   Position of Battalion Headquarters will be notified later.

          Issued at 11:30 am

          Copy No. 1. O.C. "A" Coy.
                   2. O.C. "B"   "
                   3. O.C. "C"   "
                   4. O.C. "D"   "
                   5.   Quartermaster
                   6.   Transport Officer
                   7.   Headquarters
                   8.   War Diary
                   9.   War Diary.

                           G. B. DEMPSEY. Lieut. and Adjutant.
                           24th Battalion The Manchester Regiment.

SECRET　　　　　　　　　　　　　　　　　　　　　　　　Copy No. 3

24th Battalion The Manchester Regiment
OPERATION ORDER NO. 18.

Appendix 2

Reference. 1/20,000 MONTAUBAN, MARTINPUICH Sheets.

July 13th, 1916.

I. **INTENTION**

The 4th Army will attack the enemy's second line at 3-25 a.m. July 14th., in conjunction with the French to the South and Reserve Army to the North.

II. **INFORMATION**

(a) **ENEMY**

The enemy has been greatly disorganised by our attacks. He has been forced to draw on his reserves from all parts of the front, from YPRES SALIENT, VALENCIENNES and CHAMPAGNE. These troops have been thrown into the line at the shortest notice. The LEHR Regiment (3rd Guards Division) hold the line in front of BAZENTIN-LE-GRAND WOOD with the 122nd Reserve Regt. (183rd Division) on its right and the 16th Bavarian Regt. (10th Bavarian Division) on its left. Numbers of prisoners have been captured from all these units; but so much disorganisation has been caused by the hurried arrival of reinforcements, that it cannot be stated with certainty what Regiments will be met with in or behind the German second line.

(b) **OUR FORCES**

1. The front in the enemy's line allotted to 7th Division is from S. 15. c. 15.40. to the point where the road crosses the German trenches at S. 14. a. 7.3.

2. On our right the XIII Corps is attacking the front as far as S. 18. c. 2.9. On our left the 21st Division is attacking the front as far as the South-West Corner of BAZENTIN-LE-PETIT WOOD.

3. The dividing line between the 7th Division and XIII Corps will run from point S. 20. d. 90.35. - Junction of roads S. 14. d. 90.15. to East Edge of BAZENTIN-LE-GRAND WOOD to the North East Corner of the CEMETERY inclusive.

Between the 7th Division and 21st Division S. 19. Central - Road running from East Corner of MAMETZ WOOD S. 20. a. 1.8. to road Junction S. 14. b. 1.5. - Road along East of BAZENTIN-LE-PETIT WOOD to MARTINPUICH (road inclusive to 7th Division).

III. **CONSOLIDATION**

Strong points will be established at:-

(1) S. 14. b. 2.3.
(2) S. 14. b. 65.50.
(3) S. 15. a. 25.90.
(4) Machine Gun position in Wood at S. 15. a. 10.85. to cover Cross roads.
(5) A "keep" consisting of a group of houses surrounding point S. 8. d. 2.7., arrangements being made to fire up the MARTINPUICH ROAD.
(6) Northern Corner of Wood covering CEMETERY S. 8. b. 9.1.
(7) The North end of the BAZENTIN-LE-PETIT village will be prepared for an all round defence.

The 95th Coy. R.E. prepare (1), (2), (3), and (4), two Companies 24th Manchesters Regt., Pioneers (5) and (6).
The 54th Coy. R.E. (7)
The XIII Corps will establish strong points at S. 15. c. 15.40.

Sheet 2.

and at the Northern end of BAZENTIN-LE-GRAND village (S. 15a b. 0.9
The 21st Division will form a strong point at North West Corner of BAZENTIN-LE-PETIT WOOD.

IV. DETAIL

(a) "A" and "B" Companies will prepare works (5) and (6) under command of Captain Wall. Orders to move forward will be issued by Battalion H.Q.

(b) "C" Company will work on road MAMETZ - West End of QUEENS NULLAH - N.W. of CLIFF TRENCH - S.E. to E. of MAMETZ WOOD - S. 14. a. - S. 14. b. 1.5. - Cross roads S. 14. b. 1.8. through BAZENTIN-LE-PETIT on the MARTINPUICH ROAD. The first objective being to fill in shell holes etc. and make a track passable for Artillery.

This Company to move off at 4-5 a.m. July 14th.

(c) "B" Company will remain at Headquarters in reserve.

V. (a) Dump for Battalion will be at   for tools, wire, etc.

All Battalion tools not required will be dumped by Companies at WELLINGTON DUMP and collected by tool carts when Battalion Headquarters moves forward.

(b) Two days rations including emergency rations to be carried by each man.

(c) Two bombs per man to be carried.

VI. "A" and "B" Echelon transport will remain in their present positions at 71 North and E. 18. a.

VII. Divisional Headquarters will be at MINDEN POST.

VIII. Battalion Headquarters will be at WELLINGTON REDOUBT.

Issued at 5-15 p.m.

Copy No. 1.   Commanding Officer
        2.   War Diary
        3.   War Diary
        4.   2nd in Command
        5.   O.C. "A" Coy.
        6.   O.C. "B" "
        7.   O.C. "C" "
        8.   O.C. "D" "
        9.   Transport Officer
       10.   Quartermaster.

G. B. DEMPSEY. Lieut. and Adjutant.
24th Battalion The Manchester Regiment.

S E C R E T   Copy No. 8.

24th Battalion The Manchester Regiment.
OPERATION ORDER NO. 19.

Appendix 3

18th July, 1916.

Reference MARTINPUICH, MONTAUBAN – 1/20,000.

1. The 4th Army will continue the attack tomorrow at "Zero" hour.

2. The 7th Division will capture HIGH WOOD and portion of German Switch Trench West of the Wood as far as the Central North and South line through squares M.33 and S.3., with the 33rd Division operating on the left.
    The position on the right will not be attacked.

III. "B" and "C" Companies under Capt. A.Best will act under command of G.O.C., 20th Infantry Brigade, and dig a support trench from the West Corner of HIGH WOOD to S. 3. b. 2.6.
    "A" and "D" Companies will remain at WELLINGTON REDOUBT in reserve.

IV. "B" and "C" Companies with their Lewis Gun Sections will move up by platoons this evening and bivouac for the night in the vicinity of WHITE TRENCH at an hour to be arranged by their O.C. They will move off from there one hour before "Zero" to FLATIRON COPSE.

V. All tool carts to be loaded as soon as they return from working parties. "B" and "C" Companies to pack their coats on carts before marching off.
    "A" and "D" Companies to be ready to stack their coats on orders being received for them to move off.

VI. Men should carry full equipment less pack and greatcoat.
    Waterproof sheets, two bombs and two days rations including the emergency ration.

VII. Unless otherwise ordered Companies return to WELLINGTON REDOUBT on completion of work.

VIII. During operations reports showing progress of work, situation and approximate casualties (Numbers only) should be sent to Battalion Headquarters every two hours if practical.

IX. Battalion Headquarters will be at WELLINGTON REDOUBT.
    Divisional Headquarters MINDEN POST.
    There will be an advance Battalion Headquarters, established at "Zero" hour at X. 30. a. 85.35. in WHITE TRENCH Orderlies and messages to be sent there by Companies forward of this position.

    Issued at 1-30 pm

    Copy No. 1   Commanding Officer
           2   2nd. in Command
           3   O.C. "A" Coy.
           4.   O.C. "B" "
           5   O.C. "C" "
           6   O.C. "D" "
           7   Quartermaster & Transport Officer
           8   War Diary
           9   War Diary

                G. B. DEMPSEY. Lieut. and Adjutant.
                24th Bn. The Manchester Regiment.

SECRET   Copy No. 6

24th Battalion The Manchester Regiment
OPERATION ORDER NO. 20.

Appendix 4

I. The Battalion will move tomorrow to new bivouacs. Headquarters, Lewis Gun Section, "A" and "D" Companies to field West of BECORDEL.
"B" and "C" Companies next to 54th Coy. R. E. at F. 4. a. 5.3.

II. <u>Time table</u>:— Reveille 5-30 a.m. Breakfast 6-30 a.m.
All tool carts to be packed by 7-15 a.m.
"A" and "B" Companies move off 7-30 a.m.
"C" and "D" 7-45 a.m.

III. Route for all Companies MANSEL COPSE along main ALBERT-PERONNE ROAD.

IV. Major Chadwick will proceed at 7-0 a.m. to take over Bivouac area for Headquarters, "A" and "D" Companies, from Staff Captain, 91st Brigade.
"B" and "C" will detail Officer to proceed to select Bivouac area.

V. <u>Dress</u> Marching order less packs with Greatcoats en banderole

VI. <u>Transport</u> "A" Echelon will proceed with 22nd Infantry Brigade to F. 4. c. 7.4. Tool carts will accompany their Companies.

VII. Companies will report to Headquarters when new Bivouacs are occupied.

Issued at 11-15 p.m.

Copy No. 1. Commanding Officer
2. 2nd. in Command
3. O.C. "A" Coy.
4. O.C. "B" "
5. O.C. "C" "
6. O.C. "D" "
7. Transport Officer & Quartermaster
8. War Diary
9. War Diary.

18th July, 1916.   G. B. DEMPSEY. Lieut. and Adjutant.
24th Battalion The Manchester Regiment.

Appendix 5
Copy No 6

24th Manchester Regt
Operation Order No 21

1. The enemy counter attacked XIII Corps yesterday and regained possession of a portion of DELVILLE WOOD and northern portion of LONGUEVAL.

2. To relieve pressure on XIII Corps and to assist their attack, the XV Corps will tomorrow attack HIGHWOOD and roads leading to LONGUEVAL. The 7th Division will capture the road from S.11.c.5.8. to eastern corner of HIGH WOOD with the 5th Divn on their right and 33rd on the left.

3. The 7th Divn attack will be carried out by the 20th Infy Bde and one Battalion 22nd Bde. The assault will take place at 3-35 am.
Boundaries. Dividing line between 7th & 5th Divisions S.16.a.3.9. to S.10.d.8.8. Thence to road junction S.11.c.5.8.
Between 7th & 33rd Divns S.9.c.0.0. - S.10.a.5.3 junction of tracks thence by track to S.4.d.2.8. western corner of wood.

4. B & C Coys are attached to 20th Infy Bde to assist in consolidation A. & D Coys will remain in reserve.

5. Short trenches facing eastwards have already been dug near S.10.d.8.8 & at S.10.a.5.5.

2

6. Capt A Best will command B & C Coys and take his orders from GOC 20° Inf. Bde
Tool carts of B & C Coys will remain in their present position under Capt Robertson
Reports of progress of work and situation and numbers of casualties will be sent if possible every two hours to Bn HQ.

7. Dress etc as in Operation Order no 20 df 18/7/16

8. Divn HQ at MINDEN POST
Bn HQ at E 12 b 2.2 west of BECORDEL

Issued at 9-15pm
19/7/16

Copies to all concerned

GB Dempsey
Lt + Adjt

7th Divisional Troops.

1/24th BATTALION

MANCHESTER REGIMENT (Pioneers)

AUGUST 1 9 1 6

Army Form C. 2118.

24TH BN THE MANCHESTER REGT
Vol 10

WAR DIARY
INTELLIGENCE SUMMARY

(Erase heading not required.)

24TH/13N MANCHESTER REGIMENT

VOLUME X   AUGUST 1916

Place	Date	Hour	Summary of Events and Information	Remarks and references to Appendices
ST VAST EN CHAUSSÉE	1st	10 pm	**Weather** Warm and Bright: wind light East.	
			Parades No early parade. A & D Companies paraded at 6 am and marched to Roman Camp near LA CHAUSSÉE and there filled in trenches. 2400 yds of trenches filled in by 248 O.R. in 7 hours.	(Map Ref AMIENS Sheet 17)
			B & C Companies paraded at 6 am and marched to STATION POULAINVILLE and there filled in trenches. 2444 OR. 5 hours.	
			The Alarm The Fire Alarm was blown at 8·31 pm. It is in the Bomb Billet. The following were the times:—	GBS
			Bugle Call 8·31 pm	
			Fire Engine pumping 8·36 pm	
			The Picket in position 8·39 pm	
	2nd	10 pm	**Weather** Fine and warm, wind NE by E	
			Parades 7 – 7·45 am Cyclists Parade	
			9 – 12·45 pm Company Parades	
			2 – ? Classes in Musketry, Blacksmith work, Rocket work &c	GBS

Place	Date	Hour		Summary of Events and Information	Remarks and references to Appendices
B	3rd	10 p.m	Weather	Fine and warm. Wind light Easterly	Y & S
			Work	H Companies proceeded to ROMAN CAMP, LA CHAUSSÉE to further trenches. 3400 yards filled in by 480 O Trawlers 7 hours.	
	4th	10 p.m	Weather	Fine and warm in the morning. Dull and inclined to rain in early afternoon. Wind light N.N.W	
			Inspection	The Commander of the 4th Army (Sir H Rawlinson) inspected Nos 2, 3 and 9 Companies at 11.30 am. The two Companies were attached to 91st Brigade for the occasion. The G.O.C thanked the troops for their work during the recent offensive and read out the record of each battalion. Concerning the 24th Bn. Manchester R he said they had done excellent work throughout and at BAZENTIN-LE-PETIT, after having established itself, held it against the repeated counter attacks of the enemy on the 14th July.	

Army Form C. 2118.

WAR DIARY
or
INTELLIGENCE SUMMARY
(Erase heading not required.)

Instructions regarding War Diaries and Intelligence Summaries are contained in F. S. Regs., Part II. and the Staff Manual respectively. Title Pages will be prepared in manuscript.

Place	Date	Hour	Summary of Events and Information	Remarks and references to Appendices
ST VAST	4th	10pm	Move. A & B Companies moved to E.12 (Ref: map ALBERT 1/40,000) at 2pm by motor buses. Transport followed by road at 5pm. (Operation order no 22 attached) Headquarters, C & D Companies remained in ST VAST. 2nd in Command. – Field Ambulance H.Q.	G.S. Appendix I
-"-	5th	10pm	Weather. Cooler and dull in the morning. Baths. C & D Company with headquarters attended the baths at ACQUIGNY.	G.P.S.
-"-	6th	10pm	Weather. Warm and bright. Wind light N.W. Parade. Church parade. Guard for C of England. 10-15am Non Conformist. Honours. Military Cross awarded K. 2/Lt W. SOWARD. 11th E. Surrey Regt (atta 7th Manchester) D.C.M. 14729 Pte J. HUMPHRIES. 14464 Sergt C.A. BURMAN	G.P.S.

WAR DIARY
or
INTELLIGENCE SUMMARY

Army Form C. 2118.

Place	Date	Hour	Summary of Events and Information	Remarks and references to Appendices
ST VAST	7th	10 pm	A & B Companies Work done. 7½ hours making fire trench out of trench running from DANTZIG ALLEY to BRIGHT ALLEY to NE face of MAMETZ and wiring same with low wire. Deepening the C.T. from trench to boys in trench running to BUNNY TROTCH to village.	Refmt Montauban GBS
—	8th	10am	Weather — looks but fine; wind fresh N.E. Parade — Company parades in the morning. Special classes in the afternoon. Work — A and B Companies completed front and support line NE of MAMETZ including 5 M.G. emplacements. Battalion acted as Fatigue party partly.	GBS
			Warmer. Wind fresh E.N.E. Company Parade. 9 – 12.45 p.m. {Arms Drill, Company training Coy, Physical Exercises Classes 2 – 4 p.m. {Bricklaying, Pontoon making, Carpentry &c	GBS
			Work A and B Coys, 3 Platoons prepare defence of the N face of MAMETZ. One platoon carrying party R.E.	

WAR DIARY
or
INTELLIGENCE SUMMARY

Army Form C. 2118.

(Erase heading not required.)

Place	Date	Hour	Summary of Events and Information	Remarks and references to Appendices
ST VAST	9th	10am	Weather. Wind light E. Very warm. Parade. Adjutants parade 7am. Company parades 9-12.45pm, 2-4pm. Officers and Recruits.	
			Boxing competitions were held during the evening. Semifinal and finals left to be fought on the 10th.	Yes
-"-	10th	10pm	Weather. Wind NNW. Light rain from 6am-11am, fine for remainder of day. Work. C Coy } worked 2½ hours filling 2,600 yds trench 3' x 3½' D " } near Roman Camp La Chaussée. B " } A on the G.R.	A and B Companies continued defence of M. trees MMETZ. Preparation carrying party for R.E.
-"-	11th	10p	Weather. Slight rain in early morning. Wind light N.W. Fine later in the day. Bath. C & D Companies went to bath at VAUX. Work. A and B Companies on the G.R.	

WAR DIARY
or
INTELLIGENCE SUMMARY
(Erase heading not required.)

Army Form C. 2118.

Place	Date	Hour	Summary of Events and Information	Remarks and references to Appendices
RIBEMONT	12th	10pm	Weather. Heavy mist in morning. Bright and warm during the day. Wind light N.E. Changing to N + N.W in evening. Rain during night 12th/13th.	
			News. None	
			Transport of C + D Coys Headquarters has moved onwards to RIBEMONT via QUERRIEU & PONT NOYELLES. Headquarters, C + D Coys left ST VAST at 5.30am and entrained at VIGNACOURT at 9.15am. Route – CANAPLES, FLIXECOURT, CONTÉ, PICQUIGNY, AMIENS, MÉRICOURT, Detrained MÉRICOURT at 2.45pm and marched to RIBEMONT. (Operation Order attached)	Railway AMIENS 17 GBS Appendix II
			Work. A and B Companies worked 9am to 3.30pm.	
-do-	13th	10pm	Weather. Still in the morning. Fine and warm in the afternoon. Wind 17/7/14.	
			Parades. Church parade at 10.30 am.	
			Work. A and B Companies preparing N and E faces of MAMETZ and widening C.T. on S.E face. 1 Platoon levelling gully for RE. Work hours 9 – 3.30 pm	A Coy on the E face of MAMETZ. B Coy on the N face. GBS

Army Form C. 2118.

WAR DIARY
or
INTELLIGENCE SUMMARY

(Erase heading not required.)

Place	Date	Hour	Summary of Events and Information	Remarks and references to Appendices
RIBEMONT	14th	10pm	Weather. Wind from N.N.W. Rain at midday and from 5 - 6.15 pm. Parades. B and D Companies carried out Company training in the village area. The men of both Companies went to the river to bathe in the afternoon. A and B Companies 7 platoons worked on the defences of the N. face of MAMETZ. One platoon worked on the defence of the E face of MAMETZ.	GoS
—do—	15th	10pm	Weather. Showery: Wind N.N.W. Parades. Company parades in the morning. Baths at HEILLY in the afternoon.	GoS Appendix III
—do—	16th	10pm	Weather. Wind from H.N.W. Thus during day. Heavy rain from 9pm. Work. C and D Companies moved to E 12 C.9.7 (Ref) ALBERT Combined Sheet at 5pm. Battalion HQ. unmoved at RIBEMONT. Operation Order No 24 attached. A and B Companies. Prepared defence of E face of MAMETZ and continued work on N. face. Do. Watson carried out RE 12 or collected working parties 9 - 13. 30 pm.	GoS

Army Form C. 2118.

WAR DIARY
or
INTELLIGENCE SUMMARY
(Erase heading not required.)

Instructions regarding War Diaries and Intelligence Summaries are contained in F. S. Regs., Part II. and the Staff Manual respectively. Title Pages will be prepared in manuscript.

Place	Date	Hour	Summary of Events and Information	Remarks and references to Appendices
HQ RIBEMONT A Company BECORDEL E.12.c.9.7.	17th	10pm	Weather Warm Westerly. Rain in the afternoon and evening. Work in MAMETZ. A Company No 1 platoon. Butting reserve trench ; 1 M.G. emplacement and small communication trench. No 2 platoon Constructing 2 dug outs. No 3 platoon Constructing dug out and communication trench. No 4 platoon Constructing 3 dugouts ; 2 M.G. emplacements Connecting up fire line. B Company No 5, 6 and 7 platoons opening up communication trenches in MAMETZ. N° 8 platoon carrying for R.E. C Company Nos 9, 10 and 11 platoons deepening and widening communication trench. No 12 platoon resting over. D Company Carrying loads. Deepening and cleaning trenches. No 13, 14, 15 and 16 platoons.	GBS
"	18th	10pm	Weather Warm N.N.W. Rain in morning and at night, fine in the afternoon. Work MAMETZ A Coy work to 17th B Coy " " C Coy " " Constructing FRITZ TRENCH (Near MONTAUBAN) 2/Lt A.G. MacGowan rejoined	GBS

2449 Wt. W14957/M90 750,000 1/16 J.B.C. & A. Forms/C.2118/12. 1/20,000

Army Form C. 2118.

WAR DIARY
or
INTELLIGENCE SUMMARY
(Erase heading not required.)

Instructions regarding War Diaries and Intelligence Summaries are contained in F. S. Regs., Part II. and the Staff Manual respectively. Title Pages will be prepared in manuscript.

Place	Date	Hour	Summary of Events and Information	Remarks and references to Appendices
HQ at RIBEMONT & Companies at E.12.c.9.7	19th	10pm	Weather. Rain in the morning. Fine in the afternoon. Wind fresh N.N.W. Commission. R.Q.M.S. POTTER. J. to 1044444 Proceeded to Western Command to take over Quartermaster's duties with 15th Liverpool Regt. Work. Work from 8pm to 3 am:— A Company. Constructing dug outs and L.G. emplacements, Communication trenches and connecting up shaft for Kircheo MAMETZ. B Company. Opening up Communication trenches in MAMETZ. One platoon wiring to NE face of MAMETZ. One platoon demolishing houses and carrying wire for R.E. C Company. Wiring in FRITZ TRENCH and BRIGHT ALLEY, MAMETZ. D Company. Improving FRITZ TRENCH. Dug outs commenced.	[sig]
"	20th	10am	Weather. Fine. Wind N.W. Fresh. Parade. Divine Service held at 10.30 am for C.of E. and 10.15 am for Roman Catholic. Work. Work was suspended in MAMETZ.	[sig]

WAR DIARY
or
INTELLIGENCE SUMMARY

(Erase heading not required.)

Army Form C. 2118.

Place	Date	Hour	Summary of Events and Information	Remarks and references to Appendices
—	21st	10pm	Weather. Warm. Fine. Wind N.N.W. light breeze.	
			Work. A Coy Constructing dug outs. L.G. emplacement H. side of MAMETZ.	
			B Coy Opening communication trench in MAMETZ	
			2 Platoon wiring	
			1 Platoon Clearing ground and carrying for R.E.	
			1 Platoon	
			C Coy Wiring. Revering trenches. Opening communication trenches	
			D Coy Trenching FRITZ TRENCH. Deepening and cutting bombing	
			Stoplits in CLIFF TRENCH and RAILWAY ALLEY.	
		Reinforcements	15 O.R. returned from base.	
—„—	22nd	10pm	Weather. Fine and warm. Light N.N.E breeze.	
		Work	A and B Company went to the bath ville.	
			C Company revised FRITZ TRENCH and CLIFF TRENCH. L.G. emplacement	
			and dug out constructed. Number 145 O.R. 7½ hours	
			B Company 1 Platoon Conducted bombing stop CLIFF TRENCH	
			3 Platoons revised RAILWAY TRENCH.	

WAR DIARY
or
INTELLIGENCE SUMMARY

Army Form C. 2118.

Place	Date	Hour	Summary of Events and Information	Remarks and references to Appendices
—	23rd	10hr	Weather. Fine and warm wind N. Slight rain in the evening. Working Parties. A Coy. Working in M.G. emplacement and Communication trenches. 2 Platoons opening Communication trenches in MAMETZ. 1 Platoon wiring 1 platoon clearing wreckage and carrying wire for R.E. C " Turning dug-out, revetting. Constructing M.G. emplacements. his trenches revived. D " Digging new trench near FRICOURT - MAMETZ Ry. and wiring. part of same.	
—	24th	15hr	Weather. Fine wind light N.N.E. Work. Companies rested. No work was done.	
—	25th	10hr	Weather. Fine and warm wind light N. Battalion Headquarters moved to E.12.c.9.7 (Map ALBERT Ovillers Sheet) B & C Companies left camp to dig trench (T.13.c. Map GUILLEMONT 1/20000) owing to relief of Battalion in the line not being completed, no work was done on the proposed advanced trench.	Appendix IV

Army Form C. 2118.

WAR DIARY
or
INTELLIGENCE SUMMARY

(Erase heading not required.)

Instructions regarding War Diaries and Intelligence Summaries are contained in F. S. Regs., Part II. and the Staff Manual respectively. Title Pages will be prepared in manuscript.

Place	Date	Hour	Summary of Events and Information	Remarks and references to Appendices
FRICOURT WOOD (Ref Map MONTAUBAN)	26th	10pm	Weather — Fine in the morning and afternoon. Heavy rain in evening and at night. Wind Sth. N.W.	
			Operation Order No 35 attached. The Battalion moved to FRICOURT WOOD II.	
			Working Party — A & B Companies left camp at 6pm to dig battle trench at T.13.c. West of GUITCH-L. Owing again to relief not being complete a working party could not be supplied by 22nd R.de., and no work was done.	
			Casualties — 3 men wounded in A Coy.	
			Reinforcements — 2/Lt J.P. RUSSEL rejoined	
"	27th	10pm	Weather — Generally dull with heavy rain showers. Wind N.N.	
			Work — B and C Companies left camp at 4.30 pm to dig trench at T.13.C. (Ref map GUILLEMONT 1/20,000) No work was done by D Coy. 2 Platoons C Company completed 120 yds of new trench. There was no shelling on the site of the digging, but heavy shelling occurred while the Companies were moving up.	
			Casualties — Officers nil. Other Ranks 2 killed 10 wounded 1 missing (Pvt S. Cheetham C Coy) No 14568	

WAR DIARY
or
INTELLIGENCE SUMMARY

Army Form C. 2118.

Place	Date	Hour		Summary of Events and Information	Remarks and references to Appendices
FRICOURT WOOD	28th	10am	Weather	Heavy rain showers in the morning. Bright intervals in the afternoon. Wind fresh W.N.W.	
			Work	A and D Companies left camp at 5pm for work on new trench. The work was completed, and the Companies arrived in camp 7am (29th). There was no shelling on the site of the digging. 1st Royal Welch Fusiliers provided the covering party.	Yes
			Casualties	Officers nil. Other ranks 3 slightly wounded; all remaining at duty	
—	29th	10pm	Weather	Rain throughout day. Wind light N.N.W.	
			Work	Companies rested during the day	
			Operation	Operation (on the trench No 26) postponed 48 hours.	Gas Appendix V
—	30th	10pm	Weather	Dull and squally with heavy rain	
			Work	B & C Companies left camp at 11am to dig Communication trench from YORK ALLEY through S.18.d. 30.35. to a point 80x east of the Sunken Road (Map GUILLEMONT 1/20,000) about 500 yds of trench 4'6"deep dug.	
			Casualties	One man wounded	

WAR DIARY
INTELLIGENCE SUMMARY

(Erase heading not required.)

Army Form C. 2118.

Place	Date	Hour	Summary of Events and Information	Remarks and references to Appendices
—	30th	10 pm	**Work (continued)** "D" Company left camp at 5.30 pm to continue the communication trench eastwards to T.13 c Central (They not GUILLEMONT 1/20,000). There was considerable shelling by the enemy in reply to a heavy bombardment by our artillery.	(95)
			Casualties Officer nil. Other ranks one killed, 3 wounded. No 15370 Pte J. Lee R.T.Coy reported missing. Two prisoners of the 76th R.I.R taken by A Coy.	
—	31st	10 pm	**Weather** Fine and much warmer. **Work** "B" Company left camp at 5.30 pm to work on GINCHY AVENUE etc. The enemy had counter-attacked in this sector in the afternoon and had gained a footing in our trenches. The Company was attached to 91st Inf Bde to carry up bombs and S.A.A. The other work was done.	(9Bs)
			Operations Postponed until further notice.	
			Reported missing. Pte Lee of R. Coy, reported missing, returned.	Appendix VI

MMButter Lieut Colonel
Commanding 24 Manchester Regt (Pioneers)

Appendix I

SECRET   Copy No. 7

24th Battalion The Manchester Regiment
OPERATION ORDER No. 22.

Reference map, Sheet 62.D. N.E. & AMIENS 17.

1.   "A" and "B" Companies will proceed by bus today at 2 p.m. to E.12 and will come under the orders of the C.E. XV Corps MAMETZ.
       Bivouac area to be selected by O.C. Detachment.

2.   Parade outside Headquarters 1-15 p.m.
       DRESS - Full marching order.

3.   Rations for tomorrow and cooking utensils will be carried. The Supply Train will deliver rations for 6th. at E.12 on evening of the 5th.

4.   Transport under Capt. Robertson will march at 5 p.m. this evening via POULAINVILLE & ALLONVILLE to PONT-NOYELLES, where they will report to Town Major for billets for the night.
       The march will be continued to E.12 on 6th via DERNACOURT.

       Issued at 1-10 p.m.

               Copy No. 1.   O.C. "A" Coy.
                       2   O.C. "B" "
                       3.   O.C. "C" "
                       4.   O.C. "D" "
                       5.   T.O. & Q.M.
                       6.   Capt. Robertson.
                       7.   War Diary
                       8.   War Diary.

4/8/16   G. B. DEMPSEY. Lieut. and Adjutant.
                                 24th Battalion The Manchester Regiment.

Appendix II

SECRET   Copy No. 5

24th Battalion The Manchester Regiment
OPERATION ORDER NO. 23.

REFERENCE AMIENS SHEET 17.

1. The Battalion, less two Companies, will move by train tomorrow the 12th August.
   Train leaves VIGNACOURT 7-30 a.m., arrives MERICOURT 11-30 a.m.   Billets will be at RIBEMONT.

2. Reveille tomorrow will be at 3-30 a.m. Breakfast 4-15 am Parade in MOIR STREET at 5-15 a.m.
   ORDER OF MARCH:- Headquarters, "C" and "D" Companies.
   The head of the column will be at the end house on the right of the Street.   DRESS:- Full marching order.
   MOVE OFF at 5-30 a.m.

3. Dixies will be carried to the station.

4. 2/Lieut. H.E.Braine will report at VIGNACOURT STATION at 6-30 a.m. on the 12th and will ascertain the entraining point and mark the compartments allotted.

   Issued at 5-15 p.m.

   Copy No. 1.   O.C. "C" Coy.
            2.   O.C. "D" "
            3.   2/Lieut. Braine
            4.   Headquarters
            5.   War Diary
            6.   War Diary.

                          G. B. DEMPSEY. Lieut. and Adjutant.
   11-8-16   24th Battalion The Manchester Regiment.

Appendix III

S.E.C.R.E.T.   Copy No. 6

24th Battalion The Manchester Regiment.
OPERATION ORDER NO. 24.

REFERENCE ALBERT Combined Sheet.

1. "C" and "D" Companies will proceed to E. 12. c. 9.7. to-morrow the 16th instant.

2. Parade on Church Square 4-45 p.m. Move off 5 p.m.
ORDER OF MARCH:- "C", "D". Fifty yards interval will be kept between these two Companies.
ROUTE:- BUIRE – DERNANCOURT – MIN du VIVIER – ALBERT – MEAULTE ROAD – thence along track by Railway to E. 12. c. 9.7.

3. Transport consisting of one tool wagon per Company, Canteen Cart and one Limber will proceed at 3 p.m. under orders of Transport Officer. Field Kitchens will follow the two Companies. Officers kits are to be loaded on the Limber which will be in the Church Square at 2 p.m.

4. Forward Headquarters will be at E. 12. c. 9.7.
Battalion Headquarters will remain at RIBEMONT.
Reports and returns will be rendered through Forward H.Q

Issued at 9-10 p.m.

Copy No. 1.   O.C. "C" Coy.
         2.   O.C. "D" "
         3.   Quartermaster
         4.   O.C. Detachment,
         5.   2nd in Command.
         6.   War Diary.
         7.   War Diary.

G. B. DEMPSEY. Lieut. and Adjutant.
15-8-16   24th Battalion The Manchester Regiment.

Appendix IV

S.E.C.R.E.T.   Copy No. 6

24th Battalion The Manchester Regiment
OPERATION ORDER NO. 25.

REFERENCE ALBERT COMBINED SHEET.   25th August, 1916.

1. "A" and "D" Companies with Tool Wagons and Cookers will move off at 10 a.m. to-morrow the 26th instant to FRICOURT WOOD. Tools are to be dumped and wagons returned together with the horses of Cookers to Transport.

2. Headquarters, "B" and "C" Companies, Tool Carts and Cookers, to move off at 3 p.m. "A" and "D" Tool Carts to be used to take up spare kit. Tool Carts and horses of Cookers to return to Transport.

3. Officers kits will not be taken up. The Quartermaster will arrange for Train Baggage Wagons for kits.

4. Transport will move to E. 12. c. at an hour to be arranged by Transport Officer.

5. Major Chadwick will ascertain the position for bivouacs and allot same to Companies, etc. The Transport Officer will arrange the supply of water.

6. Lewis Guns will move with Handcarts at the same time as their Companies. Band will remain with Transport.

Issued at 10-45 p.m.

Copy No. 1.   O.C. "A" Coy.
         2.   O.C. "B" "
         3.   O.C. "C" "
         4.   O.C. "D"
         5.   Quartermaster
         6.   War Diary
         7.   War Diary.

G. B. DEMPSEY. Lieut. and Adjutant.
24th Battalion The Manchester Regiment.

Appendix V

SECRET

Copy No. 7.

24th Battalion The Manchester Regiment
OPERATION ORDER NO. 26.

29th August, 1916.

REFERENCE GUILLEMONT, Sheet 1/20,000

1. INFORMATION

    The Fourth Army and French on our right are renewing the attack at "Zero" hour on August 30th.
    "Zero" hour will be at 12-55 p.m.

2. INTENTION

    The 7th Division objective is:-
    (a) The village of GINCHY
    (b) The line of the road as far N. as the Junction of PINT TRENCH and ALE ALLEY (T. 7. d. 4.0.)
    (c) ALE ALLEY to its junction with BEER TRENCH.
    The 20th Division is attacking the village of GUILLEMONT.

3. OBJECTIVE

    The 22nd Infantry Brigade are carrying out the attack Their two objectives are:-
    First:- PINT TRENCH and the village of GINCHY
    Second:- The trench running from T. 20. a. 1.3., E. of GINCHY To T. 14. a. 4.3.

4. CONSOLIDATION

    Strong points are being established at:-
    I.   T. 20. a. 1.6.
    II. T. 14. c. 5.4.
    III. Northern Edge of Trench T. 14. a. 4. 3.
    IV. Outside N.E. Corner of ORCHARD T. 13. b. 9.4.
    V.   T. 7. d. 3.2.
    VI. T. 7. d. 4.0.

    Keeps at:-
    I. T. 13. b. 8.0.
    II. T. 13. d. 8.5.

V. RESERVE

    The Battalion will remain in Reserve at FRICOURT WOOD.

VI. REPORTS

    Divisional Headquarters FRICOURT CHATEAU.
    Battalion Headquarters, FRICOURT WOOD.

    Issued at 12-35 p.m.

    Copy No. 1. O.C. "A" Coy.
           2. O.C. "B" "
           3. O.C. "C" "
           4. O.C. "D" "
           5. Quartermaster
           6. War diary
           7. War Diary.

    G. B. DEMPSEY. Lieut. and Adjutant.
    24th Battalion Manchester Regiment.

Appendix VI

S.E.C.R.E.T.   Copy No. 8

24th Battalion The Manchester Regiment
OPERATION ORDER NO. 27.

31st August, 1916.

REFERENCE MAP :- LONGUEVAL 57 c S.W.3. Edition E 1/10,000.

I.   Operations are postponed until further notice.

II. On the day of the attack the 24th Manchester Regiment has been ordered to assemble in the vicinity of MONTAUBAN, and when 7th Divisional Objective has been reached to prolong GINCHY AVENUE from PORTER TRENCH at T.13.c.55.40 to German Trench running from T.20.a.1.6. to T.14.a.40.25. which will then be our front line.

III. "A" Company will work from PORTER TRENCH to German Support Trench due EAST at T.13.d.10.45. inclusive.
     "C" Company from this point to NORTH Corner of Farm building at T.13.d.55.40. inclusive.
     "B" Company from this point to the GINCHY – MAUREPAS Road at T.13.d.95.40. inclusive.
     "D" Company from this point to nearest point of front line.

IV. The following method will be adopted to lay out trench.
     On orders being given to move out each Company will send forward 1 Officer and a small party with tapes and pickets.
     "D" and "B" will go out together and lay out their tasks from T.13.d.95.40. "D" to the EAST and "B" to the WEST.
     "A" and "C" will lay out their tasks from T.13.d.10.45. "C" to the EAST and "A" to the WEST.
     "B" and "C" Companies must be careful to meet at their junction at NORTH Corner of Farm T.13.d.55.40.
     Companies will move off 15 minutes after laying out parties in the order "D", "B", "C", "A".
     A winding trench will be dug 5 feet deep by 3 feet wide.
     On completion of tasks Companies will return to FRICOURT WOOD, reporting completion of work at report centre.

V.   Position of Report Centre will be notified later.

Issued at 4-30 pm

Copy No. 1.   O.C. "A" Coy
         2.   O.C. "B" "
         3.   O.C. "C" "
         4.   O.C. "D" "
         5.   C.R.E.
         6.   2nd in Command
         7.   War Diary
         8.   War Diary.

G. B. DEMPSEY. Lieut. and Adjutant.
24th Battalion The Manchester Regiment.

SECRET

WAR DIARY OF

24TH MANCHESTER RGT

VOLUME XI SEPT 1916

Army Form C. 2118.

WAR DIARY
or
INTELLIGENCE SUMMARY

(Erase heading not required.) **24TH In THE MANCHESTER REGT.**

Instructions regarding War Diaries and Intelligence Summaries are contained in F. S. Regs., Part II. and the Staff Manual respectively. Title Pages will be prepared in manuscript.

VOLUME XI SEPTEMBER 1916

Place	Date	Hour	Summary of Events and Information	Remarks and references to Appendices
FRICOURT WOOD. Ref Map ALBERT. Bombarded Street and MONTAUBAN 1/20,000	1st	10 pm	Weather Fine and warm. Wind light westerly. Work A and B Coys left camp 5-20 pm to work on redoubt line PORTER TRENCH C Company to work in GINCHY AVENUE. D Company rested. Casualties Killed 3 other ranks. Wounded 3rd. Missing 3. 15 wounded remained at duty; LIEUT E TKOD slightly wounded, remaining at duty. 2nd LT. T. L. SWAIN evacuated to C.C.S. suffering from sen trouble — the result of shell shock	1 C.S. Appendix I
	2nd	10.15 pm	Weather Dull and still fine. Wind N.N.W. Work Companies rested.	Yes
	3rd and 4th		Weather Fine in morning dull with slight rain in afternoon. Operations Ref Operation Orders 28. The 7th Division attacked GUINCHY and captured it. GUILLEMONT was also taken. Coincid attacked GUINCHY and the situation was observed as some of our troops and some of the enemy were in GUINCHY at the same time. The 24 MANCHESTERS meanwhile awaited	Appendix II

Army Form C. 2118.

WAR DIARY
or
INTELLIGENCE SUMMARY

(Erase heading not required.)

Instructions regarding War Diaries and Intelligence Summaries are contained in F. S. Regs., Part II. and the Staff Manual respectively. Title Pages will be prepared in manuscript.

Place	Date	Hour	Summary of Events and Information	Remarks and references to Appendices
	3rd to 4th		The order to move up to GUINCHY from their place of assembly (MONTAUBAN ALLEY nr. MONTAUBAN 1/20000) in the defence trenches of MONTAUBAN. As no definite knowledge could be gleaned concerning the situation in GUINCHY the 24th MANCHESTERS were ordered to return to Camp to FRICOURT WOOD. Arriving in Camp 2.30 a.m. on the 4th. Casualties Nil. In the afternoon of the 4th, the 20th Infy Bde of the 7th Division, was ordered to attack the portion of GUINCHY held by the enemy and so assist the troops of the 22nd Bde in GUINCHY. The 2/Manchesters remained in FRICOURT WOOD in Reserve.	GBS GBS
—	5th	10 p.m.	Weather fine; wind light northerly. Work — The Companies rested	GBS
—	6th to 7th		Weather fine. Wind N. light. Work. A, B (also 2 Companies) C & D left Camp at 4.45 p.m. for work on GINCHY AVENUE. Working hours 11-40 p.m. & 4-15 a.m. Trench from YORK ALLEY to DIAGONAL TRENCH cleared and deepened 4'6"5"6"	Appendix III

WAR DIARY
or
INTELLIGENCE SUMMARY

Army Form C. 2118.

(Erase heading not required.)

Place	Date	Hour	Summary of Events and Information	Remarks and references to Appendices
	6th to 7th	10pm	DIAGONAL TRENCH to Z Z ALLEY cleared and deepened 30yds. Z.Z ALLEY to STOUT TRENCH was entirely obliterated by shell fire. 320yds dug. 2 Platoons B Company left camp at 4.30 pm as carrying party for R.E. Worked from 1am to 3.30 am (7th) Casualties. Officers nil. Other Ranks killed 2 wounded 7 (pioneering at duty)	GS7
	8th	10pm	Weather fine and bright. Wind N changing N.E in afternoon. Work. One Company worked 7½ hours digging telephone trench from POMMIERS REDOUBT to LONGUEVAL. 100 yds dug. Specification Trench to be 6' deep. Bde HQ at S.16.d.6.1. to be A.1.d.5.8 S.22.L.05.4.0 Shafts at A.2.a.3.7.6 A.2.b.2.7.6 A.2.b.95.95 Last dug outs at S.27.c.7.9 S.27.c.15.15. S.27.b.20.75 S.27.b.25.35. 21.d.8.1 22.c.5.6. Trench to be 6" deep from S.27.b.25.35 to be 7'.6" deep.	GSA

2449 Wt. W14957/Mg0 750,000 1/16 J.B.G. & A. Forms/C.2118/12.

WAR DIARY
or
INTELLIGENCE SUMMARY

(Erase heading not required.)

Army Form C. 2118.

Place	Date	Hour	Summary of Events and Information	Remarks and references to Appendices
—	9th	10pm	Weather: Fine and warm. Breezy, light easterly. Working Parties: Four companies left camp at 5am for work on cable trench. Trench continued towards LONGUEVAL 16 S 27.b. 25.35. Casualties: Nil.	Yes
—	10th	10pm	Weather: Wind light; cooling. Dull in morning. Bright in afternoon. Working Parties: A Coy dug 195 yds trench 7'6" deep hours 5am 3pm B " " 220 " " " 6:30 – 4pm " " 35 " " 3 ft deep C " " 170 " " 7'6" " 5am to 3pm " " 70 " " 6' deep " " 75 " " 7'6" D Coy " " 270 " " 7'6" 5am to 5pm Casualties: Officers nil. Other ranks: wounded – one (shell).	Yes

Army Form C. 2118.

WAR DIARY
or
INTELLIGENCE SUMMARY
(Erase heading not required.)

Place	Date	Hour	Summary of Events and Information	Remarks and references to Appendices
— " —	11th	10pm	Weather Fine. Wind light easterly. Working Parties Four companies left camp at 5am (B Coy left at 4.30pm) for work on the aid trench. Trench completed. Casualties Officers, nil. Other ranks one (Shell) wounded	Gas Appendix N/1
FRICOURT WOOD ALBERT OISEMONT HALLENCOURT	12th	10pm	Weather Fine. Occasional light showers. Wind C/17.E. Move The battalion less transport moved by train from ALBERT to #H OISEMONT by and thence by road to HALLENCOURT. Time Table — Left camp FRICOURT WOOD 6.15am Entrained ALBERT 8.30am Arrived OISEMONT 6.30pm HALLENCOURT 9pm Transport moved by road according to Operation order no 29 attached moving at HALLENCOURT at 1pm on 14.15.	YBS
HALLENCOURT (SOMME)	13th	10pm	Weather Fine and warm. Rain at night. Wind light N.E. Parade Company parades and inspection held.	G/35

Army Form C. 2118.

WAR DIARY
or
INTELLIGENCE SUMMARY
(Erase heading not required.)

Place	Date	Hour	Summary of Events and Information	Remarks and references to Appendices
HALLENCOURT	14th	10pm	Weather Parade Fine but cooler wind N.E. light C.O's inspection at 11.30 a.m. The remainder of the day Companies were at the disposal of Company Commanders.	Appx A
—	15th	10pm	Weather Parades Fine; wind, fresh, westerly 9am Adjutants Parade Breakfast 7-45am Company Parade 9am to 12.30pm 2 to 3pm Classes in Signalling; Lewis gun etc 2 - 3 pm Lecture by Major Chadwick 3-15 to 3-45 pm	Appx B
—	16	10pm	Weather Parades Mess Fine warmer; wind Easterly; light breeze 7 - 7.45 am Adjutants Parade 9am - 12.30 pm Company Parade. The afternoon was devoted to sports. Notification received that the 7th Bn (attached to 2nd Machine Gun as a unit) will proceed to 2nd Army Area. Time and date of move to be notified later.	Appendix V Appx C

WAR DIARY or INTELLIGENCE SUMMARY

Army Form C. 2118.

(Erase heading not required.)

Place	Date	Hour	Summary of Events and Information	Remarks and references to Appendices
HALLENCOURT	17th	12pm	Weather fine. Wind S. light breeze. Rain just before midnight. None. Operation Order no 30 & 31 (Appendix VI) The Transport and Loading party moved off from HALLENCOURT to LONGPRE via WANEL at 11 p.m. The roads were in good condition	Appendix VI Yes
HALLENCOURT – LONGPRE – BAILLEUL – METEREN – ROUGE-CROIX	18th	12pm	Weather Wet. Wind S.W. Continuous fine rain. None. The battalion less transport and loading party moved off from HALLENCOURT at 12.20 a.m. and marched to LONGPRE via WANEL. Departed 5 a.m. Arrived LONGPRE STATION 1 a.m. Route ABBEVILLE – ETAPLES – BOULOGNE – CALAIS – ST OMER – HAZEBROUCK to BAILLEUL where the battalion detrained and moved off at 4.30 p.m. to billeting area at ROUGE-CROIX. Route ROUGE-CROIX – COURTE-CROIX – METEREN – CAESTRE RD. Headquarters established on CAESTRE RD at 8 p.m.	Yes
—	19th	10pm	Weather Wind S.W. Heavy showers. Parades. Ceremonial Inspection parades were held.	Yes Appendix VII

WAR DIARY
or
INTELLIGENCE SUMMARY

(Erase heading not required.)

Army Form C. 2118.

Place	Date	Hour	Summary of Events and Information	Remarks and references to Appendices
ROUGE CROIX	20th	10 pm	Weather: Rain at intervals. Boots "wear" freely N.N.E. Wind light N.N.E. Operation Order No 32. (Appendix VII) B and D Coys moved by motor bus at 11.30 am from ROUGE-CROIX to 29. d. 8. 6. (Ref. Sheet 28 S.W.) B Coy and remainder of D moved to same place by road to take over Pioneer work from 5th Bn. S.H.B.	Appendix VII
		None	1 officer and 50 other Ranks II Coy making wire dug out with 1st A.T. Coy. R.E. near PLOEGSTEERT WOOD II	Gas
ROUGE-CROIX to OOSTHOVE FARM	21st	10am	Weather: Fine. Wind light N.N.E. The battalion less B and D Coys moved by road to OOSTHOVE FARM. (Sheet 36 N.W.) Move off 9.30 am. Arrived in billets at farm 3.30 pm. Roads mostly pavé and very dusty. Route Road S of BAILLEUL — Mann BAILLEUL — ARMENTIERES Rd. — PONT D'ACHELLES — LA RUE du SAC. — LE DON — OOSTHOVE FARM. (Sheet 28 S.W. and 36 N.W.) OOSTHOVE FARM provided very good billets, comfortable all convenience	Appendix VIII
		None		Gas

Army Form C. 2118.

WAR DIARY
or
INTELLIGENCE SUMMARY

(Erase heading not required.)

Place	Date	Hour	Summary of Events and Information	Remarks and references to Appendices
OOSTHOVE FARM Sheet 36 NW B.11.d.	22nd	10pm	Weather Fine wind E.N.E. Work B + D Coys supplied 100 men 9am ⎫ for work on mine dug outs 50 " 12 noon ⎬ 50 " 4 pm ⎭ A + C Coys improved the Company billeting areas	Yes
	23	10pm	Weather Fine; wind N.E. light breeze Work B and D Coys supplied 100 men 9 am ⎫ for work on mine dug outs 50 " 4 pm ⎬ PLOEGSTEERT WOOD 50 " 12 midnight ⎭ A + C Coys improving the Company area	Yes
-"-	24	10pm	Weather Fine wind N.N.W. light breeze Work Nothing further as above.	Yes

Army Form C. 2118.

WAR DIARY
or
INTELLIGENCE SUMMARY

(Erase heading not required.)

Place	Date	Hour	Summary of Events and Information	Remarks and references to Appendices
OOSTHOVE FARM	25th	10 pm	Weather Fine, Wind light N.N.E.	
			A Coy 2 Platoons making tree standings at Transport, also cleaning and drawing up drain in transport yard	
			8 to 12.30 pm One Platoon cleared and widened two drains running into main drain D.3.a.c	
			1.30-4 pm One Platoon repairing road at Headquarters. Men constructing covered passage from cellar under HQ to Bombardment dugout.	
			B Coy & D Coy worked in shifts on dug out Hill 63	
			Shifts 8 am to 10 ff " 108 OR	
			4 pm " 10 ff " 50 "	
			12 midnight " " " 50 OR	
			C Coy Drainage in forward area	
			8 hour One platoon commenced clearing subsidiary drain TREES k	
			DESPIERRE FARM	
			One platoon " subsidiary drain GUNNER FARM k WEST HOEK	
			2 Two platoons " subsidiary drain GUNNER FARM k C.8.a 2.4 C.8.5 N of road	

WAR DIARY
or
INTELLIGENCE SUMMARY
(Erase heading not required.)

Army Form C. 2118.

Place	Date	Hour	Summary of Events and Information	Remarks and references to Appendices
—	26th	10 pm	Weather	

Warm. Wind: N.N.E. light breeze.

A Coy. One platoon 8 hours making knee thick-ups and tubs at transport yard.
One platoon cleaning deepening and widening drains at B.3.a.S.S. & B.3.a.3.S.
One platoon engaged in hutting at TROIS ARBRES.
One platoon engaged on road at Headquarters.

B & D Coy.
1 off 100 O.R. At 9am 9am
1 " 50 " 12 noonday 4pm Out Shift 63.
1 " 50 " 12 pm.   Working ordinary day

C Coy. One Platoon Cleaned & deepened DYKE from DESPIERRE FARM to TREES C.9. B.S.S. and from HOYTS FARM to U.26.b.2.3.
Two Platoons. HUNTER AVENUE new type constructed on both Sides from REGENT ST to U.27.A.8.7.
One platoon widened and levelled & drained road from Baconette to GUNNER FARM.

Divisional Damage Section (1 Platoon ATCoy)
No. 1 Squad Cleaning outdrains B.3.b. to B.4.a.
No. 2 Squad Draining around B.3a. S.S. & B.3a.3.S.

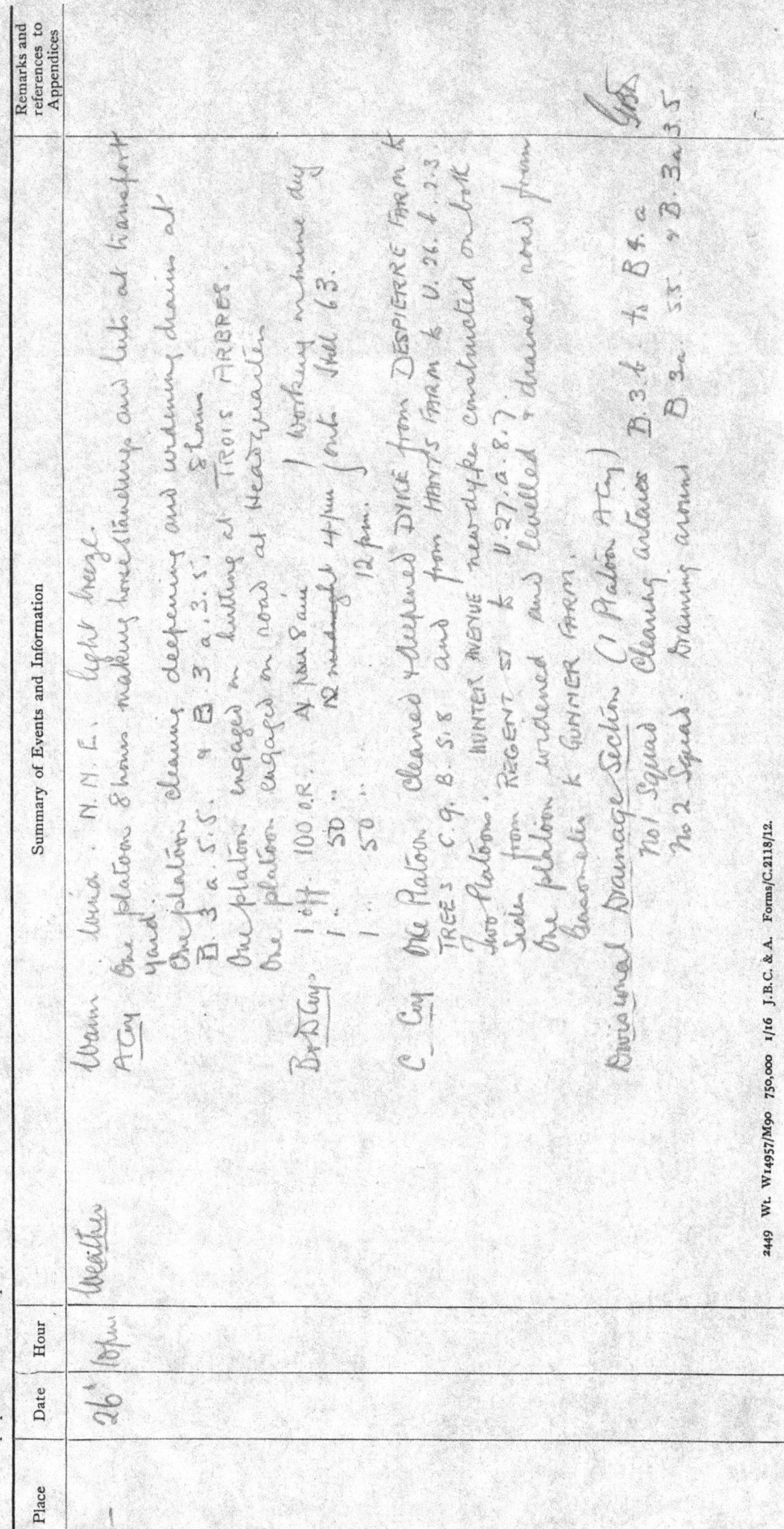

Army Form C. 2118.

WAR DIARY
or
INTELLIGENCE SUMMARY
(Erase heading not required.)

Instructions regarding War Diaries and Intelligence Summaries are contained in F. S. Regs., Part II. and the Staff Manual respectively. Title Pages will be prepared in manuscript.

Place	Date	Hour	Summary of Events and Information	Remarks and references to Appendices
---	27th	10 am	Wind frsh S.W. Rain Showers in morning and afternoon	
			A Coy. Completed construction of harness room and horse standing. Widened and deepened drains at T.28.c.2.5. Outpost on worked on huts at TROIS ARBRE. On platoon working on site drainage.	
			B+D Mined dug outs Shafts Saw - 1 off + 50 other ranks) working at hill 4 hrs 1 bgr SD } 63 man 1st 12 mdnyt-1off SD A.T. Coy. R.E.	
			C Coy. Sub drain from DEAD HORSE CORNER S.E. of HUNTER LANE. Sub drain from REGENT ST FORT to MAIN DRAIN. ESSEX FARM Cleared - ECCLES FORT - FRONT LINE - MAIN DRAIN Cleaned Sub drain GUNNER'S FARM to GASOMETER CORNER.	
			Steel Drainage Section No 1 Squad Clearing culverts B 3 b also new trench at T.27.d. + T.28.c.2.5 B 3 c 2.9 No 2 Squad Cleaned drains B 2 d.9.9 Culvert	YoS)

WAR DIARY
or
INTELLIGENCE SUMMARY
(Erase heading not required.)

Army Form C. 2118.

Place	Date	Hour	Summary of Events and Information	Remarks and references to Appendices
-"-	28/1/19		Weather. Wind light N.E.	
			Divisional Reserve Sector	
			Working Parties	
			No 1 Squad cleaning and widening drains II.4.a.0.7 - T.28.c.2.5.	
			No 2 Squad Cleared drains B.3.c.2.5. - B.3.a.1.4./ also main	
			B.2.d.9.4. - B.2.d.8.7./ drain connecting Three	
			A Company	
			One platoon cleaning and metalling road to transport yard.	
			" " widening and deepening drain at T. 28.c.2.5.	
			" " Erecting huts at S.28.b.84	
			" " draining area OOSTHOVE FARM.	
			B and D Coys constructing mine dug outs at T. 29.a.9.6.	
			Shift 8 am 1 officer and 50 or	
			4 pm " " "	
			12 midnight " " "	
			C Company Main drain from DEAD HORSE CORNER to U.21.6.37	
			PLOEGSTREERT completely cleared and cleared 1 week	(as)
			WOOD Sub drain E and N of HUNTERS AVENUE partially cleared.	
			" " from HUNTERS AVE to LE GHEER " "	
			Main dyke from ESSEX FARM to FRUIT LINE " "	

WAR DIARY
or
INTELLIGENCE SUMMARY
(Erase heading not required.)

Army Form C. 2118.

Place	Date	Hour	Summary of Events and Information	Remarks and references to Appendices
—	29th	10 p.m.	Walter	
			Work	

Cool and dull during greater part of day.

A Coy One platoon metalling road to transport yard
  "   "   Deepening and widening drains at T.28.c
  "   "   Erecting huts at S.28.b.8.7.
  "   "   Rebuilding brick wall at HQ yard. Laying drain behind HQ.

B and D Coy running dug outs 5 am   1 officer and 100 or
                                4 am   "   50 "
                                12 midnight   "   50 "

C Coy One platoon Cleaning and clearing subdrain forwards. GASOMETER
                    CORNER C.8.a.2.4. to drain (road southwards).
       One platoon Clearing main drains
                    KEEPERS HUT to 120' forward.
                    ESSEX FARM – PARK VILLA. & HUNTERS AVnue 120' forward.
                    U.21.c.3.4. to U.21.c.2.7.
       One platoon dug out drain east of HUNTERS Avnue 120' in vicinity
                    ECLES FORT.
       One platoon Sub drain 150' from REGENTS FORT.

Divisional Drainage Section (24th Manchester)
  No 1 Squad Cleaning and widening drains B.4.a 0.7 to T.28.c.2.5.
  No 2   "   "   "   "   B.3.c.2.5 – B.3.a.1.4.
                                           B.2.d.9.4 – B.2.d.8.7.

WAR DIARY or INTELLIGENCE SUMMARY

Army Form C. 2118.

Place	Date	Hour	Summary of Events and Information	Remarks and references to Appendices
-"-	30th	10am	Weather fine cool. toward light variable N.N.E.	

Working Parties

A Coy One platoon clearing and laying road at Transport Yard
" " deepening and widening drains at Fort VIII HELLES T.28.0.
S.28.b.8.4.
" " erecting huts at
" " laying drain pipes, clearing drains etc at OOSTHOVE FM.

Hdl 6.3 with 1st A.T.

B and D Coys Constructing mine dug outs at
Coy R.E.
8am 1 officer 100 other ranks
4 pm " " 50 "
12 midnight " " 50 "

C Coy One platoon clearing drain and draining road GASOMETER CORNER to GUNNERS FARM
" " clearing drain READING FORT; KEEPERS HUT to LE GHEER; ECCLES FORT & FALK VILLA
" " " EEL PIE FT to HAYMARKET.
" " Sub-drains in HUNTERS AVENUE.
" " " ECCLES FORT & ESSEX FARM.

Divn Drainage Sect. (21st N/c R.E) T.28.C.2.5; & B.4.a. 0.7.
No 1 Squad clearing drains Indycd B4.a. 2.9.
raised wooden
No 2 Squad clearing and widening drains at B.2.d 6.7.
B.2.d. 4.5.

1/10/16

A Chadwick Major
for Lieut Colonel,
STIRLING, 14th Batn MANCHRs Regt

S E C R E T. Appendix I

Copy No 7.

24th. Battalion The Manchester Regiment.
OPERATION ORDER NO. 27.

31st. August, 1916.

Reference Map- LONGUEVAL 57 c S.W.3. Edition E/10,000.

I.   Operations are suspended until further notice.

II.   On the day of the attack the 24th. Manchester Regt. has been ordered to assemble in the vicinity of MONTAUBAN, and when 7th. Division objective has been reached to prolong GINCHY AVENUE from PORTER TRENCH at T.13.c.55.40 to German Trench running from T.20.a.1.6. to T.14.a.40.25 which will then be our front line.

III.   "A" Company will work from PORTER TRENCH to German Support Trench due EAST at T.13.d.10.45 inclusive.

"C" Company from this point to NORTH Corner of Farm building at T.13.d.95.40 inclusive.

"B" Company from this point to the GINCHY-MAUREPAS Road at T.13.d.95.40 inclusive.

"D" Company from this point to nearest point of front line

IV.   The following method will be adopted to lay out trench.
On orders being given to move out each Company will send forward 1 Officer and a small party with tapes and pickets.

"D" and "B" will go out together and lay out their task from T.13.d.95.40. "D" to the EAST and "B" to the WEST.

"A" and "C" will lay out their tasks from T.13.d.10.45 "C" to the EAST and "A" to the WEST.

"B" and "C" Companies must be careful to meet at their junction at North Corner of Farm T.13.d.55.40.

Companies will move off 15 minutes after laying out parties in the order "D" "B" "C" "A".

A winding trench will be dug 5 feet deep by 3 feet wide.

On completion of tasks Companies will return to FRICOURT WOOD, reporting completion of work at Report Centre

V.   Position of Report Centre will be notified later.

Issued at 4-30 p.m.

Copy No. 1.   O.C. "A" Company.
         2.   O.C. "B" Company.
         3.   O.C. "C" Company.
         4.   O.C. "D" Company.
         5.   C.R.E.
         6.   2nd. in Command.
         7.   War Diary.
         8.   War Diary.

G. B. DEMPSEY, Lieut. & Adjutant.
24th. Battalion The Manchester Regiment.

SECRET　　　　Appendix II　　　　Copy No. 8

24th Battalion The Manchester Regiment.
OPERATION ORDER NO. 28.

2nd September, 1916.

I. The attack will take place on Sept. 3rd at 12 noon.

II. (a) That portion of Operation Order No. 27 which refers to tasks is cancelled.

(b) The task allotted to the Battalion is from NORTH Corner of Farm at T.13.d.55.40. to new front line about T.14.c.35.30.

III. For the purpose of work "A" Company will be attached to "B", and "D" Company to "C".

IV. (a) "B" Company's Sector will be from new front line to Road T.13.d.95.40. inclusive.
"C" Company from this post to NORTH Corner of Farm at T.13.d.55.40. where they will connect with the South Staffordshire Regiment.

(b) Laying out parties of one Officer and small party of other ranks will be detailed by O.C. Companies.
"B" Company will arrange to meet their Officer at Road T.13.d.95.40. and "C" Company at NORTH Corner of Farm T.13.d.55.40.

V. On completion of trench 5 feet by 3 feet Companies will return independently to FRICOURT WOOD and report there.

VI. Orders for move to point of assembly will be given later.

VII. The importance of the completion of a good communication trench should be impressed on all ranks. It is only by means of this that wounded can be evacuated, stores and ammunition brought up and touch kept with our new front line. Companies must therefore complete the work at all costs.

Issued at 3-30 p.m.

Copy No. 1.　O.C. "A" Coy.
　　　　2.　O.C. "B" "
　　　　3.　O.C. "C" "
　　　　4.　O.C. "D" "
　　　　5.　C.R.E.
　　　　6.　Commanding Officer
　　　　7.　2nd in Command
　　　　8.　War Diary
　　　　9.　War Diary.

G. B. DEMPSEY. Lieut. and Adjutant.
24th Battalion The Manchester Regiment.

Appendix III

AFTER BATTALION ORDERS BY   NO. 152
LIEUT COLONEL J. B. BATTEN COMMANDING   THURSDAY
24TH BATTALION MANCHESTER REGIMENT   7th Septr. 1916.

1. **WORK**   Cable trench to be dug by R.E. and Pioneers on following
route:- BRIGADE H.Q., POMMIERS REDOUBT -

2. **ROUTE**
A. 1. d. 5.8.	Test shaft required here.
A. 2. a. 3.7.	Test shaft required here.
A. 2. b. 2.8.	Test shaft required here.
A. 2. b. 85.90.	
A. 2. b. 95.98.	Test shaft required here.
S. 27. c. 15.15.	Test dug-out required here.
S. 27. c. 3.3.	
S. 27. c. 7.9.	Test shaft required here.
S. 27. b. 20.25.	Test shaft required here.
S. 27. b. 25.35.	Test dug-out required here.
S. 21. d. 8.1.	Test shaft required here.
S. 22. c. 25.30.	
S. 22. c. 5.6.	Test shaft required here.
S. 22. b. 05.40.	Test shaft required here.
S. 16. d. 6.1.	Brigade H.Q. in mined dug-out.

3. **SPECIFICATION**
   (a) After laying of cable, trench is to be filled in.
   (b) Test shafts to be made of mining frames.
   (c) Test dug-outs will be a test shaft with a short mined gallery leading off it.
   (d) Shafts will only go to floor of trench.
   (e) Between POMMIERS REDOUBT and Point S. 27. b. 25.35., the trench is to be 6 feet deep. Between Point S. 27. b. 25.35. and Brigade H.Q., at S. 16. d. 6.1., trench is to be 7 feet 6 ins. deep.
   (f) Between Points S. 27. c. 7.9. and S. 21. d. 8.1., there is an old cable trench which should be used.

4. **TASK**   Daily task will be 3 yards per man. Depth is to be fully
excavated; the floor may be sloped off to a point and trench
must be as narrow as possible.
On completion of tasks Platoons can march off.

5. **TIME TABLE** Companies to report tomorrow at POMMIERS REDOUBT to an
Officer of the XV Corps Signal Company (South African Signals) as
under:-

"D" Company	9-45 a.m.
"C" Company	10-0 a.m.
"B" Company	10-15 a.m.
"A" Company	10-30 a.m.

6. **DRESS**   Rifle, one bandolier, haversack and waterbottle.
Haversack ration to be carried. Dinners on return to
billets.

7. **TOOLS**   Picks and shovels, measuring rods and measuring tapes and
laying out tapes.

(Signed) G. B. DEMPSEY. Lieut. and Adjutant.

Appendix IV
Copy No. 3

2nd Battalion The Manchester Regiment
OPERATION ORDER NO. 29.

ORDERS FOR MOVE OF TRANSPORT

Transport will move with Field Companies of R.E., 7th Division, and on 12th September will pass starting point at Junction of Horse Track with the BUIRE LA VIE VILLE ROAD at 11-30 a.m.

Transport at FRICOURT WOOD will leave there at 9-0 a.m., and remainder of transport at E.12. will join them as they pass.

ROUTES:-
12th September

Horse Track just NORTH of FRICOURT-MEAULTE-BUIRE-HEILLY ROAD as far as HEILLY and thence via BONNAY and LA NEUVILLE to a bivouac just NORTH of DAOURS.

13th September

Via VECQUEMONT-AMIENS SOUTH OF THE SOMME to CROUY. Columns clearing VECQUEMONT by 8 a.m.

14th September

Tp area b. Columns clearing CROUY by 9 a.m. and destination will be notified at CROUY.

Lewis Gun Handcarts will move with Company Transport in charge of two Lewis Gunners per cart. Arrangements being made to attach each cart to a wagon.

One Limber wagon will be left behind with the Battalion to accompany the Battalion to the Station. On completion of duty this wagon will rejoin transport at DAOURS on night of 12th Sept.

Copy No. 1. Quartermaster
2. Transport Officer
3. War Diary

11/9/16

G. B. DEMPSEY Lieut. and Adjutant.

SECRET   Appendix IV
                                                      Copy No. 8

24th Battalion The Manchester Regiment
OPERATION ORDER NO. 29.

I.   The Battalion will move by train from ALBERT to OISEMENT tomorrow, the 12th.
        Parade ready to move off at 6-45 a.m.   Breakfast 6-0 a.m.
        All wagons to be packed previous to this time.
        Train leaves 9-0 a.m. and is expected to arrive at OISEMENT

II.   ROUTE TO STATION:-
        FRICOURT STATION-Track to BECORDEL-BECORDEL-ALBERT ROAD-ALBERT STATION.
        Companies will move at 100 yards interval.

III.   2/Lieut. H.E.Braine with one man per Company will leave at 6-30 a.m. and proceed to station to allot accommodation.   The men will meet 2/Lieut. Braine at H.Q.Mess at 6-0 a.m.

IV.   All boxes are to be neatly stacked in Company areas.

        Issued at 10-45 p.m., 11-9-16.
        Copy No. 1.   C.O.   Copy No. 2.   2nd in Command.
                 3.   O.C. "A" Coy.   4.   O.C. "B" Coy.
                 5.   O.C. "C" "   6.   O.C. "D" "
                 7.   War Diary   8.   War Diary.

                G. B. DEMPSEY. Lieut. and Adjutant.

SECRET.

Appendix V

Copy No. 9

24th Battalion The Manchester Regiment
OPERATION ORDER NO. 30.

1. The 24th Manchesters will move by rail to the 2nd. Army area. Zero hour and date will be notified later.

2. The Battalion, less Transport and loading party, will be formed up ready to move off at 6 hours after Zero, in the following order:- "A", "B", Band, "C", "D". The head of "A" Coy. to be opposite the main watering pond East of the village.

   Captain H. Prendergast, Lieut. W. Watson and 2/Lieut. H.E. Braine and 100 men of "D" Coy. will parade with Transport in their lines at 4-30 hours after Zero, and move off accompanied by handcarts. Two Lewis Gunners with each handcart.

3. Number of train 11. Serial number 04. Entraining Station LONGPRE. Time of departure of train 10 hours after Zero.

4. Covered van holds 8 horses or 40 men. Flat truck holds 1 G.S. wagon, and 1 two-wheeled vehicle, or four pairs of wheels in the case of limbered vehicles. Some trucks can carry two G.S. wagons.

   No men are allowed to travel in open trucks or brake vans. Horses are to be loaded unharnessed and with their nose bags round their necks. Not more than 4 men are allowed to travel in each horse truck.

5. Lamps are usually provided by the French authorities in the covered vans, but not in the Officers compartments.

6. Orders concerning rations to be carried will be notified later.

   Issued at 6-30 p.m., 16-9-16.

Copy No. 1.	C. O.	Copy No. 2.	2nd in Command
3.	O.C. "A" Coy.	4.	O.C. "B" Coy
5.	O.C. "C" "	6.	O.C. "D" "
7.	Quartermaster	8.	Transport Off'r
9.	War Diary	10.	War Diary.

G. B. DEMPSEY. Lieut. and Adjutant.

SECRET

S.E.C.R.E.T

Appendix VI

Copy No. 9

24th Battalion The Manchester Regiment.
OPERATION ORDER NO. 31.

1. The times referred to in Operation Order No. 30 are cancelled.

2. The train leaves LONGPRE at 4-45 a.m. on the 18th.

3. PARADES:- Transport, Handcarts and Loading Party will parade on Transport Ground and move off at 11-0 p.m. 17th.
The Battalion will parade as ordered at 12-30 a.m. 18th.

4. RATIONS:- Rations for 18th will be carried on the cookers and issued to Companies on the train at LONGPRE ready cooked.
Fires must be out before entraining cookers.
Rations for 19th will be carried in Supply wagons.
Refilling point tomorrow at same place as today. Supply wagons will join Battalion at Station.

5. Officers' kits etc., will be packed at Transport lines by 9-0 p.m., 17th. All tool wagons packed and returned to Transport lines before 6-0 p.m.

6. The Quartermaster will arrange to keep out enough lamps ready fitted with candles to assist in entrainment of Transport and men.

7. All ranks are reminded that they are not allowed to hang their legs out of the sides of trucks nor to get out of the train without permission.
Company Commanders will arrange for a responsible N.C.O. to be in each truck. If this order is disobeyed the sides of the truck are to be closed.

Issued at 1-0 p.m., 16-9-16.

Copy No. 1.	C.O.	Copy No. 2.	2nd in Command
3.	O.C. "A" Coy.	4.	O.C. "B" Coy.
5.	O.C. "C" "	6.	O.C. "D" "
7.	Quartermaster	8.	Transport Off'r
9.	War Diary	10.	War Diary.

G. B. DEMPSEY. Lieut. and Adjutant.

Appendix VII

S E C R E T   Copy No. 7.
             24th Battalion The Manchester Regiment
                    OPERATION ORDER NO. 32.

REFERENCE MAP, Sheet 28 S.W., and 36 N.W.

1.   "B" and "D" Companies will move tomorrow, the 20th.
     to T. 29. d. 8.6. and take over from 5th Bn. S. W. B. for
     work in BOIS de PLOEGSTREERT.   The detachment will be
     under the command of Capt. Wall.

2.   100 men of "D" Company will parade outside H.Q. Mess at
     7-0 a.m. and move by Motor Lorry.   The remainder of the
     detachment under Capt. Prendergast will parade at 8-0 a.m.
     and move by road.
             Route to be followed by these men will be the road
     running SOUTH of BAILLEUL past the Station.   They are not
     to go through the town.
             Officers kits of the detachment must be stacked
     outside H.Q. Mess by 6-45 a.m. and loaded on lorries.
             Two Company Cookers will proceed with the detachment.
             No other Transport will be taken.
             Tool carts will join these Companies on the 21st.

3.   Troops moving EAST of BAILLEUL will move by platoons
     at 100 yards interval.

4.   Battalion H.Q. will remain where they are until 9-0 a.m.
     on the 21st. when they will move up to OOSTHOVE FARM at
     B. 11. d.

     Issued at 8-45 p.m., 19-9-16.

             Copy No. 1.   Commanding Officer
                      2.   O.C. "A" Coy.
                      3.   O.C. "B" "
                      4.   O.C. "C" "
                      5.   O.C. "D" "
                      6.   Quartermaster
                      7.   War Diary
                      8.   War Diary

                    G. B. DEMPSEY. Lieut. and Adjutant.

SECRET   Copy No. 6

24th Battalion The Manchester Regiment
OPERATION ORDER NO. 33.

REFERENCE MAPS, Sheets 28 S.W. and 36 N.W.

1. The Battalion less "B" and "D" Companies will move tomorrow, the 21st., to OOSTHOVE FARM.
    ROUTE:- Road SOUTH of BAILLEUL - Main BAILLEUL - ARMENTIERES ROAD - PONT D'ACHELLES - LA RUE du SAC - LE DON - OOSTHOVE FARM.
    Transport will move in rear of the Battalion to OOSTHOVE FARM, detaching "B" and "D" Companies tool wagons and sending them on to T. 29. d. 8.6. After unloading all wagons the Transport will return to billets at PONT D'ACHELLE

2. Order of march:- Band, "C", "A".
    TIME TABLE:-
    Reveille   6-0 a.m.
    Breakfast   7-30 a.m.
    Wagons packed by   8-30 a.m.
    Parade at   9-30 a.m.

    Head of column will be at Cross Roads ROUGE-CROIX.

    Baggage wagons will be packed in the Q.M. Stores yard by 8-30 a.m.

    Issued at 9-10 p.m., 20-9-16.

    Copy No. 1.   Commanding Officer
            2.   O.C. "A" Coy.
            3.   O.C. "C" "
            4.   Quartermaster & Transport Officer
            5.   O.C. Lewis Gun Section.
            6.   War Diary.
            7.   War Diary.

                G. B. DEMPSEY. Lieut. and Adjutant.

Vol 12 Army Form C. 2118.

WAR DIARY
or
INTELLIGENCE SUMMARY

(Erase heading not required.)

VOLUME XII   1st OCTOBER 1916   24 Batt. MANCHESTER REGT.

Place	Date	Hour	Summary of Events and Information	Remarks and references to Appendices
OOSTHOVE FARM B 11 d Sheet 36 NW	Oct 1st	10pm	Weather Fine. Warm. Breeze variable light. N.N.W & N.NE. Working Parties A Coy One platoon clearing and re-laying road in transport yard " " " clearing and widening drains T.28.c " " " Erecting huts S.28.t.54. " " " Draining area at OOSTHOVE FARM. Band & D Coy Constructing mine dug outs under Hill 63, & PLOEGSTREERT WOOD. 8am 1 officer 100 other ranks 4pm 1 " 30 " " 12 midnight 1 " 50 " " C Company Rested Divisional Damage Section (St Yvesbehn (pioneers)) Rested Services Divine Services were held during to-day	Sheet 28 SW 36 NW PETIT DOUVELLES Yes

2449 Wt. W14957/M90 750,000 1/16 J.B.C. & A. Forms/C.2118/12.

WAR DIARY
or
INTELLIGENCE SUMMARY
(Erase heading not required.)

Army Form C. 2118.

Place	Date	Hour	Summary of Events and Information	Remarks and references to Appendices
—	2nd	10pm	Weather Dull some light Westerly Fine rain in morning for an hour and at night	
			Working Parties A Company Laid and metalled road at TRANSPORT YARD training area at T.28.C. Deepening and widening drains at 23rd Supply Rail HQ B.10a MG. Erecting huts at S.28.b.8.4. Erecting battalion headquarters area OOSTHOVE FARM.	
			B and D Coys Constructing mine dug outs J.14. 63.
			8 am 1 Off. 75 O.R.
			4 pm 1 Off. 45 O.R.
			12 midnight 1 Off 40 O.R.
			C Company Cleaning drains from ECCLES FORT to ESSEX FARM.
			" " S of DEAD HORSE FARM and FORT BOYD.
			" " N of "
			" " ESSEX FARM to HUNTER AV.
			Divisional Damage Section
			No 1 Squad Cleaning and widening drains at B.4a 0.10 to B.4a 6.10
			No 2 Squad Cleaning main drains J and S of D.2.d overs

WAR DIARY
or
INTELLIGENCE SUMMARY

Army Form C. 2118.

Place	Date	Hour	Summary of Events and Information	Remarks and references to Appendices
--	3rd	10pm	Weather wet and dull. Wind light N.W. Working Parties as for the 2nd Oct.	GS
--	4th	10pm	Weather Rain. Winds freshly Northerly. Working Parties. A Company Owens have standings at Nieuport. Gluing chairs at 22nd Bde HQ, rd 7.28.c. Erecting huts at S.28.b.8.4. rd B4.b. 1.4. Dramas at HQ B.11.d 6.9. B+D Coys Constructing num dug outs Sans 75" shrub tanks & officers " 45 " " " 4fm " " " 12 knights " 40 " " " C Company Clearing subdrain at London Bridge. ECCLES FORT to S.H.9. Southward & Northward FORT BOYD " " PLOEGSTREERT - LEGHEER 7.28.C.O.5 - 7.28.C. 3.2 Divisional Damage Scheme B.2.d & 22nd Bde HQ Clearing drains at	GS

WAR DIARY or INTELLIGENCE SUMMARY

Army Form C. 2118.

Place	Date	Hour	Summary of Events and Information	Remarks and references to Appendices
—	5th	10am	Weather Dull but fine. Wind, fresh, northerly	
			Working Parties	
			A Company. Moving horse standings at Transport yard from PONT D'ACHELLES. Clearing drains at 22nd Bn HQ. Erecting huts at B.4.b.4.5. Cleaning drain at B.11.d.6.6. Correcting manhole and laying pipe for drains	
			B and D Coys. Constructing mine dugouts at shell 63. T.19.b.3.8. Sans 1 officer 75 other ranks. 4pm " 1 " 45 " " 12 midnight " 1 " 40 " "	
			C Company. Clearing out drain at LONDON BRIDGE, PORT BOYD. " " C.T. No 119 at HAYMARKET " " sub drain " REGENTS FORT Kt HAYMARKET " " " PLOEGSTEERT — LE GHEER	GBD
			Divisional Drainage Section	
			Deepening and widening existing on right hand road D.15.b.57.- D.8.b.1.4. ; D.10.c.2.8.- D.10.c.4.6. ; T.2 7.d.9.1 B.10.c.4.6.;	

WAR DIARY
or
INTELLIGENCE SUMMARY

Army Form C. 2118.

Place	Date	Hour	Summary of Events and Information	Remarks and references to Appendices
-"-	6th	10pm	**Weather** Fine during day, heavy rain at night. Wind Northerly. **Working Parties** As on the 5th.	GBS

-"-	7th	10pm	**Weather** Wind northerly, fresh. Rain in afternoon and at night.
			 Working Parties
			 A Company: Work on horse standings, transport yard Fort D'ACHELLES. Clearing drain at 22nd Bde H.Q. Widening and deepening drains at T.27.d.7.2. Erecting huts.
			 B and D Coys: Work on mini dug outs.
			     Fau 1 officer 80 other ranks
			     4 pm " 45
			     12 midnight " 40
			 C Company: Cleaning out drain FORT BOYD. (Wind HAYMARKET and C.T. 15 FRONT LINE PLOEGSTEERT to LE-GHEER HARNAVE.
			 Divisional Drainage Section: Deepening and clearing drains B.15.6.6.7. - B.8.6.1.4. B.10.C.2.8. - B.10.c.4.6. T.27.d.9.1.
				GBS

Army Form C. 2118.

WAR DIARY
or
INTELLIGENCE SUMMARY
(Erase heading not required.)

Place	Date	Hour	Summary of Events and Information	Remarks and references to Appendices
—	9th	10/am	Weather Dull Wind S.W. Great.	
			Working Parties A & C Coys rested	
			B " Coy. - found 3 parties or mines dug out 1 off. FS	
			" " " 4S	
			" " " 40 Other Tanks	
			Divine Service C. & D Coys and nonconformist services were held	4 BS
—	10th	10am	Weather Dull ; Wind West Clearing SW. fresh	
			Working Parties A Coy Erecting horse standings transport lines	
			Cleaning drains at 22nd Bde HQ.	
			Erecting huts at D.1.c.8.3. and B.11.b.2.2	
			Cleaning moat at HQ and opening drain	
			B and D Coys Constructing mine dug outs onto Rau 1 officer 8S Otherranks	
			4/am 1 " 4S "	
			12midday 1 " 40 "	
			C Coy Cleaning and conducting subalterns in advance of HAYMARKET	
			clearing NAPPAVE near CHESHIRE FARM and drain ROEGSTEERT - LOUQUET - BERTHE	
			at 100	
			Divisional Drainage Section No. 1 Squad deepening channel at B.5.a.3.6 -	4 BS
			B.5.a.8.7	
			No. 2 Squad deepening and clearing channel at	
			D.10.c.2.8 - B.10.c.4.6 B.10.c.1.7 - B.10.c.3.5.	

WAR DIARY
or
INTELLIGENCE SUMMARY

Army Form C. 2118.

(Erase heading not required.)

Place	Date	Hour	Summary of Events and Information	Remarks and references to Appendices
—	10th	10am	Weather. Wind South west. 20 mph. Quality. Working Parties. A Company. One platoon roofing horse standings at transport yard " " " widening and deepening drains around 22A Brigade HQ. " " Completed repair of huts at B 1.c.8.3 " " Drains now set out above farm. B and S Coy. Constructing mine dugout Hill 63. Officer Esplanade Saw 45 Lieut. 40 " Boatwright. C Company. Cleaning and clearing the MARDAVE ? near CHESHIRE AVE. Constructing drain LONG AVENUE from Via Poo AVENUE to Tor Line. Divisional Drainage section. Cleaning and completing widening outlay B5 a 3.6 – 3.5 a 8.7 " " " B 15 c.7 – B 8 b 1.4. " " deepening " " B 10 c.75 – B.10.c 4.6 " " B.10 c.1.7 – B.10.c 3.5 " " B.10 c.3.5 – B.10.6.5 ?	
—	11th	15pm	Weather. Wind H.S.W. Strong. 30 mph. Working Parties. As on the 10th.	

2449 Wt. W14957/Mgo 750,000 1/16 J.B.C. & A. Forms/C.2118/12.

WAR DIARY
or
INTELLIGENCE SUMMARY

Army Form C. 2118.

Place	Date	Hour	Summary of Events and Information	Remarks and references to Appendices
	12/4	10pm	Weather Right wind S.W. fine but dull	
			Arighing Parties	
			A Company. Begann drain to moat OOSTHOVE FARM "Rooting" horse standings hardcort lines PONT D'ACHELLES working with Burrowdale Scrounge Company. Conducting new dug out at Hill 63. T.19.6.38.	
			B & D Company	
			Company Cleaning to HARNAVE from CHESHIRE MEDIA before line drain from CHESHIRE AV – LANCASHIRE SUPPORT from Southward. R.V.27.a.7.3.	
			" from BARRIER and LANCASHIRE SUPPORT " LONG AVENUE from NA POO AVENUE & PORTHOLE	
			Divisional Drainage No 1 Squad Clearing and widening attaine round Camp B.3.c.8.4. New pipe and breakculvert leation made at B.3.c.8.4.	
			No 2 Squad Clearing drains B.15.6.5.7 – B.86.14.	
			Attached A.G.g Clearing drain S side ground B.10.c.3.0 – B.15.b.r.2. B.10.c.0.6. – B.N.6.6.6. B.10.c.3.0.9.5 – B.9.c.7.4. B.3.d.0.4.	Gas

WAR DIARY
or
INTELLIGENCE SUMMARY

Army Form C. 2118.

Place	Date	Hour	Summary of Events and Information	Remarks and references to Appendices
OOSTHOVE FARM B11c (Sect 36 NW)	13/k	10am	Weather: Fresh wind S.W. Dull.	
			Working Parties:	
			A Coy Cleaning & deepening drains at PAPOT (3 platoons) Stratford Av." Group B.4.d.9.4.; repairing huts B.1.a.6.3. ¾ (1 plat) (5 men)	
			Rubble pathways at transport yard.	
			C. Coy Cleaning drains:—	
			(1) LONG AV – NARDO AV – front line	
			(2) Sub drain BARKENHAM AV.	
			(3) Sub Drain of RESERVE FARM	
			(4) CHESHIRE AV.	
			B9 D Coys Noise dugouts under 1st Aus. Tun Coy R.E.	
			Divl Drainage Sec ① Cleaning culverts at B.3.c.9.8. & B.3.c.7.6. & drains round camp B.3.c.8.4.	J.H.M.
			② Cleaning drain B.15.b.5.7. – B.8.b.14.	

WAR DIARY
or
INTELLIGENCE SUMMARY

Army Form C. 2118.

Place	Date	Hour	Summary of Events and Information	Remarks and references to Appendices
OOSTHOVE FARM B.11.c (Sheet 36 N.W.)	14th	10 P.M.	Weather - Fresh wind S.W. Fine but Dull. Working Parties:- A Coy. Clearing deepening drain at PAPOT (3 platoons). Enlarged 2 Trench Dumps at B.10.a.6.5 (1 plat). Repaired 7 Huts B.1.a.6.4 (1 pl). Built 4 pathways at transport yard (1 coy). C. Coy. Clearing out Spr. Ost. BIRKENHAM M. (2) at LANCASHIRE SUPPORT FARM. B.9.D Coy.:- Mined dugouts under 7th Mx. Tun. Coy R.E. 2nd Drainage Sec:- (1) Clearing drain at B.3.c.8.4. Making culvert at B.3.c.8.4 + new spur good [illeg] (2) Clearing drain B.9.d.2.6 - B.9.c.4.8	

2449 Wt. W14957/M90 750,000 1/16 J.B.C. & A. Forms/C.2118/12.

Army Form C. 2118.

WAR DIARY
or
INTELLIGENCE SUMMARY
(Erase heading not required.)

Instructions regarding War Diaries and Intelligence Summaries are contained in F.S. Regs., Part II. and the Staff Manual respectively. Title Pages will be prepared in manuscript.

Place	Date	Hour	Summary of Events and Information	Remarks and references to Appendices
OOSTHOVE FARM (B.11.c Sheet 36NW)	15th	10AM	Weather Colder, some showers. Wind Good Surf. Working Parties A & C Coys. roads B&D Coys on more dugouts under plank team & R.E. Divine Service Coy E & Newcomers services to be at 6PM. Coys at T.19.c.6.3. for B&D Coys.	
	16th	10AM	Weather. Wind W. Slight showers. Working Parties A Coy (1) Completed Jarvis at PAPOT (1/Plk) (2) Commenced Sawing camp at B37.d.9.6.6pm (3) Complete shuttle pathways at transport pad (5am) (4) Making Dugout at R.2.a.9.9. (6 mns) (5) Erected M.Hs at NIEPPE C Coy Continued work as on Saturday. B&D Coys Divl Drainage Section (1) New culverts at B.3.c.84 7B9.7.8.11 (2) Cleaning & deepening drain B15.d57-B8.b14	

WAR DIARY
INTELLIGENCE SUMMARY
(Erase heading not required.)

Army Form C. 2118.

Place	Date	Hour	Summary of Events and Information	Remarks and references to Appendices
OOSTHOVE FARM (B.11.c Sh36NW)	17th	10 p.m	Weather Cold & start; wind W. Working Parties: A Coy continued clearing & improving drains (3 platoons). Erecting huts at Artillery Camp (1 platoon). Working Dugout at N.2.d. B Coy Dr moved Dugouts under 9 & 1st Aus Tun. Coy. C Coy Clearing out drains.	J.S.P.W.
	18th	10 p.m	Weather Fine. Wind W. Working Parties Coys continued work on mined Dugouts, erecting huts & clearing drains.	(1) BARKENHAM Av-post (2) LANCASHIRE SUPPT F.Ad (3) Vistas 4 dugouts in easterly direction J.S.P.W.
	19th	10 p.m	Weather Some showers. Easterly wind. Working Parties Coys commenced work as previous day but were recalled about 11 AM on getting warning order to move. Move Orders Preliminary move orders attached.	Appendices 1 and 2. J.S.P.W.

WAR DIARY or INTELLIGENCE SUMMARY

Army Form C. 2118.

Place	Date	Hour	Summary of Events and Information	Remarks and references to Appendices
	20th		The Bn. Entrained in Operation Order No.1 attached.	9.31.M
	21st		route BAILLEUL - HAZEBROUCK - ST POL - DOULLENS - BELLE ÉGLISE. Belle Église was reached about 4.40 AM 21st inst. The Bn. detrained & marched via VARENNES - BOUZINCOURT & ALBERT to TARA HILL B. Bn. H.Q. attd to 4th Can. Div.	9.31.M
Pt W30c S.3			Bouzincourt reached a camp of hutments at W.30.c.S.3.	
(Shot 57D)	29th 10 p.m.		Corps (named) 4.45 P.M. working strength 400 (incl 2000 yds at COLT AVENUE cleaning of 5 fire) 750 yds of trench. Working parties returned about 1 a.m.	9.31.M
	23rd 10 p.m.		Wet & cold, little wind. Corps (named) as previous night; about 1200 yds of COLT AVE. cleared & deepened. Trench boards laid in a portion of COLT AV. 2 huts erected in camp	9.31.M

WAR DIARY
or
INTELLIGENCE SUMMARY

Army Form C. 2118.

Place	Date	Hour	Summary of Events and Information	Remarks and references to Appendices
TARA HILL W30.c.3.3 Sheet 57D	24th	10 PM	Weather Wet & cold. Wind light S.E. Work A.T.C. Coys. Rested. B & D Coys. Paraded 4.45 pm; carrying wood boards into position in COLT AVENUE; returned to camp about 2.30 a.m. Casualties 1 wounded (accidentally) & 1 missing (returned to camp 2.15 am)	J.S.H.W.
	25th	10 PM	Weather Wet & cold. Wind light S.E. Work B Coys paraded 4 PM; deepening & widening 10TH STREET for 115-0yds. 3 Platoons carrying wood boards; returned to camp about 2.15 am. 1 hut erected in camp. Casualties Nil. N.C.O & 3 men worked at Divl HQ 7 hours.	J.S.H.W.
	26th	10 PM	Weather Showers. Wind Easterly, fresh. Work 300 men paraded 4.45 p.m., carrying wood boards from army into position in 10th St.; laying wood boards, clearing & leaving #10th St.; returned to camp 1.30 am. Casualties Nil. 1 N.C.O. & 12 men worked at Divl HQ 7 hours (civ.)	J.S.H.W.

Army Form C. 2118.

WAR DIARY
or
INTELLIGENCE SUMMARY
(Erase heading not required.)

Instructions regarding War Diaries and Intelligence Summaries are contained in F. S. Regs., Part II. and the Staff Manual respectively. Title Pages will be prepared in manuscript.

Place	Date	Hour	Summary of Events and Information	Remarks and references to Appendices
TARA HILL W.30.c.53 Sheet 35JD	27th	10 PM	Weather Showery & cold. Wind E. Fresh. Work 1 hut erected in camp Coys rested	H.C.R.N.
	28th	1 PM	Weather Slightly warmer. Wind SE fresh Work 20 O.R's worked 7 hours at Divl HQ Coys (300 O.R's) paraded 4.45 PM, cleaned up roads & 675 yds of 10th STREET; also carried trench boards & met then in position; returned to camp about 2 am. Casualties 1 man slightly wounded by H.E. shell	H.C.R.N.
	29th	10 AM	Weather Cold Showery Wind NE fresh Working Parties As on the 28th	Appendices 3 and 4 GOS
-/-	30th	10 AM	Weather Showery Wind NE. Working Parties trainers Appendix 29K	GOS

Army Form C. 2118.

WAR DIARY
or
INTELLIGENCE SUMMARY

(Erase heading not required.)

Instructions regarding War Diaries and Intelligence Summaries are contained in F. S. Regs., Pa II and the Staff Manual respectively. Title lges will be prepared in manuscript.

Place	Date	Hour	Summary of Events and Information	Remarks and references to Appendices
X.11.a Sheet ALBERT (Contour)(leaf)	31st	10 p.m	Weather fine warmer. Shower in afternoon. Wind Easterly. Working Parties 200 O.R. reported at X.9.b for work cleaning 10 K STREET. With 11th Field Coy R.E. at 5 p.m 150 " for work with 101st Field Co. R.E. on COLT AVENUE. Reported at X.9.T. 5:30 p.m. Casualties: Officer nil. Other ranks 1 killed 4 wounded. The battalion moved to to X.11.a. (ALBERT Contours Sheet) Transport moved to area W.24 on N side of ALBERT - BAPAUME RD. (Order No 3)	11th Fd.Cy R.E. at 5 p.m X.9.T. 5.30 p.m GBS

J.H. Chadwick Major
Commanding 24th Northumberland Regt.

Appendix 1

No. 11

SECRET   24th Battalion The Manchester Regiment
PRELIMINARY MOVE ORDERS
19th October, 1916.

1. The Battalion will be ready to move at 4 p.m.

2. Tool wagons will be packed by 4 p.m. Company Mess Baskets to be carried on tool wagon.

3. Officers valises will be collected by wagon starting at 2/Lieut. Russel's Detachment. This wagon will reach Q.M. Stores by 3 p.m. "B" and "D" Companies will be ready for loading not later than 2 p.m.

4. Blankets will be rolled in bundles of 10 and ready for collection at 3 p.m.

5. Sufficient camp kettles for cooking en route will be carried by the men.

6. Rations for consumption tomorrow (20th) will be carried on the fore portion of the field kitchens.

7. Lewis Gun carts will be loaded and sent to Transport by 3 p.m.

8. Gum boots will be returned to Q.M. Stores by 3 p.m.

Issued at 12-15 pm.

Copy No. 1.   Commanding Officer
         2.   Quartermaster
         3.   Transport Officer
         4.   Lewis Gun Officer
         5.   Medical Officer
         6.   O.C. "A" Coy.
         7.   O.C. "B" "
         8.   O.C. "C" "
         9.   O.C. "D" "
      10.   2/Lieut. Russel
      11.   War Diary
      12.   War Diary.

(Signed) A. St. G. WALSH. 2/Lieut. and Acting Adjutant.

Appendix 2

SECRET

OPERATION ORDER NO. 1
BY MAJOR J. H. CHADWICK
COMMDG. 24TH BATTALION MANCHESTER REGT.

Map Reference. France Sheet 36 N.W.
1/20,000.

19th October, 1916

1. The Battalion will entrain at BAILLEUL to-morrow (20th instant)

2. Hour of departure 12 noon.

3. Transport will reach BAILLEUL STATION at 9 a.m. They will leave Transport lines at 6-30 a.m.

4. Captain Prendergast and 100 Other Ranks of "D" Company will form the loading party and will join the Transport at 6-15 a.m. They will form the unloading party on arrival at destination.

5. The remainder of the Battalion will move at 7-45 a.m. at intervals of 100 yards between half Companies.

6. ORDER OF MARCH:—
   (1) Headquarters and Band
   (2) "A" Company
   (3) "C" Company
   (4) "B" & "D" Companies (less Capt. Prendergast and 100 Other Ranks).

7. "B" Company and "D" Company (less Capt. Prendergast and 100 Other Ranks) will join the column at Road Junction B. 4. b. 8.6.
   O.C. "A" Company will arrange for 2/Lieut. Russel's detachment to join the column.

8. 2/Lieut. Braine will accompany the Transport and allot accommodation on the train.

9. 2/Lieut. Wilkins will be in command of details left behind, and will hand over camps and stores to O.C., 7th Divisional Salvage Company.

10. Details left behind will be attached for rations to the 7th Divisional Salvage Company.

ISSUED AT 7-0 p.m.

Copy No. 1. Commanding Officer
     2. Quartermaster
     3. Transport Officer
     4. Lewis Gun Officer
     5. Medical Officer
     6. O.C. "A" Coy.
     7. O.C. "B" "
     8. O.C. "C" "
     9. O.C. "D" "
    10. 2/Lieut. Russel
    11. 2/Lieut. Wilkins.
12 & 13. War Diary.

(Signed) A. St. G. WALSH 2/Lieut. and Acting Adjutant.

Appendix 3

24th Battalion The Manchester Regiment
OPERATION ORDER NO. 2

Copy 89

30th October, 1916.

Reference Map. ALBERT COMBINED SHEET

1. The Battalion will move to the Camp at X. 11. a.

2. Transport will move to an area in W. 24, on the North side of the ALBERT – BAPAUME Road.

3. 2/Lieut. Braine and advance party of 1 N.C.O. and 3 Other Ranks will take over the new Camp from 50th Canadian Battalion. He will proceed at once to X. 11. a.

4. ORDER OF MARCH:—
   1. Headquarters and Band
   2. "D" Company
   3. "B" Company
   4. "C" Company
   5. "A" Company

   An interval of 100 yards willbe left between half Companies.

5. ROUTE:— This will be given in a subsequent order.

6. Blankets (rolled in bundles of 10) and Mess Baskets and Officers valises will be handed in to Q.M. Stores by 8-0 a.m.

7. 2/Lieut. Wilkins will hand over tents and shelters to Camp Commandant at TARA.

8. Date and time of move will be communicated to those concerned.

Issued at 11-0 a.m.

Copy No.	
1.	Commanding Officer
2.	O.C. "A" Company
3.	O.C. "B" "
4.	O.C. "C" "
5.	O.C. "D" "
6.	Quartermaster
7.	32nd Division
8.	4th Canadian Division
9.	War Diary
10.	War Diary.

G. B. DEMPSEY Lieut. and Adjutant.

SECRET

24th Battalion The Manchester Regiment (Pioneers)

SUPPLEMENTARY TO OPERATION ORDER NO.2.

With reference to para 8 Operation Order No. 2, the Battalion will move at 10 am on the 31st Oct

30-10-16   G. B. DEMSEY. Lieut. and Adjutant.

SECRET   Appendix #4   Copy No. 8

24th Battalion The Manchester Regiment
OPERATION ORDER NO. 3.

31st October, 1916.

1. (a) On a date to be notified later the Reserve Army is to attack North and South of the River ANCRE.
   (b) II Corps, consisting of 18th, 19th, 32nd, 39th and 4th Canadian Divisions, in the initial stages of the operation is to capture PYS, IRLES, ACHIET LE PETIT, MIRAUMONT, and the line of the MIRAUMONT-BEAUCOURT Sur ANCRE Road.

2. In the first phase the 4th Canadian, 18th, 19th and 39th Divisions are to gain the following objectives:-

   <u>4th Canadian Division</u> <u>First Objective</u> Approximate line M. 14. d. 10.85.- M. 7. d. 8.4.- M. 7. a. 15.05. and thence along COULLEE Trench to R. 12. c. 1.9.
   <u>2nd. Objective</u> M. 7. b. 5.1. to R. 5. d. 60.25.

   <u>18th Division 1st Objective</u> GRANDCOURT Trench from R. 12. c. 1.9. to R. 16. a. 8.8.
   <u>2nd Objective</u> Line R. 5. d. 60.25.- Cross Roads at R. 5. b. 5.4.- Railway bridge at R. 5. a. 5.5. and thence along Railway to R. 4. d. 1.1.
   <u>3rd Objective</u> MIRAUMONT.

   <u>19th Division 1st Objective</u> GRANDCOURT Trench R. 16. a. 88- R. 15. b. 70.95 - R. 15. a. 6.1. and thence to R. 15. c. 05.95.- R. 14. b. 90.15 - R. 14. b. 80.05. and thence a line running approximately R. 14. b. 3.3.- R. 14. a. 2.5.
   <u>2nd Objective</u> Line of Railway from R. 4. d. 1.1. to bridge at R. 8. c. 4.5. and thence to R. 8a. c. 20.
   <u>3rd Objective</u> Line of MIRAUMONT-BEAUCOURT sur ANCRE Road from Cross Roads at R. 4. b. 25.20 to R. 8. a. 2.2. and thence to R. 8. c. 2.0.

   <u>39th Division 1st Objective</u> Line of River ANCRE from R. c. 2.0. to Q. 24. b. 1.3. and crossings at THE MILL (R. 13. a. 2.7.) and BRIDGE Road (Q. 13. b. 85.40).

3. There will in each case be a halt of approximately 1 hour after the capture of the 1st and 2nd Objectives and the times for continuing the advance against the 2nd and 3rd Objectives will be respectively-
   (i) Zero plus 1 hour 28 minutes
   (ii) Zero plus 3 hours 24 minutes.

4. PRELIMINARY MOVES OF 32nd DIVISION

   32nd Division (less Artillery) will move on the day preceeding the attack to positions in bivouac as follows:-
   <u>14th Inf. Bde.</u>   X. 7. Central.
   (with 1 Section 206th Fd. Coy. R.E. and 1 Company 24th Manchester Regt. Pioneers).

   <u>96th Inf. Bde.</u>   X. 9. c. and 8. d.
   (with 1 Section 218th Fd. Coy. R.E. and 1 Coy. 24th Manchester Regt. Pioneers)

   <u>97th Inf. Bde.</u>   USNA HILL
   Divl Engrs (less 1 Fd. Coy. R.E. and 2 Sections).
   March table will be issued later.
   219th Fd. Coy. R.E. will remain in its present position at LA BOISSELLE, and 24th Manchester Regt.(Pioneers, less

Sheet 2.

two Companies, will remain at X.11.a. till the morning of the day of the attack.

5. STATE OF READINESS

At 2 hours after Zero hour on the day of the attack, the units of the 32nd Division will be ready to move as follows:-
14th & 96th Inf.Bdes. Groups at ½ hours notice, which will be altered later to 10 minutes notice.
97th Inf.Bde. Divl Engineers and 24th Manchester Regt. (Pioneers) less 2 Coys. at 1 hours notice, which will be altered later to ½ hours notice.

6. FIRST MOVES OF 32nd DIV. ON DAY OF ATTACK

(a) As soon as the rear Bde. of the 18th Div. moves forward preparatory to attacking MIRAUMONT, the 96th Bde. Group will move forward under orders from the Division via the ALBERT-POZIERES Road (or across country 150 yards North and parallel to this Road-X.3.b.-X.4.a.-R.34.a. to a position of readiness in the area R.28.c., whence it can be moved forward to the valley South of MIRAUMONT.

(b) As soon as the 96th Bde. Group is ordered forward from the vicinity of R.28.c., the 14th Bde. Group will be moved up to take its place, following one or other of the following routes:-
 (i) OVILLERS-COURCELETTE Road to R.34.c. and thence via R.34.a. to R.28.c.
 (ii) X.1.b.-X.2.a.-R.32.c.-R.32.b.-R.33.a.- R.27.c.

(c) In the event of the situation permitting it both Bde. Groups will move up simultaneously by the routes given to positions of assembly about R.28.c. and R.27.c.

(d) 97th Inf. Bde. Group, assembled at USNA HILL, will be moved up to the vicinity of X.9.c. and X.8.d. so soon as this area is vacated by the leading Bde. Group, and again 97th Bde. Group will in time replace the leading Bde. at R.28.c. when these move forward.

7. TASK ALLOTTED TO 32nd DIV.

The task allotted to the 32nd Division is the capture of PYS, IRLES and ACHIET LE PETIT, so soon as MIRAUMONT is captured.

8. INTENTION

The G.O.C. intends to employ the 96th Inf. Bde. on the right to attack PYS, and the 14th Inf. Bde. on the left to attack IRLES. These villages will be captured and strong posts established at points on their far side. The 97th Inf. Bde. will be held in reserve for the subsequent capture of ACHIET LE PETIT.

9. R.E. AND PIONEERS

The Section of a Fd. Coy. R.E. and Company of Pioneers attached to each of the 14th and 96th Inf. Bdes. will not be thrown into the attack with the assaulting Battalions; they will be retained in a position of readiness and brought forward under orders from the Bde. after the position has been captured to assist in the work of consolidation.

In order to keep the attacking troops clear of hostile Artillery fire directed from the map and at the same time to adapt new defences to the lie of the ground, troops

Sheet 3.

will, when consolidating positions gained, avoid so gar as possible old trenches.

10. PRISONERS OF WAR Prisoners of War will be sent to X. 9. b. 9.5. through Battalion H.Q.

11. MISCELLANEOUS (-) No papers will be carried by Officers and Other Ranks taking part in the attack except the 1/20,000 Trench Maps showing the German trenches, Sheets 57 D S.E., N.E., and 57 C. N.W., S.W. or special map "K17 - M21". All messages and reports will refer to one or other of these maps. The hectograph sketches may be taken.

(b) Men are not to fall out to bring back wounded.

(c) Any guns captured which are in danger of being lost again, must be rendered useless by damaging the sights and breach mechanism. Captured machine guns must be collected.

(d) Administrative instructions have been issued separately under G.S. 758/5 of 24th October, 1916, copies of which have been issued to the Officers concerned.

12. "C" Company (Lieut. Wood) will be attached to 14th Bde.
"A" Company (Lieut. Bateman) to 96th Bde.
"B" and "D" Coys. (Capt. Wall) to move under orders of 32nd Division.

13. Each Company will carry 2 Lewis Guns and magazines.

14. Tools will be carried in the ratio of 2 shovels to 1 pick, each N.C.O. and man to carry one tool.
Each N.C.O. and man will carry 6 sandbags.

Issued at 3.30 p.m.

Copy No. 1. Commanding Officer.
2. O.C. "A" Company
3. O.C. "B"   "
4. O.C. "C"   "
5. O.C. "D"   "
6. Quartermaster
7. 32nd Division.
8. War Diary
9. War Diary

G. B. DEMPSEY. Lieut. and Adjutant.

WAR DIARY or INTELLIGENCE SUMMARY

Army Form C. 2118.

Vol 13

VOLUME XIII   NOVEMBER 1916   24TH MANCHESTER REGT.

Place	Date	Hour	Summary of Events and Information	Remarks and references to Appendices
X IIA. Map ALBERT Combined Sheet	Nov. 1st	10 p.m.	**Weather.** Fine. Wind light westerly. Shower in evening. **Working Parties.** A Company. Cleared 200 yards of trench (COLT TRENCH). Dug 4 new dump holes and completed 4 others. 75 other ranks 4 hours work. B Company. Training and clearing COLT NERVE. 80 other ranks 6 hours. C Company. Cleared 10" STREET and dug Sump holes. 80 other ranks 6 hours. D Company. Cleared 10" STREET and dug Sump holes. 93 other ranks 6 hours. **Casualties.** Killed nil. Wounded Officers nil - other ranks 2.	Map Ref K11- M 28. 905
	2nd	10 p.m.	**Weather.** Rain. Dull. Wind S.W. **Working Parties.** A Company. Worked 5 p.m. to 11.30 p.m. Cleared 10" Street and laid trench boards. 40 men Constructed dug out. B Company and D Company. Worked 7.15 p.m. to 11.30 p.m. 30 men Cleared COLT AVENUE. 24 men erected bridges over hurdles. 23 men erected O.P. near COLT AVENUE. 5 men working on AID POST. 28 men carrying material. C Company. 25 men worked 4 hours - ammunition dump. Casualties Officers nil. Other ranks 3 wounded.	905

WAR DIARY
or
INTELLIGENCE SUMMARY

(Erase heading not required.)

Army Form C. 2118.

Place	Date	Hour	Summary of Events and Information	Remarks and references to Appendices
X 11 a	3rd	10pm	Weather Wind light S.E. Fine. Slight rain at night.	
			Work Companies rested except a party of 25 x/C Coy working on an ammunition dump and 32 to Bn HQ. D Company was attached to 32nd Bn HQ from the 3rd inst inclusive	M.1
			Casualties Nil	
			Commission No 41334 L/C A. Smith proceeded to England for Commission in T.F. Lancs Fusiliers.	Yes
"	4th	8pm	Weather Fine during day. Rain at night. Wind S.E. Fresh.	
			Work A Company rested. B and E Coys supplied 150 men for draining and hand boarding 10th STREET. C Company supplied 25 men at 32 Bn to erecting huts 20 men at POZIERES Dump 20 " " Dump (S.A.A.) at X Bat. 20 " " (S.A.A.) at R.32 W.6.B	Yes
			Casualties Nil	

Carville

Army Form C. 2118.

WAR DIARY
or
INTELLIGENCE SUMMARY
(Erase heading not required.)

Place	Date	Hour	Summary of Events and Information	Remarks and references to Appendices
X11a	5th	10pm	Weather - cold but fine. Wind strong S.E. Ground much drier. Work - 40 men laying heavy boards DEATH VALLEY A Company B Company - 30 men cleaned OUTPOST. Communication trench C Company - Aromatic 4th Av D Company - Rested Casualties - Officers nil - Other ranks 3 slightly wounded	Yes
→	6th	10pm	Weather - Wind strong westerly. Rain and cold. Work A Company - 24 men worked clearing trenches & digging sump. 44 men to build breastworks - no work done owing to Shell fire B Company } Rested C Company } 85 men working on S.H.A dumps under 32nd Divn! D Company - 100 men to build emplacements across valley & to clean up A trench. No work done owing to enemy barrage. Casualties - Officers nil. Other ranks nil.	MM 2 Yes

Army Form C. 2118.

WAR DIARY
or
INTELLIGENCE SUMMARY

(Erase heading not required.)

Instructions regarding War Diaries and Intelligence Summaries are contained in F. S. Regs., Part II. and the Staff Manual respectively. Title Pages will be prepared in manuscript.

Place	Date	Hour	Summary of Events and Information	Remarks and references to Appendices
X.11.a.	7th	10pm	**Weather** Strong westerly wind; much rain. **Work** A Coy Rested. B Coy Left camp 5.30 pm; cleared 100 yds of mud & pulled sandbags. C Coy As previous day. D Coy cleared trench & taken in DEATH VALLEY; built 80 yds of sandbag wall.	App 3
	8th	10pm	**Casualties** Officers — Nil; Other ranks — 1 wounded **Weather** West to south west wind; some rain **Work** C Coy finishing S.A.A dumps; & 25 men erecting huts etc at Div H.Q.	AH gM
	9th	10pm	Other boys rested **Weather** Cold, wind lighter. **Work** As previous day; in addition C Coy had 30 men on RE Depots near AVELUY. **Casualties** Officers Nil — 1 OR wounded in camp by fragment of Anti-Aircraft shell.	AH M AH M

Army Form C. 2118.

WAR DIARY
or
INTELLIGENCE SUMMARY

(Erase heading not required.)

Instructions regarding War Diaries and Intelligence Summaries are contained in F. S. Regs., Part II. and the Staff Manual respectively. Title Pages will be prepared in manuscript.

Place	Date	Hour	Summary of Events and Information	Remarks and references to Appendices
X.11.a	10th	10PM	**Weather** Light S.W wind, warmer. **Work** C Coy 28 men at Divl HQ; also new S.A.A Dump. 15 O.Rs worked as carrying party 2 hrs for Can.R.Es at CORPSE DUMP. Otherways Rest.	
	11th	10PM	**Weather** Dull, light southerly wind. **Work** 300 men paraded 5.30 pm to dig new communication trench in square X.14.8 from old front line to captured position in square X.14.a.3. Returned to camp without doing any work owing to hostile barrage. C Coy Rests. 25 men enemy hut at Divl HQ; parties at new SAA Dump & (2) at R.E Dumps near NEUVY. **Casualties** Officers - nil O.Rs - 1 wounded.	

Army Form C. 2118.

WAR DIARY
or
INTELLIGENCE SUMMARY
(Erase heading not required.)

Place	Date	Hour	Summary of Events and Information	Remarks and references to Appendices
X11a	12th	10 PM	Weather Cold; wind S. Work 200 men paraded 5.30 PM. Dug new trench (see Previous Day) for 300 yds length 4½-5 ft deep. C Coy Rested. Casualties Officers – nil ORs – 1 wounded (HE shell)	JSJM
	13th	10 PM	42 wounded remaining at duty (HE shell) Weather Dull; thick mist in morning; wind S.E. light. Work C Coy 80 men working on RE dumps near AVELUY 15 " " " " near MOUQUET FARM 15 " " " " near POZIÈRES. Other Coys rested.	JSJM

2449 Wt. W14957/M90 750,000 1/16 J.B.C. & A. Forms/C.2118/12.

WAR DIARY or INTELLIGENCE SUMMARY

Army Form C. 2118.

Place	Date	Hour	Summary of Events and Information	Remarks and references to Appendices
X-11-a	14th	10 P.M.	Weather Colder; wind light N-NE. Work. 1 Officer & 100 O.R's (A Coy) reported at POZIÈRES DUMP at 5 P.M; remained there owing to non arrival of R.E officers & guides. Owing to damage to H.E & gas shells, left dump at 7.30 P.M & returned to camp, men suffering from effects of gas. C Coy. 1 Officer & 100 O.R's went to replace them; owing to misunderstanding failed to meet R.E's & returned to camp. Set out again about 10.15 P.M; deepened new communication trench (Lee work for 12th) from 3' to about 5'; carried & fitted trench boards. Bydleys Poches. Casualties 1 Officer & 20 O.R's wounded, gassed — 2 other ranks wounded — 1 other rank wounded — shell shock } all remaining with unit.	App 4. AESBW

WAR DIARY
or
INTELLIGENCE SUMMARY

(Erase heading not required.)

Army Form C. 2118.

Place	Date	Hour	Summary of Events and Information	Remarks and references to Appendices
X.11.a.	15th	10 pm	Weather: Cold, ground drier. Wind N-NE. Work: B Coy, 1 Offr & 50 O.Rs carried & laid 5-16" ordinary track from DESTREMONT FARM - COLT AX. 10ff.30 O.Rs finished laying duckboards in new communication trench (MANCHESTER AV.) D Coy 10ff 930 O.Rs out 7 hours, no work done owing to the men & others being no covering party out. Casualties – Nil	J.S.W.
X.11.a	16th	10 pm	Weather: Cold but clear. Slight frost. Work: 1 Off & 120 O.Rs (80 A Coy, 40 C Coy) paraded 4 PM to dig forward sap from new front line; after reviewing for Ky hr under very heavy M.G & shell fire, returned work not completed. The party was also bombed from a hostile sap. 1 Off & 30 O.Rs (C Coy) carrying & laying 300 yds (one) of ordinary on mule track; work suspended; but owing to MG & shell fire. 10ff 5 O.Rs wounded. Casualties 1 O.R wounded (HE) remaining with unit.	M.A.E.S. J.S.W.

WAR DIARY
or
INTELLIGENCE SUMMARY

Army Form C. 2118.

Place	Date	Hour	Summary of Events and Information	Remarks and references to Appendices
THIEPVAL WOOD.	17th	10 PM	Weather Bright/clear; frosty.	
			Move The Battalion (less Transport & Band) moved to Ouposts at the S end of THIEPVAL WOOD; Operation order attached.	App 5.
			Work A Coy 25 O.Rs. B Coy 10 Offr & 100 O.Rs. Left camp 5.10 P.M; worked 8.15 P.M - 12 midnight C Coy 10 Offr & 25 O.Rs. arrived back 1.15 A.M. Workdone 500 yds D Coy 10 Offr & 93 O.Rs. of 6ft cable trench.	App. 6.
			Casualties — Nil.	
	18th	10 PM	Weather Milder, some rain.	
			Work A Coy left camp 4.45 P.M. reported to 56 K.B Dr HQ; carried 30 boxes of bombs to new front line; cleared latter & put in two steps for 90'; returned at 2.10 A.M.	J.S.G.N.
			C Coy left camp 4.45 P.M; 1 Offr & fwy story party at R.S.d.4.4 3 Offrs fwy out front R.8.d 3.2.k to R.8.d 2.k.0.k. carried up 60 boxes of Bombs & T.M. Ammn.	

Army Form C. 2118.

WAR DIARY
or
INTELLIGENCE SUMMARY
(Erase heading not required.)

Instructions regarding War Diaries and Intelligence Summaries are contained in F. S. Regs., Part II. and the Staff Manual respectively. Title Pages will be prepared in manuscript.

Place	Date	Hour	Summary of Events and Information	Remarks and references to Appendices
THIEPVAL WOOD			B⁰ D⁰y's. Left camp 5.0 PM & reported to 7th B⁰s HQ; guides from there did not know the way; owing to darkness & the rough cut up nature of the ground the work was not gone; returned to camp about 2 AM Casualties – Nil – O.R's 1 wounded	
	19th	10.0 am	Message of Appreciation received from G.O.C 4th Canadian Divn. Weather Milder. Some rain. Work A.Coy 87 O.Rs } Left camp 3.0 PM; returned between 2.15 AM & 5.0 AM. B.Coy 102 O.Rs } Work done digging new fire trench with C.Coy 116 O.Rs } 4 strong points, from about R.14.A.17 to about D.Coy 83 O.Rs } R.14.C.5.0 Casualties – Nil. Prisoners – 2 Prisoners were taken by the working party; 1 wounded & 1 unwounded.	

Army Form C. 2118.

WAR DIARY
or
INTELLIGENCE SUMMARY
(Erase heading not required.)

Place	Date	Hour	Summary of Events and Information	Remarks and references to Appendices
THIEPVAL WOOD	20th	10 A.M.	Weather Fine, proved very muddy. Work 10AM 400 O.R's (25 per Coy) left Camp 4 P.M. returned 1.15 a.m.; work done - New trench (see previous day) deepened & improved. 10AM 4.50 O.R's (A Coy) carried 100 french mats from about 400 yds So of ST PIERRE DIVION to new communication trench & placed them in position. 2.0PM 54.150 O.R's (B.C & D) carried 75 trench boards, deepened 750 yds of new communication trench, from about 3 ft to about 5ft 6in; put in 7 traverses. Casualties Officers 1 wounded, remaining with unit, other ranks 2 wounded.	J.S.P/W.
	21st	10AM	Weather Thick mist in morning clearing later; warm & clear later. Work Rested.	J.S.P/W.
	22nd	10AM	Weather Thick mist in morning; warm & clear later. Move B⁰ moved to huts & bivouacs in MAILLY WOOD WEST; fun then order attached. Casualties O.Rs 2 wounded & remaining on duty.	J.S.P/W.

Army Form C. 2118.

WAR DIARY
or
INTELLIGENCE SUMMARY

(Erase heading not required.)

Instructions regarding War Diaries and Intelligence Summaries are contained in F. S. Regs., Part II. and the Staff Manual respectively. Title Pages will be prepared in manuscript.

Place	Date	Hour	Summary of Events and Information	Remarks and references to Appendices
MAILLY WOOD W. P-17.6.	23rd	10PM	Weather. Clear, cold. Work. Cleaning camp etc. Casualties — Nil.	A.S.H.P.W.
	24th	10PM	Weather. White frost, some rain later. Work. Coys rested; Commanding Officer inspected the Bn. Casualties — Nil.	A.S.H.P.W.
	25th	10PM	Weather. Heavy & continuous rain. Work. Some drains dug in camp. Casualties — Nil.	A.S.H.P.W.
	26th	10PM	Weather. Fine; very wet underfoot. Work. Coys 125/30 Casualties — Nil.	A.S.H.P.W.

Place	Date	Hour	Summary of Events and Information	Remarks and references to Appendices
	27th	10PM	**Weather** Damp cold, no wind. **Work** A Coy 120 all ranks worked 4½ hrs, cleaning & dredging 6TH AV. for 200 yds, 2 pumps worked, 4 frames made & fitted with expanded metal; returned to camp about 3.30 PM. B Coy 125 other ranks worked & his camp supplied seed boards, cleaning 150 yds of WALKER AV. C Coy Nos. Resting. 12 men worked on horse standings in camp. **Casualties** A Coy 6 O.R.s wounded (H.E. Shrapnel) 1 O.R accidentally wounded.	A.S.H/M
	28th	10PM	**Weather** Damp cold, no wind. **Work** A Coy 45 men worked 4½ hrs carrying party for R.E.'s 1 Off + 58 men ... ... cleaning SIXTH AV. B Coy Nos. C Coy 2 Offs + 125 O.R.s cleared comprised engineers. WALKER AV. 100 yds. First made-late. D Coy 2 Offs + 113 O.R.s went out for night work, came under heavy bombardment of gas shells; 11 men detained aft. A. remainder ordered back to camp, all more or less affected by gas.	A.S.H/M

Place	Date	Hour	Summary of Events and Information	Remarks and references to Appendices
MAILLY WOOD M.	29th	10PM	**Weather** Slight frost; thick mist in morning; no wind.	
			Work B Coy 2 Offrs & 119 ORs worked 5½ hrs; completely clearing WALKER AV. Laid trench mats along whole length.	
			D Coy Rested.	
			M Coy 4 Offrs & 223 ORs worked 2¾ hrs (night); dug 410' new narrow fire trench, average depth 3' - 3' 6"	
			Casualties — Nil.	
			Msgs of appreciation received from GOC 19th Div.	
	30th	10PM	**Weather** as 29th.	
			Work A Coy Rested.	
			D Coy 2 Offrs & 93 ORs worked 6 hours cleaning, deepening & enlarging trench mats in LEAVE AV.	Mk 9...
			B & C Coy worked 4½ hrs (night); 4 Offrs & 231 ORs; fire steps made, trench deepened, 2 new sections dug (of new front line)	
			Casualties O.R. — 1 killed, 2 wounded (by snipers)	

WAR DIARY
or
INTELLIGENCE SUMMARY

Army Form C. 2118.

Place	Date	Hour	Summary of Events and Information	Remarks and references to Appendices
			Honours — The following NCO's & men were awarded the Military Medal for gallantry in the field.	J.S.S.M.
			14249 Sergt Howarth E.	
			14375 L/c (A/Sgt) O'Neill J.	
			14239 Sergt Taylor J.	
			14034 L/Sgt Lowry W.	
			14047 L/c Bond J.	
			14706 L/c Turner T.	
			14729 Pte Humphrey J. D.C.M.	
			14719 " Taylor M.	
			14804 " Hudson E.	
			15238 " Haslam S.	

SECRET   Copy No. 7

OPERATION ORDER NO. 4.
BY MAJOR J.H. CHADWICK COMMANDING
24TH BATTALION THE MANCHESTER REGT.

Appendix 1

3rd November, 1916.

1.   In continuation of 24th Bn. The Manchester Regt., Operation Order No. 3, of 31st October, 1916, in the attack against PYS the objective of the 4th Canadian Division and the 96th Brigade will be approximately the line running from M. 9. a. 63 - M. 2. d. 35 - G. 31. d. 5.1.

2.   The 14th Brigade, detailed to attack IRLES, will advance at the same time as the 96th Brigade and will take up a line from about M. 1. b. 85.85. through trench running W.N.W. from G. 31. d. 51 and trench running N.W. from L.36.d.5.4 to connect with the right of the 18th Division at L. 35. b. 44 and will halt for 30 minutes on this line before continuing its advance.

3.   The dividing line between 4th Canadian Division and 32nd Division will be the road running M. 13. b. 1.0 - M. 7. d. 75.70 - Cross Roads M. 2. c. 65.10 - Bridge at M. 2. d. 65.80 (inclusive to 4th Canadian Division)

         Issued at 11-30 a.m.

Copy No. 1.   C. O.   Copy No. 2.   O.C. "A" Coy.
         3.   O.C. "B" Coy.   4.   O.C. "C" "
         5.   O.C. "D" "   6.   Quartermaster
         7.   War Diary   8.   War Diary

(Signed) G. B. DEMPSEY. Lieut. and Adjutant.

SECRET
Appendix 2.

Copy No. 1

OPERATION ORDER NO. 5.
BY MAJOR J.H. CHADWICK COMMANDING
24TH BATTALION MANCHESTER REGIMENT

6th November, 1916.

1. During Operations "C" Company will draw rations from the 14th Infantry Brigade and "A" Company from the 96th Infantry Brigade.

2. Battalion H.Q. will be at the 32nd Divisional H.Q.

Issued at 3-15 p.m.

Copy No. 1. O.C. "A" Company
       2. O.C. "B"   "
       3. O.C. "C"   "
       4. O.C. "D"   "
       5. Quartermaster
       6. War Diary
       7. War Diary.

G. B. DEMPSEY. Lieut. and Adjutant.

SECRET

Appendix 3

Copy No. 3

OPERATION ORDER NO. 6.
BY MAJOR J.H. CHADWICK COMMANDING
24TH BATTALION MANCHESTER REGIMENT.

7th November, 1916.

1.   During the attack 1 Section 218th Coy. R.E. and "A" Company 24th Battalion Manchester Regiment (Pioneers) will be in the Ravine in R. 17. a.

2.   The order of march of the 96th Brigade Group from X. 9. c. to R. 28. c. will be as follows:-
- 2nd R. Innis. Fus.
- 16th Lanc. Fus.
- 16th North'd. Fus.
- 15th Lanc. Fus.
- 96th M.G. Coy.
- 1 Section 218th Fd. Coy. R.E.
- "A" Coy. 24th Manchester Regt. (Pioneers)

3.   Brigade H.Q. and Report Centre will be as follows:-

(a) When Brigade is in position in bivouac -
    Bde. H.Q. and Report Centre about X. 9. c.

(b) When Brigade is in position of readiness -
    Bde. H.Q. and Report Centre about R. 28. c.

(c) When Brigade is in position of assembly -
    Bde. H.Q. and Report Centre about R. 11. c.

Issued at 3-50 p.m.

Copy No. 1.   Commanding Officer
        2.   O.C. "A" Company
    3. & 4.   War Diary.

A. St. G. WALSH. 2/Lieut. and Acting Adjutant.

SECRET

Appendix 4

SECRET.   Copy No. 7.

OPERATION ORDER NO. 6A.
BY MAJOR J.H.CHADWICK COMMANDING
24TH BATTALION MANCHESTER REGIMENT.

14th Novr. 1916.

Operation Orders Nos., 3, 4, 5, and 6 are cancelled.

Issued at 11.30 a.m.

```
Copy No. 1.    Commanding Officer.
        2.    O.C. "A" Coy.
        3.    O.C. "B"  "
        4.    O.C. "C"  "
        5.    O.C. "D"  "
        6.    Transport Officer & Quartermaster.
    7 & 8.    War Diary.
```

A.St G.WALSH.   Lieut. and Acting Adjutant.

SECRET Copy No. 8

**OPERATION ORDER No.7 BY
MAJOR J.H. CHADWICK COMMANDING
24TH BATTALION MANCHESTER REGT.**

16th November, 1916.

REFERENCE - FRANCE 57 D. S.E., 1/20,000

1.   The Battalion will move tomorrow (17th November0 to THIEPVAL WOOD.

2.   TIME TABLE   (a) Reveille 6-30 a.m.
                    (b0 Breakfast 7-0 a.m.
                    (c0 Field Kitchens, Tools, Blankets and Officers Mess Baskets to be ready by 8-30a.m.
                    (d(Battalion to move at 9-30 a.m.

3.   DRESS:- Marching order. Steel Helmets will be worn.

4.   ROUTE:- Valley to BAILIFF WOOD, LA BOISELLE, Cross Roads W. 18. b. Central, AVELUY WUARRY, AUTHUILLE.

5.   ORDER OF MARCH:- H.W., 'C' Company, 'D', 'A', 'B'. An interval of 100 yards between half Companies.

6.   Lewis Gunners will join the Transport at W. 24. b. leaving the Camp at 8-30 a.m.

7.   Orders for movement of Transport will be issued separately.

8.   2/Lieut. Braine will proceed to take over new Camp at 9-0 a.m.

    Issued at 11-30 p.m.

    Copy No. 1. Commanding Officer
            2. O.C. 'A' Coy.
            3. O.C. 'B' "
            4. O.C. 'C' "
            5. O.C. 'D' "
            6. Wuartermaster & Transport Officer
            7. Lewis Gun Officer
        8 & 9 War Diary.
           10 2nd In Command.

    A. St. G. WALSH 2/Lieut. and Acting Adjutant.

S E C R E T   Copy No 7

Appendix

OPERATION ORDER NO. 8.
BY MAJOR J.H. CHADWICK COMMANDING
24TH BATTALION MANCHESTER REGT.

17th November, 1916.

REFERENCE, FRANCE 57 D. S.E.

1.   The Battalion will be attached to the 19th Division for Operations to-morrow (18th instant)

2.   **W O R K :-** To dig a switch line from about R. 13. b. 9.8. to about R. 14. b. 5½.3½.

3.   DRESS:- Fighting order, less greatcoats, as detailed in previous preliminary instructions.

4.   TOOLS:- Each man to carry a shovel, and every alternate man a pick in addition.

5.   The Battalion will be ready to move at half an hours notice after 9-15 a.m.

6.   Captain Wall with two runners will report to G.O.C., 57th Brigade at R. 26. b. 3.3. by 9-0 a.m. to-morrow as liaison Officer between 57th Brigade and the Battalion and to reconnoitre the position of the new trench when G.O.C., 57th Brigade considers the situation admits of reconnaissance

7.   Two Lewis Guns with magazines will be attached to each Company.

                Issued at 11-15 P.M.

Copy No. 1. C. O.   Copy No. 2. 2nd in Command
        3. O.C. 'A' Coy.   4. O.C. 'B' Coy.
        5. O.C. 'C' '   6. O.C. 'D' '
7 and 8. War Diary

                                                          A. St. G. WALSH 2/Lieut. & A/Adjutant.

Appendix 7

The following message has been received from the G. O. C., 4th Canadian Division:-

4th Canadian Division
G-14-1

Major Chadwick,
O.C., 24th Battalion
Manchester Pioneer Regt.

Dear Major Chadwick,

I wish to express to you my regret that your Battalion is to-day leaving this Division, and I take this opportunity of conveying to you and all ranks of your Unit my appreciation of the excellent work done while attached to us.

The thoroughness and keenness with which your work has been consistently carried on has been brought to my attention, and I would particularly thank you for the capable way in which you met the situation on the night of the 14th instant, when with a party of the 10th Field Company Canadian Engineers, your party was gassed near Pozieres.

Yours very sincerely,

(Signed)   D. WATSON   Major-General,
Commanding 4th Canadian Division."

The following reply has been despatched:-

"G. O. C.,
4th Canadian Division.

Sir,

I wish to thank you for your kind letter of appreciation of the work of the 24th Manchester Regiment while attached to your Division.

I has been a great pleasure to work with your Engineers who consistently showed the greatest consideration for us, and the regret at the separation is mutual.

I have the honour to be, Sir,
Your obedient servant,

(Signed)   J. H. CHADWICK,   Major,
18-11-16   Commanding 24th Bn. The Manchester Regiment.

SECRET   Copy No. 8

OPERATION ORDER NO. 9 BY MAJOR J.H. CHADWICK COMMANDING 24TH BATTALION MANCHESTER REGT.

21st November, 1916

REFERENCE, FRANCE 57 D. S.E. 1/20,000 or 57 D. 1/40,000.

1. The Battalion will move to-morrow (22nd Nov) to P. 17. b.

2. TIME TABLE:- Reveille 5-30 a.m. Breakfast 6-0 a.m.
Sick Parade 6-30 a.m.
Blankets will be carried to Motor lorry at Q. 36. c. 7.6. by 7-0 a.m.
Officers valises and Mess baskets to be stacked by sentry box at 8-0 a.m.
Field Kitchens to be ready to move at 8-0 a.m.
Move off 9-0 a.m.

3. ORDER OF MARCH Headquarters, "D" Coy. "A" Coy, "B" Coy, and "C" Coy.
200 yards interval between Companies.

4. ROUTE:- Road to Q. 36. c. 5.2., Cross the ANCRE at MILL (Q. 36. c. 1.6.) MESNIL, Q. 22. b. 38, ENGLEBELMER, P. 24. c. 20.95, P. 17. b. Central

5. DRESS:- Marching order. Shrapnel helmets will be worn.

6. O.C. "C" Coy. will detail an Officer to march in rear of the column and collect stragglers.

7. Attention is called to 7th Divisional March Orders dated 13-11-16, which must be strictly complied with.

ISSUED AT 6-0 p.m.

Copy No. 1. C/mdg Officer   Copy No. 2. 2nd in Command
        3. O.C. "A" Coy.   4. O.C. "B" Coy.
        5. O.C. "C" "   6. O.C. "D" "
        7. ~~O.C. Transport Off'r~~   8 & 9. War Diary

(Signed) A. St. C. WALSH, 2/Lieut. and Acting Adjutant.

19th Division, No. 221.

Headquarters,
    4th Canadian Division.   Novr 23, 1916.

        Will you please convey my thanks to the 24th Bn. Manchester Regiment (Pioneers) for the excellent work they did during the few days that they were attached to the 19th Division, especially in the construction of the new line on the night of the 19/20th instant west of GRANDCOURT.

        This line was 800 yards long, with three Strong Points, and was finished in a night in close proximity to the enemy, and I regard it as a fine bit of pioneering.

                              (Sgd) H. Bridge.
                                Major-General
D.H.Q.   Commanding 19th Division.
22/11/16.

24th Manchester Regt.
    Forwarded.

                The G.O.C. has read this with much pleasure.

                (Sgd) W. Wingfield.
28/11/16.   A.A. & Q.M. 7th Division.

Army Form C. 2118.

WAR DIARY
or
INTELLIGENCE SUMMARY

(Erase heading not required.)

Vol XIV   December 1916.

2/4 "B" Manchester Regt.   Vol 14

Place	Date	Hour	Summary of Events and Information	Remarks and references to Appendices
MAILLY WOOD WEST P.23.6.17 Sheet 57.D.S.E.	1st	10pm	Weather frosty & thick mist. Work A Coy 2 Offrs & 75 O.R. worked 4½ hrs (Day); cleaned & deepened 150' LEAVE TR. B.C.D Coys Resting. Casualties — Nil	H.S.H.W.
	2nd	10pm	Weather Slight frost & mist. Work A Coy 1 Offr 106 O.R. worked 4½ hrs (Day); cleared 500' of trench from SUNKEN RD K.R.E. Dump. D Coy 2 Offrs 82 O.R. worked 4½ hrs (Day); camp handed over, improved 200 yds new front, & comm. trench from Pt 5.9 to Pt 2.6 (Q.5.d) B Coy 2 Offrs 110 O.Rs cleared 150' LEAVE TR & laid road over; camp meets improvements & rifle range wars C Coy Resting. Casualties Nil	H.S.H.W.

WAR DIARY or INTELLIGENCE SUMMARY

Army Form C. 2118.

Place	Date	Hour	Summary of Events and Information	Remarks and references to Appendices
	Dec 3rd	10pm	**Weather** Slight frost; no wind. **Work** B'y Coy's 30 Offrs 1960 R cleared & deepened 110 yds (completed) & 285 yds (partly finished) of communication tr. 60 yds of new gun trench improved. Worked 4 hrs (Day); Locality STATION AVE. A & D Coy's 3 Offrs 180 ORs worked 4½ hrs in Left B'y Area. 1 Coy deepened and widened 300 yds new front line. 1 Coy carried trench material frames for R.E.'s, staked water from Essex & Stephens 100 yds new comm. trench. **Casualties** — 1 wounded (O.R.)	J.H.W.

WAR DIARY
or
INTELLIGENCE SUMMARY
(Erase heading not required.)

Army Form C. 2118.

Place	Date	Hour	Summary of Events and Information	Remarks and references to Appendices
	Dec 4	10 A.M.	Weather: Slightly milder; no wind. Work: A Coy 20 ptrs 100 hrs worked 4 hrs (day); cleaning SIXTH AV. & carrying mats & frames; undergrdspace ext. 100 ft. new branch off SIXTH AV. D Coy 16 ptrs 760 O.R. worked 4½ hrs; carrying & deepening new front line night. B Coy's 40 ptrs 1760 O.R. worked 4½ hrs & digging 625' new comm: trench from BEAUCOURT TR to HUCK TR. Aus & Sept 4'; out 12 hrs. Casualties — 1 O.R. wounded.	J.S.H.W.
	Dec 5	10 A.M.	Weather: Mild milder; ground very sticky. Wind light, E. Work: A Coy 9 D Coy worked 4 (day); 20 ptrs 171 O.R. 1 carried frames, leads &c. C.I & E.A also 40 mats, improved new C.T & fire trench. B Coy 2 Offrs 85 O.R. worked 3½ hrs (night) on new C.T to HUCK TR. C Coy Rested. Casualties — Nil.	J.S.H.W.

WAR DIARY
or
INTELLIGENCE SUMMARY
(Erase heading not required.)

Army Form C. 2118.

Place	Date	Hour	Summary of Events and Information	Remarks and references to Appendices
	Dec 6	10 P.M.	Weather Mild. Wind Northerly. Ground very sticky. A Coy 1 Off. 94 O.R. 4 hours. Improved 200 yds. Cont. avenue, revetted 30 yards, drained 100 yds and deepened by 2 feet. Just another 500 yds. Rested. B Coy C Coy 2 Offs. 97 O.R. 4 hours. Deepened & 5'6". 400 yards of new C.T. from STATION AVENUE. D Coy 1 Off. 78 O.R. 4 hours. Cleaning up T.L. also emptg. stone water supply. Kept getting no last 400 yds done after arrival also drained bays. Casualties 1 killed 1 wounded.	P
	Dec 7	10 P.M.	Weather Mild. No mist. Slight snow in morning. Ground very wet. A Coy Rested. B & C Coys 2 Offs. 109 O.R. 4 hours. Work in new C.T. to Front Trench. 5 x 8' yards deepened to 6 feet. 4 Offs. duty with 2 Offs. Ground very soft and caving continually. D Coy 1 Off. 75 O.R. 4½ hours. Revetting and cleaning bay for forward trench. 12.00 tunnelling aust. for General Bay wet. Casualties Nil.	T.

2449 Wt. W14957/Mgo 750,000 1/16 J.B.C. & A. Forms/C.2118/12.

WAR DIARY
or
INTELLIGENCE SUMMARY

Army Form C. 2118.

(Erase heading not required.)

Place	Date	Hour	Summary of Events and Information	Remarks and references to Appendices
	Dec 6	10 PM	Weather. N.E. Wind Northerly. Ground very sticky. <u>A Coy</u> 1 Off 94 O.R. 4 hours. Inturned 300 yards Sixth Avenue revetted 30 yards, drained 100 yards and deepened by 2 feet another 150 yards. <u>B Coy</u> Rested <u>C Coy</u> 2 Off 97 O.R. 4 hours. Deepened 6'3" – 6'. 450 yards of new C.T. from STATION AVENUE <u>D Coy</u> 1 Off 96 O.R. 5 hours. Clearing new F.L. also carrying trench gratings and laid 40 of same. Some revetting done with sandbags. Casualties. 1 killed 1 wounded; both in "C" Coy	
	Dec 7	10 PM	Weather Mild. No wind. slight rain in morning. Ground very wet. Work <u>A Coy</u> Rested <u>B & C Coy</u> 2 Off 188 OR 4 hours. Work on new C.T. to Muck Trench 525 yards deepened to 6 feet. 4 ft wide at top. Ground very soft and crumbly, continually falling in. <u>D Coy</u> 1 Off 75 OR 4½ hours. Lengthing and clearing new fire trench. 1200 Sandbags carried from Beaumont Hamel Avent. Casualties. Nil.	

WAR DIARY
or
INTELLIGENCE SUMMARY
(Erase heading not required.)

Army Form C. 2118.

Place	Date	Hour	Summary of Events and Information	Remarks and references to Appendices
	Dec 8	10 PM	Weather - Mild Wind S.W. Rainfall 1 day. W.L. A Coy 1 Off 950 O.R. W/ line. Clearing and deepening trench from III AVENUE to Batt HQ. to Trench work carried B Coy 2 Offs 207 O.R. 4 hrs New C.T. 6-pick trench whilst remainder 6/f deep with duckboard 50 yards. Also 50 ft of trench 10 Fire Bays finished. 400 Sandbags carried up. Casualties 1 Killed (C Coy)	
	Dec 9	10 PM	Weather Mild and wet. Wind S.W. Rifles. A Coy 1 Off 95 OR W/ line. Carried up 45 Frames 75 sheets C.I. and 20 Trench Gratings. Cleaning III AVENUE B Coy 1 Off 100 O.R. 4 hrs. Renewing 50 yds ? New C.T. 6 pick TRENCH deepened 1 bay. 2 hrs fire bays made and revetted falling in. where had lay aground many ? C Coy Rests D Coy 1 Off. 76 OR W/line carried 40 trench gratings ? Off III AVENUE C.T. from E AGNES & 76 deepened to 6ft. Casualties N.L.	

WAR DIARY

or

INTELLIGENCE SUMMARY

(Erase heading not required.)

Army Form C. 2118.

Instructions regarding War Diaries and Intelligence
Summaries are contained in F. S. Regs., Part II.
and the Staff Manual respectively. Title Pages
will be prepared in manuscript.

Place	Date	Hour	Summary of Events and Information	Remarks and references to Appendices
	Dec 12	10 PM	Weather — Cold and Wet. Snow in the morning.	
			Work — A Coy. 1 Off 58 OR. 4 hrs carried stores to Old German F.L. and partially cleared and act of VI AVENUE which was deplorable condition	
			B Coy 1 Off 98 OR 4 hrs clearing STATION ALLEY which was waist deep in mud.	
			C Coy 1 Off 98 OR 4 hrs. Trench Mats and XPM carried to forward dumps. Attempted to clear TANK ALLEY which was flooded	
			D Coy rested. Casualties — Nil	
	Dec 13	10 PM	Weather — Dull overcast some rain. Wind S	
			A Coy 1 Off 60 OR 4 hrs. Rain carried so far and so thick C.I. remainder cleared 80 yds of trench east of WAGON ROAD from CRATER LANE to FL carried up materials but flood then	
			B Coy 1 Off 9 OR 4 hrs carried and fixed 6 frames in 150 yds of STATION ALLEY cleared waist fit frames and 50 yds partially cleared	
			C Coy rested	
			D Coy 1 Off 60 OR 4 hrs cleared 150 yds of FL and fixed 10 frames the rain was bad then	
			Casualties — Nil	

WAR DIARY or INTELLIGENCE SUMMARY

Army Form C. 2118.

Place	Date	Hour	Summary of Events and Information	Remarks and references to Appendices
	Dec 14	10 P.M.	Weather: Wet.	
			A.Coy 19/7. 6 O.R. 48 hrs. 50 shells C.I. and 50 Frames carried to CANS TR. for R.E. 70 yds of trench east of WAGGON ROAD from CRATER LANE to 7L cleared ready for [traffic].	Appx 1.
			B.Coy Rested.	
			C.Coy 19/7. 76 O.R. 48 hrs. 100 yds of TANK ALLEY 48 hrs. 100 yds of TANK ALLEY cleared out to half depth. 200 yds of STATION ALLEY cleared out to half depth. 6 frames fixed.	
			D.Coy 19/7. 61 O.R. 120 yds of E AVE. cleared. 60 shells C.I. + 30 frames carried up. 15 frames fixed and 8 mels laid.	27
			Casualties – Nil	
	Dec 15	10 P.M.	Weather: Rain at intervals. Wind – slight. S	
			A.Coy 19/7. 1.8. O.R. at hrs. Trench E of WAGGON ROAD. 140 yds cleared and 30 Trench mats laid.	
			B.Coy 19/7. 104 O.R. 48 hrs. 113 frames + 48 shells C.I. carried up. 6 frames fixed with [bolts] and [duckboards]. STATION ALLEY	
			C.Coy 19/7. 11 O.R. 48 hrs. 30 yds of trench 8 frames and 40 shells C.I. carried up to frame post 200 yds of TANK ALLEY cleared.	
			D.Coy 19/7. 46 O.R. 48 hrs. 6 frames carried up into D AVE. shells C.I. + sandbags to within 100 yds. Shells C.I. 6 frames fixed. 9 Retaining wall.	
			Casualties.	
			3 O.R. (C.Coy.)	

WAR DIARY
or
INTELLIGENCE SUMMARY

Army Form C. 2118.

Place	Date	Hour	Summary of Events and Information	Remarks and references to Appendices
Martin Puich	Dec 16	10 AM	Fate and Rain. Suse at Times. Wind S.S.W.	
			A Coy Rested	
			B Coy 1 Off. 26 OR. where. Carried 200 Drums 48 picks & Pcks 17 planks	
			1 from fatigue parties 200 yds J STATION ALLEY cleared	
			1 Off. 21 OR. at the X P.M. Front and 300 yds J TANK ALLEY	
			photograph chart	
			1 Off. 51 OR. at the 8 From 130 Half G.I. carried and fixed. 8 OYS	C
			D Coy 44 Ave cleared and made land	
			Casualties — Nil	
Martin Puich	Dec 17	10 AM	Cold and overcast. No wind.	
			A Coy 100 yds J VII AVE. cleared 74 Drums fat'd in. 23 frame carried	
			to do. Same XPM SE OA	
			B Coy 1 Off. 2+O.R. 45 hrs So ft STATION ALLEY cleared 8 frame filled	ST
			9 from 250 fi of Planking 40 Plcks XPM carried up	
			C Coy 1 Off. 40 OR when 250 yds J TANK ALLEY cleared & deepened	
			12 O from fixed	
			Casualties — Nil	

WAR DIARY
or
INTELLIGENCE SUMMARY

(Erase heading not required.)

Army Form C. 2118.

Place	Date	Hour	Summary of Events and Information	Remarks and references to Appendices
Martin Wood	Dec 18	10 P.M.	Batt. Report moved from S.	
			A.Coy. 1 Off - 60 OR. 4 hrs - 33 Trench mats carried up to CAGE TRENCH, in which 10 frames incidental were filled. 50 yds of Trench cleared. (?) Front mats carried to HAWSER DUMP.	
			B.Coy 1 Off. 79 OR. 4 hrs. 30 yds of STATION ALLEY filled with U-frames and not etc. Sand and further sags of Revetment stuff stowed for frames. 30 frames, 35 planks.	
			(2) 10th Corps Mobile X.M carried up.	
			C.Coy Diary	1 Off. 63 OR. 4.15 hrs. 10 frames, 2.5 sheets XPM. 100ft I Ranking carried up to TI AVE. 4 frames filled. 50 yds of Trench cleared.	
				4-5 R.Dudley and G.O.R. proceed to I St. Eloi.	
			D.Coy.	Passed all ? night - from S.	
	Aug 19	10 P.M.	Maurette Huts	C.H.O.	
			A.Coy	1 Off. 56 OR. 4 hrs. 100 yds of NEW CUT cleaned and 10 frames fitted for Trench mats carried to HAWSER DUMP. 20 U frames carried up to NEW CUT.	
			B.Coy	Rested.	
			C.Coy	1 Off. 70 OR. 4 hrs. 30 yds of TANK ALLEY cleared. 3 shelters, also 30 sheets XPM. 34 frames, 3 sheets XPM, half of 5x5 carried up.	
			D.Coy	1 Off. 63 OR. 4 hrs. 30yds of TI AVE cleaned. 105 frames filled. Ribbons.	
			* 3 scouts carried up Barb wire for post-R.E. works Batt. Reinforcement arrived but at Batt. MANLY WOOD. Among the lads 3 relief of NOTCH HUTS have been cleaned & swept by the day forces reinforcement by 10 OR from A Coy.	
				Conn. Oben. N.C	

Army Form C. 2118.

WAR DIARY
or
INTELLIGENCE SUMMARY
(Erase heading not required.)

Instructions regarding War Diaries and Intelligence Summaries are contained in F. S. Regs., Part II. and the Staff Manual respectively. Title Pages will be prepared in manuscript.

Place	Date	Hour	Summary of Events and Information	Remarks and references to Appendices
	20th	10PM	Weather — Bright & clear. No wind.	
			Work — Coys. did 3 hours Coy training; also instruction in M.G. bombing & signalling	J.S.H.M.
			Casualties — Nil.	
	21st	10PM	Weather — Wet, strong westerly wind; heavy rain at night.	
			Work — Lectures on bombing, M.G. & signalling	J.S.H.M.
			Casualties — Nil.	
	22nd	10PM	Weather — Westerly wind; very cold; C of E. Xmas services held in camp.	J.S.H.M.
			Work — As previous day. Casualties — Nil	
	23rd	10PM	Weather — Cold. Ground very bad underfoot.	J.S.H.M.
			Work — As previous day. Casualties — Nil	
	24th	10PM	Weather — Slightly milder; some rain.	
			Work — As previous day; working parties in camp erecting Nyson huts this day & previous days.	J.S.H.M.
			Casualties — Nil	

Army Form C. 2118.

WAR DIARY
or
INTELLIGENCE SUMMARY
(Erase heading not required.)

Place	Date	Hour	Summary of Events and Information	Remarks and references to Appendices
	25th	10PM	Christmas Day. Weather. Milder; strong westerly wind. The day was observed as a holiday; roast pork Christmas pudding provided for dinner, & extra ham for tea in addition to usual rations. Casualties — Nil.	J.S.M.
	26th	10PM	Weather. Clear & bright; no wind. Work. A & D Coys - Rested. B & C Coys dug 300 yds new assembly trench from (night) r BEAUCOURT TR. towards MUCK TR. to S of ST. Assembly. Casualties — O.R's — 1 wounded.	A.S.H.M.
	27th	10PM.	Weather. Milder; slight frost at night. Work. A Coy worked 3¾ hrs (day), 17 men carrying; 61 cleaning CAKE TR. B Coy worked 4 hrs (night) putting in head mats & digging sortie steps in new assembly trench. C Coy Rested. D Coy cleared trench, carried, & sandbagged, in WALKER AV. 4 hrs (day)	A.S.H.M.

2449 Wt. W4957/M90 750,000 1/16 J.B.C. & A. Forms/C.2118/12.

WAR DIARY
or
INTELLIGENCE SUMMARY

(Erase heading not required.)

Army Form C. 2118.

Place	Date	Hour	Summary of Events and Information	Remarks and references to Appendices
	28th	10AM	W.E.F. (period covering tour)	

A Coy. 1/A/4 53 OR moved to hutments (Nissen) e CAMP TR. cleared soggy ready for U frames & revetment. Carried 130 U frames 920 duckboards, 450

B Coy. Rest.

C Coy. 20 ffr. 94 Oth. men. Men washed tubs (myth) & new coffee Hy March. (Sea frames day.) cleared stuck lynx & carried 1/34 coats. completed assaulting steps & trench mortar alongs with depth.

D Coy. 10Ap. 44 OR carried (cany) from Quarry Dump to WALKER AVE 50 mats, 40 frames 436 duckboards, to CAMP TR. 60 ducks 220 frames

Casualties — Nil.

WAR DIARY or INTELLIGENCE SUMMARY

Army Form C. 2118.

Place	Date	Hour	Summary of Events and Information	Remarks and references to Appendices
	29th	10PM	**Weather** – Fine; rain at intervals; westerly winds. **Work** A Coy 1 Off 40 O.R. 4 hrs (Day) on CAMP TRACKS, HMM Track at water (ATISV 24 in places); filling in shell holes 4 hrs (night) on CAMP TRACKS, clearing & filling caused by artillery; clearing and general night work which had to be taken with down during the daytime. B Coy 1 Off 20 O.R. 4½ hrs (Day) on BEAUCOURT TR & HARDWICK TR clearing & laying mats. C Coy Rested D Coy 1 Off 30 O.R. worked 6½ hrs (night) digging new road along portion of CRATER LANE which was obliterated **Casualties** – O.R's 2 wounded (our own shell fire) + 1 wounded remaining at duty) 1 Prisoner taken. Joffre	
	30th	10PM	**Weather** – Rain at intervals; westerly winds. **Work** A Coy 1 Off 39 O.R. worked 3¾ hours (Day) on CAKE TR, also carrying for R.E. +14 men draining WAGGON RD. B Coy 1 Off 88 O.R. worked 3½ hrs (Day) on TANK ALLEY & STATION ALLEY filling in trench X911	

WAR DIARY
or
INTELLIGENCE SUMMARY
(Erase heading not required.)

Army Form C. 2118.

Place	Date	Hour	Summary of Events and Information	Remarks and references to Appendices
	31st	10 P.M.	C Coy 1 Off 92 O.Rs worked 4 hrs (night) on new assembly trench (continuation of STATION ALLEY); cleared out undrained storm & seepage out water.	
			D Coy 1 Off 35 O.Rs worked 7½ hrs (night) on new portion of CRATER LANE (see 29 ft); sides had fallen in, in several places, & the trench was 2 feet deep in water; trench baled, undrained & deepened, ready for frames.	
			Casualties — Offrs — Nil; O.R — 1 wounded.	
			Weather: Heavy Rain at intervals; westerly wind	
			Work A Coy 1 Off 40 men worked 4½ hrs (day) carrying, pumping water out of CAKE TR; new piece of trench dug at entrance to CAKE TR; widening CAKE TR.	
			B Coy 1 Off 83 O.Rs worked 4 hrs (day); draining, widening & re-setting HARDWICK TR.	
			C Coy Rested	
			D Coy 1 Off & 30 O.R's (in 2 reliefs) worked 9½ hrs/day) on new portion of CRATER LANE (see 30ft); carried up material re-cleared out trench & re-sited all but about 10 ft.	
			Casualties — Nil	

4th. Canadian Division.

A. 42-71.

Appendix 1.

24th. Bn. The Manchester Regt.
(7th. Divisional Pioneers).

Under authority granted by His Majesty the King, the General Officer Commanding-in-Chief has awarded No. 3122 Sergt. E.B. WHITE, 24th. Bn. Manchester Regt, the MILITARY MEDAL. (Authority Fifth Army HR/411/441 dated 4/12/1916., Second Corps DC/1032 of 6/12/1916).

11/12/16.
(Sd). X X X X   Capt. D.A.A.G., for
Lieut. Colonel, A.A. & Q.M.G.

==========

IInd. Corps No. D.C.1467.   7th. Div. No. R/45/24.

7th. Division.

The Corps Commander has awarded the MILITARY MEDAL to the following :-

24th. Battalion, The Manchester Regiment.

No. 14069 Sergeant J. BUCKLEY.
No. 14060 L/Sergt. (Cpl). F. GRUNDY.
No. 14457 Sergeant. W. RAYNOR.
No. 14034 L/Sergt. (Cpl). W. LAMBERT. (Bar to M. M.)
No. 14153 Sergeant F. RYAN.
No. 14375 L/SERGT. (Cpl). J. PERCIVAL.

(Sd).   XXXXX XXX   Captain,
D.A.A. & Q.M.G. IInd. Corps.

9-12-1916.

24th. Bn. Manchester Regt.

For your information and retention.

(Sd). W. WINGFIELD. Lieut. Col.
A.A.& Q.M.G. 7th. Division.

Divnl. H.Qrs.
13th. Dec. 1916.

Army Form C. 2118.

Vol 15

WAR DIARY
or
INTELLIGENCE SUMMARY

(Erase heading not required.) January 1917 24th (S) Bn. The Manchester Regt. (Pioneers)

VOL XV

Place	Date	Hour	Summary of Events and Information	Remarks and references to Appendices
MAILLY WOOD-W P23.c.5.7 (Sh57D)	Jan 1st	10 AM	Weather Mild; westerly wind. Coys rested. Casualties — Nil	J.A.W
	Jan 2nd	10 PM	Weather Mild; westerly wind. Work A Coy. 1 Offr & 2 O.R. worked 3¾ hrs (day); making hughes covering french mats; 6 O.R. (day) 2½ [hrs] repairing mine dugouts, remainder widening, deepening & refirming new trench. B Coy. 10ff 890.R worked 3½ hrs (day); 1 Offr 100R 2½ hrs (night); 1½ Offr carrying, 3 clearing & fitting mats & chairs in BEAUCOURT TR. C Coy. 1 Off 85 O.R. worked 3½ hrs (night); clearing, widening, improving new continuation of STATION ALLEY. D Coy. 1 Off 35 O.R. worked 1½ hrs on CRATER LANE 4 30 NEW MUNICH. Casualties — Nil.	J.A.W
	Jan 3rd	10 PM	Weather Mild; westerly wind. Work A Coy 1 Off 65 O.R. worked 3½ hrs (day); carrying mats & chairs, CT, XPM stores, completing new piece of CAKE TR; wired 200 mats. B Coy 1 Off 27 OR worked 3 hrs (night); carried mats & laid 130 yds of new outer hand track to K35.d.6.1. B Coy 1 Off 40 OR worked 3 hrs (day); carrying & laying mats & chairs & clearing in BEAUCOURT TR.	

WAR DIARY or INTELLIGENCE SUMMARY

Army Form C. 2118.

Place	Date	Hour	Summary of Events and Information	Remarks and references to Appendices
	4th	10 PM	C Coy 1 Offr 39 O.R. worked 3½ hrs (night) re-clearing continuation of STATION MUFF	
			D Coy 1 Offr 38 O.R. worked 4½ hrs (day); cleared 50' NEW MUNICH TR.	
			Casualties 1 Offr wounded, 2 O.R. wounded. Reinforcements 6 Offrs joined	
			Weather Mild & clear; no wind.	
			Work A Coy 1 Offr 65 O.R. worked 3½ hrs (day); making hurdles & covering mats, carrying materials; cleared growth 6" CAME TR.	
			1 Offr 29 O.R. worked 3 hrs (night); completed overland track (see previous night); nearly half length double mats.	
			B Coy 1 Offr 55 O.R. worked 3½ hrs (day); cleared 100 yds BEAUCOURT TR.; laid 10 mats.	
			C Coy 1 Offr 40 O.R. worked 3½ hrs (night); carried up 275 mats from various dumps for A Coy's overland track.	
			D Coy 1 Offr 38 O.R. worked 4 hrs (day); 1 Offr 29 O.R. worked 60' NEW MUNICH TR. 12 trestles 24 mats laid; carried up 45 trestles 78 mats.	
			Casualties — Nil.	

WAR DIARY
or
INTELLIGENCE SUMMARY
(Erase heading not required.)

Army Form C. 2118.

Place	Date	Hour	Summary of Events and Information	Remarks and references to Appendices
	5th	10 PM	Weather: Bright, colder. Wind light W. Work ACoy 10ft 48 O.R's worked 3½ hrs (day); carried 140 mats RUMMY DUMP to CRATER LANE; made 65 hurdles; ground 120 mats. 10ft 44 O.R's worked 2½ hrs (night) carried up 40 mats, completed duckwalk along CAKE LANE (120 mats); carried 20 frames, 30 hurdles 770 mats. BCoy 10ft. 82 O.R's carried, laid 30 mats; cleared 30' BEAUCOURT TR. CCoy Rests. 3¾ hrs (day) DCoy 2ft 37 O.R's worked 6 hrs (day); carried up 20 frames, cleared & completed 35' NEW MUNICH TR. Casualties — Nil	[signature]
	6th	10 PM	Weather: Dull. Wind light W. Work ACoy 10ft 30 O.R worked 3½ hrs on CAKE TR; cleared 50 to 68ft. 7.6ft (night) BCoy 2ft 32 O.R worked 3½ hrs (day) on BEAUCOURT TR; carried up & laid 19 mats & 22 chairs, picked what had fallen in during night. CCoy 10ft 80 O.R. worked 4 hrs (day) on 250' BEAUCOURT TR. cleaning & laying out. DCoy 10ft 38 O.R worked 4 hrs (day) on NEW MUNICH TR. cleaning work etc. Casualties — Nil	[signature]

WAR DIARY or INTELLIGENCE SUMMARY

Army Form C. 2118.

Place	Date	Hour	Summary of Events and Information	Remarks and references to Appendices
	7th	10PM	**Weather** Frosty in morning; clear; no wind. **Work** D Coy 2 Offr 41 O.R.'s carried 10 mats & 930 yds; completed 30 yds NEW MUNICH TR. Cleared a further 25 yds. Remainder Rested. **Divine Services** C of E services held in Camp. **Transport** for last 13 nights 265 waggons carried 120 mats per night, AUCHONVILLERS – GREEN DUMP. **Casualties** – Nil	
	8th	10 PM	**Weather** Frost; wind W.N.W. light; later stormy & very rain. **Work** A Coy 1 Offr 13 O.R. worked 3½ hrs (night) on CAKE TR, clearing & fitting 1 Offr 32 O.R. worked 1½ hrs (night), laid overland track to Jn of LAGER ALLEY & NEW MUNICH TR from existing track. B Coy 2 Offr 94 O.R. worked 3½ hrs (day) on BEAUCOURT TR. C Coy 1 Offr 42 O.R. worked 2½ hrs (night) laid overland track towards Jn 83 from end of STATION ALLEY; 78 mats carried & laid. 1 Offr 40 O.R. worked 4 hrs (day) on BEAUCOURT TR. D Coy 1 Offr 28 O.R. worked 3½ hrs (night); carried 60 mats, QUARRY DUMP 1 Offr 30 O.R. worked 3½ hrs (day) on NEW MUNICH TR. – CAKE TR.	

WAR DIARY
or
INTELLIGENCE SUMMARY

(Erase heading not required.)

Army Form C. 2118.

Place	Date	Hour	Summary of Events and Information	Remarks and references to Appendices
	9th	10 AM	**Weather** Dull; westerly wind.	
			Work A Coy 1 Off 190 O.R. worked 4 hrs on CAKE TR.	
			B Coy 2 Offs 92 O.R. worked 3½ hrs (day) carrying 287 mats GREEN DUMP to fr of STATION ALLEY & HARDWICK TR.	
			C Coy 10 Off 39 O.R. worked 1½ hrs (day) on BEAUCOURT TR; withdrawn for bombardment.	
			10 Off 40 O.R. worked 2 hrs (night) laid track along side of STATION ALLEY, 101 mats.	
			D Coy 10 Off 34 O.R. worked 4 hrs (day) on NEW MUNICH TR & WALKER AVE. clearing, revetting & laying mats.	
			10 Off 31 O.R. worked 2¾ hrs (night) carrying 70 mats as previous night.	Att. I
		Casualties — Nil.	
	10th	10 PM	**Weather** Fine, changing later to rain, westerly wind.	
			Work A & D Coys 3 Offrs & 240 O.R. laid an assembly tape as in para 3 of Operation Order no 10.	
			B Coy 2 Offs & 84 O.R. (night) carried mats from GREEN DUMP towards BEAUCOURT TR; withdrawn owing to shell fire.	
			C Coy ratio	
			Prisoners 7 Off, H. CLARK, Sergt F. BUCKLEY & 2 men took 25 prisoners (armed).	
			Casualties Nil. O.Rs 3 wounded; 1 missing & 1 wounded (left duty).	

2449 Wt. W14957/M90 750,000 1/16 J.B.C. & A. Forms/C.2118/12.

WAR DIARY
or
INTELLIGENCE SUMMARY
(Erase heading not required.)

Army Form C. 2118.

Place	Date	Hour	Summary of Events and Information	Remarks and references to Appendices
	11th	10 PM	Weather Dull; little snow. Was misty.	
			Work A&D Coys carried out work of Operation Orders no 10. speak; left M.T.1. camp 10.15 A.M. waited & hrs for fatigue.	
			B Coy #20/ft 40(6) O.R worked - 3 hrs (night) laying 110 x trench	
			from STATION ALLEY towards JcT 24 in MUCK TR. left camp 12 noon, waited 3 hrs for fatigue.	
			C Coy 2 offrs 76 O.R worked 2 hrs (night) laid 120' more of track above.	Staff
			Casualties — OR's 2 killed, 4 wounded.	
	12th	10PM	Weather Wet & cold	
			A&B Coys Rested. 1 off 24 OR B Coy worked 3½ hrs revmg mats at AUCHONVILLERS	
			C Coy 20/ft 58 O.R's worked 3 hrs (night); carrying mats from GREEN DUMP; tightening & improving track & ft/tr (see above)	
			1 off 40 men A Coy at AUCHONVILLERS YARD, unloading wagons.	Staff
			Casualties — Nil.	

WAR DIARY or INTELLIGENCE SUMMARY

Place	Date	Hour	Summary of Events and Information	Remarks and references to Appendices
	13th	10am	Weather wretchedly cold.	
			Work 2 Offrs 32 O.R's (A) patrolled & repaired roads as under, 4¾ hrs (Day).	
			(1) MAILLY - SUCRERIE RD (2) AUCHONVILLERS - BEAUMONT RD	
			(3) HAMEL - AUCHONVILLERS RD	
			3 Offrs 76 O.R's (D) worked 7hrs & 3½ hrs (Day & night) on BEAUMONT HAMEL tramway.	
			repaired track, laid 2 new rails in broken places	
			cleared track, relaid rails for 30yds.	
			2 Offrs 73 O.R's (B) worked 5 hrs (night), carried 65 mats from quarry	
			to Pt 93 & branched there, owing to intense darkness	
			impossible to lay track.	
			3 Offrs 50 O.R's (C) carried 41 mats from various points on STATION RD to	
			GREEN DUMP, too dark to again to lay track	
			20 O.R RE Yard BEAUSSART	
			4 Offrs 40 O.R (A) — AUCHONVILLERS STN working on road in BEAUMONT HAMEL	
			12 OR wiring mats	
			Casualties — Nil.	

Place	Date	Hour	Summary of Events and Information	Remarks and references to Appendices
	14th	10 PM	**Weather** Cold; wind light S.W. **Work** A Coy as previous day. B Coy 2 Offs 500 OR worked (at night) on track from pt 93 to tramlines No 12 post. No 2 trench laid; carried up 42 bombs to from CRATER LANE C Coy 2 Offs 480 OR worked (at night) clearing enemy companying STATION ROAD. D Coy 3 Offs 780 OR worked & the (night) & shots shifted in tramway. **Casualties** Offrs — 1 wounded remainder of batt; 1 O.R. wounded	Staff
	15th	10 PM	**Weather** Milder; wind light S. A Coy as previous day. B Coy 2 Offs 340 OR worked 3 hrs (night); carried 105 mats from QUARRY DUMP & laid them along LAGER ALLEY, connecting with previous nights work. C Coy 2 Offs 420 OR worked 3½ hrs (night); carrying 85 boards, GREEN DUMP to HARDWICK TR. DUMP. D Coy as previous day. **Casualties** — 6 Rs wounded	Staff

WAR DIARY
or
INTELLIGENCE SUMMARY

Army Form C. 2118.

Place	Date	Hour	Summary of Events and Information	Remarks and references to Appendices
	16th	10 pm	Weather Cold, slight frost, wind light S.E. Work A Coy as previous day. D Coy as previous day; 2 offrs 74 O.R. worked 4½ hrs laid 20 yds rails & prepared 40 yds chalk digging. B. Coy Rested Casualties — Nil	Yo/M
	17th	10 pm	Weather Some snow in early morning; Dull & cold. Work A Coy as previous day. D Coy as previous day; track now completed to BEAUMONT HAMEL Dump; ready for laying rails B Coy 1 offr 28 O.R. worked 2½ hrs (night); carried & laid 28 mats; carried up a further 28. C Coy 2 offr 30 O.R. worked 2½ hrs (night); 25 mtrs laid his track now joined up 16ft 24; 25 mtrs laid from M83 towards R.I.C.30. Casualties Nil	A.F.W.

WAR DIARY or INTELLIGENCE SUMMARY

Army Form C. 2118.

Date	Hour	Summary of Events and Information	Remarks and references to Appendices
18th	10AM	Weather was light NNW; slight falls of snow throughout the day.	
		Work: A Coy as previous day.	
		D Coy as previous day.	
		B Coy carried up 62 mats from QUARRY DUMP, laid them along LAGER ALLEY; track now complete from Coy HQ mer pt 93 along LAGER ALLEY to beyond pt 56. 2 Offrs 70 ORs & belongings.	
		C Coy 2 Offrs 30 ORs worked 24 hrs night; carried to work from HARDWICK TR. & laid them from pt 83 towards Jn of RAILWAY TR. & HUCK TR.	
		Casualties — 1 O.R. wounded	
19th	10PM	Weather slight frost, as previous day	
		Work A Coy as previous day	
		D Coy as previous day.	
		B Coy 1 Offr 40 OR. } worked 24 hrs (night) completing work at	
		C Coy 2 Offrs 50 OR's } C Coy of previous night. No work carried of date.	
		Casualties Nil.	

WAR DIARY
or
INTELLIGENCE SUMMARY
(Erase heading not required.)

Army Form C. 2118.

Place	Date	Hour	Summary of Events and Information	Remarks and references to Appendices
Warloy	20th	10pm	C.O.; Adjt, as previous day. Work A Coy as previous day D Coy as previous day B Coy } Rested C Coy } During the whole of this month owing (1) to the long marches, sickness, mainly sore feet due to the constant marching through the mud & (2) to the large number of men detached for various duties, e.g. Corps signals Buried Cables, found Water Supply, unloading party at BEAUSSART, railhead Tramway Maintenance etc., the number of men available for ordinary work has been very small. Specimen Parade state attached. For the first 4 nights for 6 nights a week, 2 G.S. waggons were employed carrying trench bomb stores from AVELUY VILLIERS to Quarry Dump & Acheux Dump; average 120 bombs a night ofJSMM	A/k II

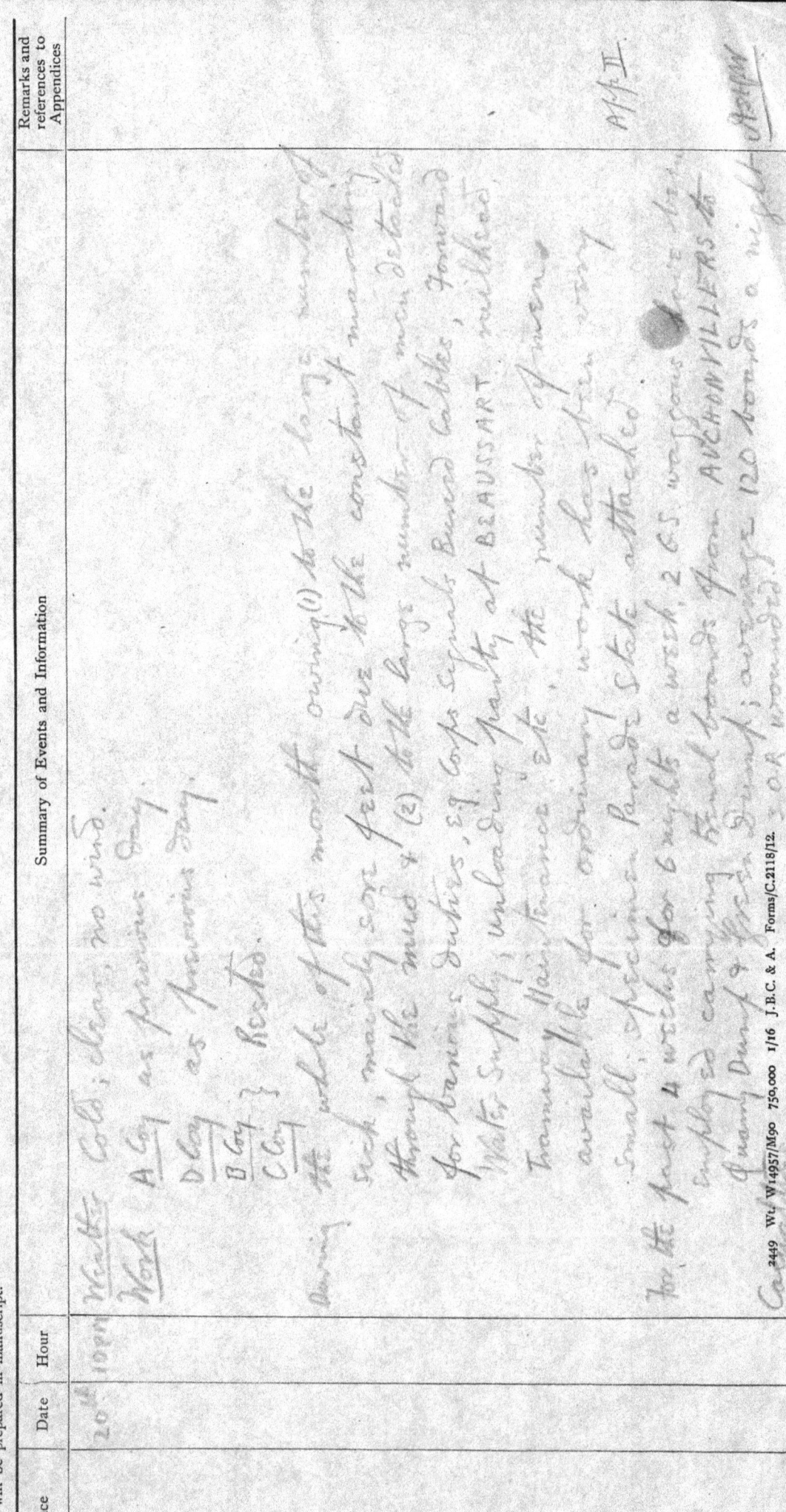

WAR DIARY
or
INTELLIGENCE SUMMARY

Army Form C. 2118.

Place	Date	Hour	Summary of Events and Information	Remarks and references to Appendices
	21st	10PM	Weather as previous day.	
			A Coy. Road parties rested.	
			C.Coy. Rested	
			B.Coy. 2 offrs 80 O.R. worked 1¾ hrs (coy); Coy 220' track from WHITE CITY towards SUCRERIE; 2 dug in pit for wire pits sinks	ASMR
			Casualties - Nil.	
	22nd	10PM	Weather cold, slight thaw during day. Freezing again at night.	
			A Coy Road patrols (3) as previously; 40 O.R at AUCHONVILLERS for unloading Railway Waggons.	
			D Coy on tramway; repairs 2 places, laid 66yds. to 380 80'. Laid track for carrying 150'.	
			C Coy Cleared & deepened 250' of SOUTHERN AVE.	
			B Coy Cleared 30" SIXTH AVE, ready for U frames; ready for U frames; cleared 40'; carried bundles & frames from AUCHONVILLERS.	ASMR

WAR DIARY
or
INTELLIGENCE SUMMARY

Army Form C. 2118.

Place	Date	Hour	Summary of Events and Information	Remarks and references to Appendices
	23	10PM	**Weather** Hard frost; wind light N.E. **Work** A Coy as previous day. B Coy reveted 18' of SIXTH N.E.; improved French; carried twighs, frames & troops from BLUE DUMP. C Coy Cleaning SOUTHERN AVE; started sinking revetting. D Coy had completed 60' T Tramway; No 80320078 with bricks. **Casualties** — Nil **Honours & Rewards** 2/Lt H. CLARK & LIEUT (a/Capt) R.W. BATEMAN awarded the Military Cross. 14108 Ssergt G.W. Greenwood & 14277 L/Cpl E. Jones awarded the Military Medal.	A.J.H/m
	24	10PM	**Weather** Close & frosty; fresh wind N.E. **Work** A Coy as previous day. B Coy erecting huts & making road in camp. C Coy ½ Coy MAILLY WOOD F loading pinewood materials improving camp. ½ Coy improving Z land of BERTRANCOURT. D Coy on Tramway laid last 150' of 27# track & ballasted 150'. Cas. Nil	A.J.H/m

Army Form C. 2118.

WAR DIARY
or
INTELLIGENCE SUMMARY

(Erase heading not required.)

Instructions regarding War Diaries and Intelligence Summaries are contained in F. S. Regs., Part II. and the Staff Manual respectively. Title Pages will be prepared in manuscript.

Place	Date	Hour	Summary of Events and Information	Remarks and references to Appendices
	25th	10PM	Weather. Bright clear. Hard frost. Work. A Coy as previous day. B Coy. Made fire steps facings in SOUTHERN AVE. Progress very slow owing to hard frost. C Coy. 12 O.R. erecting huts in camp. 1/2 Coy MARLYWOOD & as previous day 1/2 Coy BERTRANCOURT D Coy Prepared trucks for ballasting tramway & Ballast To 200'. Casualties — Nil	9.50PM
	26th	10 PM	Weather as previous day. A Coy as previous day. B Coy as previous day; 10 trays, now ready for earthing, & partly done. C Coy as previous day. D Coy Ballast 150' tramway, made sludge & cleared stones for 2nd track. Casualties — Nil	9.50PM

WAR DIARY
or
INTELLIGENCE SUMMARY

(Erase heading not required.)

Army Form C. 2118.

Place	Date	Hour	Summary of Events and Information	Remarks and references to Appendices
	27	10 PM	**Weather** Bright fair weather continued had frost **Work** A Coy as previous day. C Coy as previous day. B Coy continued work on watering Standings in S. side of SOUTHERN AVE. between BASIN WOOD & WATERLOO BRIDGE. 2 days work. 15 holes YPM 20 angle iron & two steps arriving from EUSTON DUMP. D Coy Ballasted 150x with broken brick, laid broad gauge tramway to Loading stage. **Casualties** — Nil	W.R.M.
	28th	10 PM	**Weather** Continues hard frost, wind NE **Work** A Coy as previous day. C Coy as previous day (Party working in camp roads) B Coy started firesteps in YELLOW LINE for 200 N from RED COTTAGE. D Coy Ballasted 150' with broken track. **Casualties** — Nil	W.R.M.

WAR DIARY
or
INTELLIGENCE SUMMARY
(Erase heading not required.)

Army Form C. 2118.

Place	Date	Hour	Summary of Events and Information	Remarks and references to Appendices
	29th	10PM	Weather as previous day.	
			Work. A Coy as previous day.	
			C Coy as previous day.	
			B Coy continued work on 10 foredays in YELLOW LINE	
			Casualties — Nil.	
			D Coy on tramway: ballasting & spoken track	A.S.J.M.
	30th	10 PM	Weather continued hard frost, wind light NE	
			Work. A Coy as previous day.	
			C Coy as previous day.	
			B Coy continued work on YELLOW LINE, where RED COTTAGE & STAFF COPSE.	
			D Coy on tramway: 150 x ballast to in broken track.	
			Casualties — Nil.	A.J.M.
	31st	10 PM	Weather as previous day.	
			Work. A Coy Road patrols as previously.	
			10AM 40 OR working in AUCHEN MILLERS yard unloading wagons.	

WAR DIARY
or
INTELLIGENCE SUMMARY

(Erase heading not required.)

Army Form C. 2118.

Place	Date	Hour	Summary of Events and Information	Remarks and references to Appendices
			B Coy continued work on YELLOW LINE: completed & laying ready to C Coy ½ Coy improving "Z" Camp BERTRANCOURT mostly sticky ½ Coy improving camps MAILLY WOOD & road. D Coy (½) on tramway; 120x follas Fes ½ Coy rested Casualties — 2 O.R. wounded in camp result of an accident with Lewis Gun.	ASH/W

Sgd. Maj.
andg (124 (S) B: The Manchester
Regt
(4 Divisional Pioneers)

SECRET

Copy No. 5

OPERATION ORDER NO. 10 BY LIEUT COLONEL J.H. CHADWICK COMMDG. 24th BATTALION THE MANCHESTER REGT.

REFERENCE:- REDAN Sheet, 1/5,000

1. On the 11th January the 7th Division will capture:-
   (a) MUNICH TRENCH from its Junction with LEAVE AVENUE at Q. 6. c. 6.3. to its Junction with LAGER ALLEY at K. 36. c. 3.6. (exclusive)
   (b) LAGER ALLEY from K. 36. c. 1.5. (~~inclusive~~) to K. 35. d. 5.6. When captured this trench will form a defensive flank.

2. Zero hour will be communicated to those concerned.

3. About 10-30 p.m. on 10th January an assembly tape will be laid from ~~Junction of NEW MUNICH TRENCH and PRITCHARD TRENCH at Q. 6. c. 20.95~~ Q.6.c.25.70 to K. 35. d. 5.6. This must be completed by 12-0 midnight.
   (a) 2/Lieut. Barton will lay the tape from Q. 6. c. 25.70 to Q. 6. a. 15.20.
   (b) 2/Lieut. Clark from Q. 6. a. 15.20 to K. 35. d. 85.05 (WAGGON ROAD ~~inclusive~~) (exclusive).
   (c) Captain Bateman from K. 35. d. 85.05 (WAGGON ROAD inclusive) to K. 35. d. 5.6. (6)

4. When the objective has been captured:-
   (a) "A" Company (Capt. Bateman) will wire from K. 36. c. 1.5. to K. 35. d. 1.7., the wire to be 50 yards in front of the fire trench and specially thick for a distance of 50 yards on each side of WAGGON ROAD.
   (b) Three platoons "D" Company (2/Lieut. Clark) will lay a track of trench gratings from Junction of CAKE TRENCH and NEW MUNICH TRENCH to LAGER ALLEY at K. 35. d. 7.5. They will also make strong points in LAGER ALLEY at:-
   K. 35. d. 90.45.
   K. 35. d. 7.5.
   K. 35. d. 5.6.

5. Forward dumps of material for consolidation have been formed along CAKE TRENCH from Q. 5. b. 20 to its Junction with NEW MUNICH TRENCH.

6. 2/Lieut. Clayton with two runners will report to Brigade Headquarters at Q. 17. a. 8.2. by 8-0 a.m. on the 11th January.

7. Two runners will report at the Headquarters of the 1/3rd Durham Field Coy. R.E. in MAILLY MAILLET by 9-0 a.m. on the 11th January.

8. Reports to Battalion Headquarters at OLDHAM CAMP.

9. No papers or maps to be carried.

ISSUED AT 2-15 p.m., 10-1-17.

Copy No. 1. Commanding Officer   Copy No. 2. O.C. "A" Coy.
         3. O.C. "D" Coy.   4. 2/Lt. Clayton
         5. War Diary   6. War Diary.

(Signed) A. St. G. WALSH. Lieut. and Adjutant.

Army Form C. 2118.

2/6 Bn The Manchester Regt.
(7th Provisional Pioneers)

Vol 16

WAR DIARY
or
INTELLIGENCE SUMMARY
(Erase heading not required.)

Vol XVI   16/8/1917.

Place	Date	Hour	Summary of Events and Information	Remarks and references to Appendices
MAILLY WOOD WEST P.23.b.5-7 Sheet 57º SE	1st	10PM	Weather Wind changed to N.W. in morning & slight thaw set in; later wind came back to N.E. & thaw ceased. Work A Coy 10ff 40 O.R. at AUCHONVILLERS unloading wagons in yard. 2ff 25 O.R. patrolling roads & repairing (1) AUCHONVILLERS – BEAUMONT HAMEL & STATION RD & GREEN DUMP (2) MAILLY – SUCRERIE RD. (3) AUCHONVILLERS – HAMEL RD as far as Ovil Boundary B Coy on "yellow line" from RED COTTAGES northwards; completed & revetted 2 fire bays; remainder ready for revetting. C Coy ½ Coy Improving 2 Camp BERTRANCOURT; 5½ hrs 45 O.R. ½ Coy unopened MAILLY WOOD 3 Comps; 7½ hrs 44 O.R. D Coy 73 O.R worked 7½ hrs on tramway; ballasted 250' with broken brick. Casualties – Nil.	ASH
	2nd	10PM	Weather Hard frost; wind light N.E. Work A Coy as previous day.	

Place	Date	Hour	Summary of Events and Information	Remarks and references to Appendices
	3rd	10PM	B Coy Work on "Yellow Line" as previous day: 9 bays now completed. C Coy as previous day D Coy as previous day continued hair cut. Casualties — Nil.	A.H.M
			Work. A Coy as previous day. B Coy to Coy rest fee. C Coy continued work on yellow line. Work commenced to new fire bays. Rest remainder continued to new fire bays. D Coy Moved to AUCHONVILLERS (cellars) unpacked marked out BEAUMONT HAMEL to AUCHEN. work, track marked out BEAUMONT HAMEL to AUCHEN. VILLERS : 27 5/85 An Chestre reported broke track. Casualties — Nil	
	4th	10PM	Weather as previous day. Work A Coy as previous day. B Coy continued work on Pugg. trays, 1 overseen & ready for nothing.	A.H.M

Place	Date	Hour	Summary of Events and Information	Remarks and references to Appendices
			Coy't Coy refrans 2 Coy of BERTRANCOURT ½ Coy rests. 12 OR went 115 Trench mats.	
			D Coy continued work on hangar. Artillery to 125° (now complete); Infantry group 108° & steel; steel. 270 yds. 107 × 400 R ← A Coy & D Coy (all) returned based 107 × 400 R from AUCHONVILLERS	
			Casualties — Nil	
	5th	10PM	Weather Continued frost, cold wind N.E. Move The Battalion moved to Billets at BEAUQUESNE not Operation order attended, in which for PUCHEVILLERS substitute BEAUQUESNE (owing to lack of accommodation in Gorenoy)	M.I
			Casualties — Nil Reinforcements — 3 A/N 10 O.R joined Bn.	

Army Form C. 2118.

WAR DIARY
or
INTELLIGENCE SUMMARY

(Erase heading not required.)

Instructions regarding War Diaries and Intelligence Summaries are contained in F. S. Regs., Part II. and the Staff Manual respectively. Title Pages will be prepared in manuscript.

Place	Date	Hour	Summary of Events and Information	Remarks and references to Appendices
BEAUQUESNE	6th	10PM	Weather as previous day. Coys resting; equipment to be cleaned; inspections to B. Casualties – Nil.	9.15PM
	7th	10PM	Weather Bright clear; hard frost. A Coy erecting Nissen huts at VAL DE MAISON } Classes in L.G. B Coy 1 hrs mtg drill; inspection } Signalling in the C Coy & D Coy 2 hrs mtg drill; 1 hrs wiring practice } afternoon Lectures to Officers & N.C.Os in evening Casualties – Nil.	
	8th	10PM	Weather as previous day. A Coy as previous day. B Coy constructing between gas blanket trenches in the village (6 hrs) C Coy { 2 hrs mtg drill & musketry; 1½ hrs wiring (afternoon force) O.C } Afternoon & evening as previous day. Casualties – Nil.	9.15PM
	9th	10PM	Weather as previous day. Work & Training as previous day. Casualties – Nil	Steele

Army Form C. 2118.

WAR DIARY
or
INTELLIGENCE SUMMARY

(Erase heading not required.)

Instructions regarding War Diaries and Intelligence Summaries are contained in F. S. Regs., Part II. and the Staff Manual respectively. Title Pages will be prepared in manuscript.

Place	Date	Hour	Summary of Events and Information	Remarks and references to Appendices
P	10th	10.0 p.m	Trenches: as previous day. A Coy. ½ Coy erecting Nissen Huts; ½ Coy as O.O.D. Coy.] Afternoon + evening: as previous day. Football Matches in afternoon. B. Coy: as previous day. C. Coy: do. D. Coy: do. Cavallino — Nil.	M/115/16
	11th	10.0 a.m	Trenches: hideous; slightly thaw. Divine services were held in the morning; Football Matches in the afternoon. Cavallino: Nil.	M/115/16

WAR DIARY or INTELLIGENCE SUMMARY

Army Form C. 2118.

Place	Date	Hour	Summary of Events and Information	Remarks and references to Appendices
Canaples	12th	10.0 a.m.	Twenty four hours clear during day. Training: A & B Coys. { 2 hours Class Order Drill musketry; 1 Ph training. Afternoon Classes for Non Commnd Signallers } C Coy { Cleaning Nissen huts } D Coy. Evening Relation education lectures in huts. Casualties: Nil. Weather: Milder; Clear.	[illegible signatures] Classes for Stretcher Bearers, Runners, etc afternoon. Nature of Winners Lectures evening.
Canaples	13th	10.0 p.m.	Training A & B Coys { 2 hours Class Order Drill musketry; 1 Ph training. Afternoon Classes for Non Commnd Signallers } C Coy { Cleaning Nissen huts } D Coy. Casualties: Nil. Weather: As previous day.	1 platoon CANAPLES, 1 platoon MARIEUX, 3 platoons PUCHVILLERS [illegible] 1 Platoon CANAPLES, " MARIEUX, " PUCHVILLERS, " LA VICOGNE [illegible signatures] Stretcher Bearers, Cleaners previous day. National Winners Service 2 runners. Lecture to Officers in evening.

WAR DIARY
or
INTELLIGENCE SUMMARY

(Erase heading not required.)

Army Form C. 2118.

Place	Date	Hour	Summary of Events and Information	Remarks and references to Appendices
Lucheux	1/14	10.0 p.m	Weather: Slight thaw during day; freezing at night. Training — A & B Coys { Morning 2 hr. Class over Gas musketry; training. Afternoon Classes for team leaders & section leaders. Heat { C Coy. Erecting Nissen huts. { CANAPLES, MARIEUX, PUCHVILLERS, LA VICOGNE } D Coy. as 12th. Casualties: Nil.	Stables Canteen Classes Recreation Lecture to officers men in evening
Lucheux	15th	10.0 p.m	Weather: As previous day. A, B & D Coys — as previous day. C Coy Erecting Nissen Huts { CANAPLES, MARIEUX, RUBEMPRÉ, RAINCHEVAL } Casualties: Nil.	Classes & Lectures as previous day

Army Form C. 2118.

WAR DIARY
or
INTELLIGENCE SUMMARY

(Erase heading not required.)

Place	Date	Hour	Summary of Events and Information	Remarks and references to Appendices
	16th	10.0 p.m.	Weather: Heavy snow. Battalion parade chief in morning. B Coy preparing Divisional Parade issued near VAL DE MAISON. Clean section as previous day. Casualties: Nil	
	17th	10.0 p.m.	Weather: Mild & misty. The Division paraded near VAL DE MAISON for inspection by GENERAL NIVELLE Commander in Chief French Armies. Casualties: Nil	
	18th	10.0 p.m.	Weather: Mild. Divine Service was held during the morning. Battalion Cross Country Run in morning.	

WAR DIARY
or
INTELLIGENCE SUMMARY

Army Form C. 2118.

Place	Date	Hour	Summary of Events and Information	Remarks and references to Appendices
Inventrie: Suct.	19th	10.0 am	Training: C Coy. — morning 3/2 hr. Musketry - firing on Range under Coy. arrangements — afternoon 2 hr. — Lecture (Open Fence) by Major W. — evening 2 hr. — Lecture (Open Fence) by Major W. D Coy. — morning 2½ hr. Section rushing 3 1/2 hr Close Order Drill & Physical — afternoon — Drill — evening 2 hr. — Night march. Inventring A Coy. Erecting Latrines & Athletic Bench in Village B Coy. Erecting Nissen Huts w. RAINCHÉ VAL & VAL DE MAISON Casualties Nil. Weather Wet.	Strictly Room Signallers — Lewis Gunners Chosen during day as for ASHPR previous day
	20th	10 am	Training C Coy. as D Coy. previous day D Coy. " C " " Working Party 17 as previous day B Coy. 17 as previous day Casualties Nil	as for day ASHPR previous day

WAR DIARY
or
INTELLIGENCE SUMMARY

(Erase heading not required.)

Army Form C. 2118.

Place	Date	Hour	Summary of Events and Information	Remarks and references to Appendices
BEAUQUESNE	21st	10PM	Weather - Mild. Coys cleaned up billets & prepared for move. Casualties - Nil.	
MAILLY-MAILLET	22nd	10PM	Weather - Some showers; ground very wet underfoot. More "B" moved to billets at MAILLY-MAILLET, see attached location order. Casualties - Nil.	Appx III Appx IV
	23rd	10PM	Weather as previous day. Coys cleaned billets & did inspections &c. Casualties - Nil.	
	24th	10PM	Weather as previous day. Work. Nong. 4 Offrs 118 O.R. worked 4½ hrs (day) carrying boards for A.LEMONVILLERS & laid a duckboard track through WHEEL POST trench at K36.C.17	Appx V

WAR DIARY
or
INTELLIGENCE SUMMARY

(Erase heading not required.)

Army Form C. 2118.

Place	Date	Hour	Summary of Events and Information	Remarks and references to Appendices
	24th (cont)		B Coy 3 Off. 82 O.R. worked 3½ hrs (day) carried up stores & 171 Trench boards from BEAUMONT HAMEL; laid along CRATER LANE N.E. from Q6 a 2.8.	
			C Coy 4 Off. 124 O.R. worked 4 hrs (day); carried up boards & laid 330 yds of track along WALKER AVE.	
			D Coy 4 Off. 125 O.R. worked 4 hrs (day) carried boards by train to AUCHONVILLERS; 200 in all. Reld 3 Coys 7th Bn for care of FRASER ALLEY. Drant. made at CRATER LANE, 150 mds.	
			Transport (section moved) to BEAUSSART.	
			Casualties - Nil.	
	25th	10pm	Weather Damp. very misty day. Lifted for about 2 hrs in the afternoon.	AsfRM
			Work A Coy worked about 4½ hrs (day) clearing & making fafalites SERRE RD from SUCRERIE to old German front line.	
			D Coy	

Army Form C. 2118.

WAR DIARY
or
INTELLIGENCE SUMMARY
(Erase heading not required.)

Place	Date	Hour	Summary of Events and Information	Remarks and references to Appendices
			B Coy & 1 Pltn. AUCHONVILLERS unloading waggons & working in yard. 1 Pltn. working at Divl School VAUCHELLES. 1 Pltn. working in R.E. workshops BEAUSSART. 1 Pltn.} worked 4 hrs (Day) cleaning WAGON RD. Casualties – Nil.	
	26th	10 PM	Weather: Bright & clear, mild. Work B Coy 3 Pltns AUCHONVILLERS, VAUCHELLES, BEUSSART. A.C.D Coys. worked 4 hrs (Day) Cleaning WAGON RD. & 1 Pltn B Coy S. 100' now completed & road temp'ly not top. the 12' 250' totals cleared © Cleaning anywhere BEAUMONT HAMEL–AUCHONVILLERS RD. (20 br) Casualties – Nil. Command – Lt. Col. J. H. Chadwick appointed to command R.E. B?.	

2449 Wt. W14957/M90 750,000 1/16 J.B.C. & A. Forms/C.2118/12.

WAR DIARY
or
INTELLIGENCE SUMMARY

(Erase heading not required.)

Army Form C. 2118.

Place	Date	Hour	Summary of Events and Information	Remarks and references to Appendices
	27th	10PM	Weather Mild. Bright clear, no wind. Wd. B Coy Parties at VAUCHELLES, AUCHONVILLERS, BEAUSSART ½ Coy repaired 200' BEAUMONT HAMEL - AUCHONVILLERS road. C & D Coys worked 5 hrs on WAGON Rd, clearing & making thoroughfare for artillery up to CRATER LANE. 3 ramps made. A Coy to 17th Bde. Casualties — Nil.	[signature]
	28th	10PM	Weather as previous day. Wd. B Coy parties as previous day. ½ Coy clearing mud & filling shell holes on AUCHONVILLERS - BEAUMONT HAMEL road. C Coy + 17th Bde worked 6 hrs under 19th Div repairing SERRE road in neighbourhood of German front line; bridge made over trench. Work greatly delayed by constant traffic.	[signature]

WAR DIARY
or
INTELLIGENCE SUMMARY

Army Form C. 2118.

Place	Date	Hour	Summary of Events and Information	Remarks and references to Appendices
			06 9th Bty Staff 1/4MF) worked 6 hours on STATION road; about 4 sec; clearing mud & filling holes with rubble & brick.	Asthr
			Casualties — Nil.	

H. Chadwick Lt. Col
cmdg 2/4th (r) Bn
The Manchester Regt.
(9th Divisional Reserve)

SECRET   Copy No.

OPERATION ORDERS BY
LIEUT COLONEL J.H. CHADWICK COMMANDING
24TH BATTALION MANCHESTER REGIMENT.

4th February, 1917.

REFERENCE, FRANCE 57 D.

1. The Battalion will march to-morrow (5th Feby.) to PUCHEVILLERS.

2. Route:- ACHEUX-LEALVILLERS-RAINCHEVAL-PUCHEVILLERS

3. Order of march:- Band, Headquarters, 'A' Company, 'B' Company, 'C' Company, 'D' Company.
An interval of 200 yards will be observed between Companies throughout the march.

4. The Quartermaster and 9 Other Ranks will proceed at 8-0 a.m. to take over billets.

5. TIME TABLE:-

      Reveille   6-30 a.m.
      Breakfast   7- 0 a.m.
      Dinner   10-30 a.m.

Blankets, Officers Valises and Company boxes to be at Q.M. Stores at 8-30 a.m.
Transport will march at 11-20 a.m., and join the Battalion on the MAILLY-FORCEVILLE Road (P.22.a.3.2.)
Battalion will march at 12-0 noon.

6. Lieut. Braine will collect stragglers.

ISSUED AT 6-30 p.m.

Copy No. 1.	C.O.	Copy No. 2.	2nd in Command.
3.	O.C. "A" Coy.	4.	O.C. 'B' Coy.
5.	O.C. 'C' '	6.	O.C. 'D' '
7.	Q.M.	8.	T.O.
9.	L.G.O.	10.	M.O.
11.	Camp Commandant (For information)		
12 & 13.	War Diary		

A. St. J. WALSH, Lieut. and Adjutant.

24th Battalion The Manchester Regiment. (Pioneers)

INSTRUCTIONS FOR FORTHCOMING REVIEW

App^x II

REFERENCE FRANCE. Sheet 57 D.

1. The 7th Division will be inspected by General NIVELLE Commander-in-Chief of the French Army, at about 10-30 a.m. on Saturday February 17th.

2. The Parade Ground is half a mile N.E. of VAL DE MAISON from about N. 30. d. 3.3. to about N. 25. a. 9.3.

3. The troops will be drawn up facing SOUTH and will be in position by 10-0 a.m.
The 24th Battalion THE MANCHESTER REGIMENT will be in mass formation on the left flank.

4. Lewis Gunners and H.Q. Pioneers will be in the ranks.
Signallers with slung rifles and flags and Stretcher Bearers without stretchers will be drawn up in line in rear of the Battalion.
Signallers on the right and Stretcher Bearers on the left.

5. Eight pack animals, each carrying two ammunition boxes, and the two limbered wagons for Lewis Guns will be drawn up in rear of the Signallers and Stretcher Bearers.
Pack animals (in line) on the right and limbered wagons on the left.

6. Dress and equipment will be as follows:-
   (a) Officers will not wear swords or carry sticks, but will wear revolvers and field glasses.
   (b) Company Commanders will not be mounted.
   (c) Other Ranks will wear leather jerkins over the tunic and under the belt.
   (d) EQUIPMENT:- Drill Order, which will be taken to mean, belt, side arms and rifle only.

7. The Adjutant, accompanied by markers, will be on the Parade Ground by 9-15 a.m.

8. The Battalion will fall in facing N in the RUE de l' EGLISE in the following order:-
From the right, "A", "B", "C", "D", Signallers, Stretcher Bearers, Transport.
The right of "A" Company will be at the Orderly Room.

9. The Battalion will be ready to move at 8-45 a.m.

(Signed) A. St. G. WALSH, Lieut. & Adjt
16th Feby. 1917.   24th Battalion The Manchester Regiment.

App^x III

SECRET   Copy No. 11

OPERATION ORDERS NO. 12 BY
LIEUT COLONEL J.H. CHADWICK COMMANDING
24TH BATTALION MANCHESTER REGIMENT.

REFERENCE. FRANCE, Sheet 57 D.   21st February, 1917.

1. The Battalion will move to-morrow, 22nd instant, to MAILLY MAILLET.

2. ROUTE :- RAINCHEVAL-ARQUEVES-LEALVILLERS-ACHEUX-FORCEVILLE.

3. ORDER OF MARCH :- Headquarters, Band, "A" Coy., "B" Coy., "C" Coy., "D" Coy., Transport.
   An interval of 200 yards between Coys. will be kept throughout the march.

4. DRESS :- Full Marching Order. Shrapnel helmets will be worn.

5. The Quartermaster and 9 Other Ranks will proceed at 8-9 a.m. to take over billets.

6. TIME TABLE :- Reveille 6-30 a.m.   Breakfast 7-30 a.m.
   Blankets rolled by sections and Officers
   Valises to be at Q.M. Stores by 7-30 a.m.
   Mess baskets to be at Q.M. Stores by 8-30 a.m.
   The Battalion will march at 9-15 a.m.; the head of the column will be at H.Q. Mess in the Rue de l'Eglise.

7. 2/Lieut. Holt and 12 Other Ranks will remain behind to hand over present billets.   They will rejoin the Battalion at MAILLY MAILLET.

8. Lieut. Brains will march in rear and collect stragglers.

ISSUED AT 3 pm.

Copy No. 1. Commanding Officer
         2. 2nd in Command.
         3. O.C. "A" Coy.
         4. O.C. "B" "
         5. O.C. "C" "
         6. O.C. "D" "
         7. Quartermaster
         8. Transport Officer
         9. Medical Officer
        10. Lewis Gun Officer
        11 &12. War Diary.

(Signed) A. St. G. WALSH, Lieut. and Adjutant.
         24th Battalion The Manchester Regiment.

Div. No.
/51/A.
26/2/1917.

APPENDIX IV.

24th. Battalion The Manchester Regiment.

The following is an extract from List No. 123 of "Appointments, Commissions, etc.," approved by the Field Marshal Commanding-in-Chief, dated 17th. February, 1917.

SERVICE BATTALION.

Manchester Regiment.

24th. Battn.:- Temp. Major J.H. Chadwick to command Bn. and to be Temp. Lieut. Colonel, vice Capt. (Temp. Lt. Col.) J.B. Sutton, (invalided), 2nd. January, 1917.

(Sd) E. De C. Harris St. John, Major,
A.A.G. to G.O.C., Fifth Army.

22/2/1917.

Army Form C. 2118.

2/4th (2) Bn Manchester Regt
(T.F.) as Pioneers

WAR DIARY
or
INTELLIGENCE SUMMARY
(Erase heading not required.)

Vol XVII

Place	Date	Hour	Summary of Events and Information	Remarks and references to Appendices
MAILLY MAILLET	1/3/17		Weather – Damp, cold	
			Work – BEAUMONT HAMEL – AUCHONVILLERS road; 1 Plt "A" Coy repairing & clearing	
			STATION Rd A Coy (1 Pl/s 1 N.C.O) 8 hours clearing mud, filling	
			D Coy holes with rubble & brick	
			2 G.S. wagons carrying brick.	
			SUCRERIE-SERRE Rd C Coy 6 hours, clearing 300×5'	
			B Coy (1Lt/3 platoons) 3 mud & filling holes	
			2 G.S. wagons carrying brick	
			BEAUSSART 1 Plt working in Divl R.E. yard,	
			AUCHONVILLERS 1 Plt unloading wagons.	
			1 Plt. returned from work at VAUCHELLES.	
			Casualties – Nil.	
	2nd		Weather Frost at night. Damp throughout day; no wind	
			Work BEAUMONT Road } A&D Coys as previous day	
			STATION Road }	
			SERRE Road C Coy (B Pl/s 2 Plts) as previous day	
			BEAUSSART & AUCHONVILLERS parties as previous day	
			Casualties Nil.	

Army Form C. 2118.

WAR DIARY
or
INTELLIGENCE SUMMARY

(Erase heading not required.)

Place	Date	Hour	Summary of Events and Information	Remarks and references to Appendices
	3		Weather as previous day.	
			Work A Coy 1 plh. working BEAUMONT ROAD near otherwise line (chang SUNKEN ROAD).	
			3 plhs (with an inf party) worked 6½ hrs clearing & repairing STATION RD.	
			D Coy worked 6 hours clearing & repairing SERRE RD.	
			C Coy	
			B Coy 2 plhs	
			B Coy 2 plhs worked on R.E. yard at AUCHONVILLERS & BEAUSSART.	
			Casualties — Nil.	A.S.G/W
	4.		Weather Rather colder.	
			Work as previous day; in addition 350 infy working on BEAUMONT ROAD.	
			Casualties — Nil.	A.S.G/W

Army Form C. 2118.

WAR DIARY
or
INTELLIGENCE SUMMARY.
(Erase heading not required.)

Place	Date	Hour	Summary of Events and Information	Remarks and references to Appendices
	5.		Weather: Some snow during night; then during day; wind light NE	
			Work: A Coy 1 Plt on SUNKEN ROAD clearing & repairing 265 yards camp; light track	
			A Coy 3 Plts } on STATION ROAD clearing & repairing & D Coy } 265 yards camp; light track (6½ hrs)	
			C Coy } on SERRE ROAD clearing & repairing B Coy 2 Plts } (6 hrs) Inf Party 300 men under 24th March R. officer clearing & repairing BEAUMONT road 465 yards camp; light track BEAUSSART-AUCHONVILLERS	
			B Coy 2 Plts working on R.E. yards	
			Casualties — Nil.	

Army Form C. 2118.

WAR DIARY
or
INTELLIGENCE SUMMARY.
(Erase heading not required.)

Place	Date	Hour	Summary of Events and Information	Remarks and references to Appendices
	6.		Weather fine; ground very muddy. Wind light N.E. Work as previous day, except no Infantry on BEAUMONT road & parties on SUNKEN road & STATION road. Casualties – Nil.	A.S.R.M.
	7.		Weather fine; slight frost. Wind strong E. & very cold. Work chiefly draining & repairing former roads. { STATION Road D Coy, A Coy Hqrs. (4th) & 100 Infy. { SERRE Road C Coy Q.4 B Coy { SUNKEN Road 1/4th Roy Parties working in R.E. workshops & yards at BEAUSSART & AUCHONVILLERS. Casualties – Nil.	A.S.R.M.
	8.		Weather slight frost; some snow. Wind light E. Work clearing & draining former roads. { SERRE Road D Coy, ¾ A Coy, ½ B Coy & C Coy { SUNKEN Road 1/4th A Coy loading sleepers at COLINCAMPS 1/4th. Parties as previous day. Casualties – Nil.	A.S.R.M.

Army Form C. 2118.

WAR DIARY
or
INTELLIGENCE SUMMARY.
(Erase heading not required.)

Instructions regarding War Diaries and Intelligence Summaries are contained in F. S. Regs., Part II. and the Staff Manual respectively. Title pages will be prepared in manuscript.

Place	Date	Hour	Summary of Events and Information	Remarks and references to Appendices
	9		Weather As previous day.	
			Work BEAUMONT HAMEL road clearing, 1st Acty/Cy COLINCAMPS doing loading shelters, mbags, 2/7th Cy SERRE Road clearing, repairing Beauchich stores (D Coy, ¾ C Coy, ¾ A Coy, ½ B Coy) 6-7 hrs	
			BEAUSSART } Working in R.E. yard & workshops. 2 Plns B Coy	9.55 p.m.
			AUCHONVILLERS }	
			Casualties — Nil.	
	10		Weather Slight frost at night, than sunny day; wind light N.E.	
			Work as previous day.	
			Casualties — Nil. Reinforcements 3 O/Rs joined	9.55 p.m.
	11		Weather Milder; wind light S.E.	
			Coys rested; Divine Services held during the day. The Bn. was beaten in the Final of the Divisional Football cup by the 1st S. Staffs R, 5 goals — 0. Casualties — Nil	9.55 p.m.

A5834 Wt.W4973/M687 750,000 8/16 D.D.&L.Ltd. Forms/C2118/13.

WAR DIARY
or
INTELLIGENCE SUMMARY.

Army Form C. 2118.

(Erase heading not required.)

Place	Date	Hour	Summary of Events and Information	Remarks and references to Appendices
	12		Weather Mild.	
			Work Beaumont Hamel Road; clearing & repairing 1 Plt. A Coy	AM/2
			Success-Serre-Puisieux Road; clearing & repairing with track	
			stone & sleepers. (6 hrs) D Coy & B Coy. ½ C Coy. ¾ A Coy.	
			Cohencamps Siding; loading sleepers & stone into carts of S. wagons	
			1 Plt. C Coy.	
			Beaussart to Auchonvillers. working on R.E. yards: two kitchens. 2 Plt B.	AM/M
			Casualties — Nil.	
	13		Weather Mild, wind light N.W.	
			Work as previous day. Casualties — Nil.	
			Honours & Awards — 14170 a/R.S.M. Moor E. awarded Italian Bronze Medal	AM/M
			for Military Valour	
	14		Weather as previous day.	
			Work as previous day.	AM/M
			Casualties — Nil.	

Army Form C. 2118.

WAR DIARY
or
INTELLIGENCE SUMMARY.
(Erase heading not required.)

Instructions regarding War Diaries and Intelligence Summaries are contained in F. S. Regs., Part II. and the Staff Manual respectively. Title pages will be prepared in manuscript.

Place	Date	Hour	Summary of Events and Information	Remarks and references to Appendices
	15		Weather. Slight frost at night; mild & bright during day, wind S. by W.W.	
			Work. SERRE-PUISIEUX road. Repairing & draining 2 trackers & putting 6 trs. of 200 infantry camping tracks.	
			A Coy (Capt M.M.), B Coy (Major Mᶜ—), C Coy (Capt Roff), 1 Pltn D Coy	
			BEAUMONT road — 1 Pltn C — Repairing & draining 265 approximately	
				works 1 Pltn D Coy
			COLINCAMPS — 1 Pltn — Carrying stores & taking up from trench trestles 1 Pltn C Coy	
				1 Pltn C Coy
			BEAUSSART — } Worked in R.E. Yard's workshops 2 Pltns B Coy	Appx
			AUCHONVILLERS — }	
			Casualties — 1 O.R. killed	
	16		Weather as previous day	
			Work. SERRE - PUISIEUX road — } As previous day. SUNKEN road Repairing 1 Pltn A Coy	Appx
			COLINCAMPS — sidings }	
			BEAUSSART }	
			AUCHONVILLERS }	
			Casualties — Nil	

Army Form C. 2118.

WAR DIARY
or
INTELLIGENCE SUMMARY.

(Erase heading not required.)

Place	Date	Hour	Summary of Events and Information	Remarks and references to Appendices
	17		Weather: Bright, clear, mild, wind light NW. Heavy Infantry; A & D Coys c&y tpls. 1/4th & B Coys. 114 drifts & 2 tents camping Brett. SERRE-PUISIEUX road. 6 hrs COLINCAMPS Sdg. Road: D 35 wagons with stuff for 436 with road metal. BEAUSTART AUCHONVILLERS — Working in R.E. yard & workshops EUSTON DUMP — 1/2 B Coy. Casualties — Nil	ASM
	18		Weather: Mild + fine. Wind fresh W. B Coy moved to PUISIEUX see O.O attached; camp formed of tents + tarred shelters + a few dugouts & cellars for a short time. NM/- Work Coys worked on PUISEUX-BUCQUOY road in the afternoon. BEAUSSART COLINCAMPS Sdg. EUSTON DUMP } Working in R.E. yards & workshops Casualties — Nil 1/2 B Coy. A&D Coy	ASM

WAR DIARY
or
INTELLIGENCE SUMMARY.

Army Form C. 2118.

Place	Date	Hour	Summary of Events and Information	Remarks and references to Appendices
PUISIEUX L.20.a.38 Maps 57D N.2 57C N.W.	19		Weather Colder, some rain	
			Work PUISIEUX-BUCQUOY road cleaning and draining & preparing A Coy, B Coy (less 2 pltn) C Coy (less 1 pltn). D Coy. 6 hrs work. COLINCAMPS Siding ⎫ BEAUSSART ⎬ Loading wagons; working in R.E. yards MAILLY SGT. ⎪ 4 workshops. 2 pltn B Coy EUSTON DUMP ⎭ 1 pltn C Coy.	A.H.M.
			Casualties — Nil	
	20		Weather Some rain; cold. Wind fresh N.W.	
			Work as previous day	
			Reinforcements — 18 Officers joined. Casualties — Nil.	A.H.M.
	21		Weather as previous day	
			Work PUISIEUX-BUCQUOY road Repairing & draining 1 Pltn A Coy; D Coy; C Coy 6 hrs work. 1 Pltn C Coy 6 hrs work. BEAUSSART ⎫ Loading wagons; working in R.E. yards 10 Pltn 4.30 R EUSTON DUMP ⎬ & workshops. B Coy 1 Pltn C Coy & a part of B Coy rejoined. Casualties — Nil	Appx

Army Form C. 2118.

WAR DIARY
or
INTELLIGENCE SUMMARY.
(Erase heading not required.)

Instructions regarding War Diaries and Intelligence Summaries are contained in F. S. Regs., Part II. and the Staff Manual respectively. Title pages will be prepared in manuscript.

Place	Date	Hour	Summary of Events and Information	Remarks and references to Appendices
	22		Weather Fine; slight frost. Wind light N.W. Work PUISIEUX-BUCQUOY road. 4 Coys. 5-10 O.R's worked 6 hrs repairing, cleaning & draining. Trench laid; sumps dug. Casualties - Nil.	Aspen
	23		Weather as previous day Work as previous day also working in BUCQUOY; erecting horse troughs ground at L.3.K.45.80. 700 feet (2 B°s) repairing road PUISIEUX & BLAINZEVILLE. Casualties - Nil	Aspen
	24		Weather Fine; wind light variable N.W.-N.E. Work PUISIEUX-BUCQUOY-COURCELLES road; 4 Coys. left small parties worked 6 hrs sawing & repairing. 2 B°s & 29's (about 700 men) worked about L.54 hrs. Horse troughs erected at L.3.K.45.95, L.3.K.45.80, F.23.d.5.4. 2 Complete, 2 partially done. Also worked on 300x MBLAINZEVILLE-ACHIET-LE-GRAND road. More 2 Coys (M D) moved to F.28.A.68. Casualties - Nil.	Aspen

Army Form C. 2118.

WAR DIARY
or
INTELLIGENCE SUMMARY.
(Erase heading not required.)

Place	Date	Hour	Summary of Events and Information	Remarks and references to Appendices
	25		Weather as previous day. Work as previous day, but Inf'y party 300 men only. Casualties - Nil	Appx/r
	26		Weather Mild, some rain. Wind freshen. Work as previous day for A+D Coys & Inf'y party. Most B&C Coys moved to camp at COURCELLES HALTE, BHQ moved to A+D Coys camp. Casualties - Nil.	Appx/r
ABLAINZEVILLE 27 F.28.A.68 Sheet 57DNE 95FCNW			Weather Colder, some rain. Work B&C Coys (14/5 +/4th each) worked 6 hrs clearing drainage & repairing MAMELINCOURT – MAISON ROUGE road; 1/4th clearing road in COURCELLES – Lt-COMTE. A+D Coys worked 6 hrs on BUCQUOY–COURCELLES road a further work on horse troughs. Casualties - Nil	Appx/r

WAR DIARY
or
INTELLIGENCE SUMMARY

Army Form C. 2118.

Place	Date	Hour	Summary of Events and Information	Remarks and references to Appendices
	28		Weather as previous day, slight falls of snow. Work B & C Coys as previous day. A & D Coys 350 mtrs on POISIEUX – COURCELLES & ABLAINZEVILLE – ACHIET-LE-GRAND roads. Artillery worked 6 hrs on overhead track by side of road for country & guns, cut gaps in wire in front of BUCQUOY & commenced ramps. Casualties – Nil.	
	29		Weather cold, some rain. Work B & C Coys worked 6 hrs clearing & repairing ERVILLERS – MORY road. D Coy worked 6 hrs clearing & repairing PUISIEUX-ACHIET-LE-GRAND road & continued work on track about A Coy had 2 hours on that road, then moved to COURCELLES. HALTE Casualties – Nil.	
	30		Weather cold, quiet, slight fall of snow. W.S.W. Work A, B & C Coys worked 6 hrs clearing & draining ERVILLERS – MORY road 178 mtrs also on this road. Improved main water in COURCELLES.	

Army Form C. 2118.

WAR DIARY
or
INTELLIGENCE SUMMARY.

(Erase heading not required.)

Place	Date	Hour	Summary of Events and Information	Remarks and references to Appendices
	31		Work (a) D Coy & Bns worked on PUISIEUX-COURCELLES road. General repairs with 20 Inf.	
			1 offr & 80 men repairing BUCQUOY-ESSARTS-BIENVILLERS road.	Appx
			B Coy & 150 men also worked on and widened track near BUCQUOY & HÉBUTERNE.	
			Casualties - Nil.	
			Weather Slightly cooler. Some rain that W and S.W-W.	
			Work A & C Coys with 8 Coys Inf repairing ORVILLERS - MORY road.	
			D Coy & 180 Inf on front line; small parts also on MIRAUMONT-VILLE - ACHIET-LE-GRAND road.	Appx
			Casualties - Nil.	

FK Chadwick, Lieut Col
cmdg 24th (s) Bn The Manchester Regt
(1st Army Pioneers)

SECRET Copy No. 11

OPERATION ORDER NO. 14 BY
LIEUT COLONEL J.H. CHADWICK COMMANDING
24TH BATTALION THE MANCHESTER REGIMENT.

REFERENCE MAP, 57 D. N.E.

1. The Battalion (less special working parties detailed by C.R.E., and Q.M. Stores and Transport Personnel) will move to PUISIEUX tomorrow, 18th March, 1917.

2. 2/Lieut. Anderson will proceed forthwith to arrange accommodation with the Town Major of PUISIEUX.

3. TIME TABLE:-
    Reveille   4-30 a.m.
    Breakfast   5-30 a.m.
    Tool wagons loaded   6-0 a.m.
    Blankets (in rolls of 10) to be
    at Q.M. Stores by   6-30 a.m.
    Officers valises and Mess Baskets
    at Q.M. Stores by   7-0 a.m.
    Move off   7-30 a.m.

4. DRESS:- Full marching order. Steel helmets will be worn.

5. TOOLS:- Each man will carry one tool; picks and shovels in ratio of one to two. A few saws and hammers will be carried.

6. TRANSPORT:- The Field Kitchens and L.G. limbers and H.Q. limber will accompany the Battalion. The remainder will remain in its present position.

7. ORDER OF MARCH:- H.Q. and Band, "A", "B" (less special parties), "C" and "D" Coys.
    An interval of 200 yards between platoons will be kept throughout the march.

8. All ranks must be warned of the danger of contamination of food and water, particularly of food that comes into contact with the ground.

9. Lieut. Braine will proceed at 6-0 a.m. to allot accommodation.

ISSUED AT 10-0 p.m., 17-3-17.

Copy No. 1. Commanding Officer
        2. O.C. "A" Coy.
        3. O.C. "B" "
        4. O.C. "C" "
        5. O.C. "D" "
        6. Quartermaster.
        7. Transport Officer.
        8. Lewis Gun Officer.
        9. 2/Lieut. THORP.
       10. War Diary.
       11. War Diary.

(Signed)   A. St. G. WALSH,   Lieut. and Adjutant.
            24th Battalion The Manchester Regiment.

SECRET

Copy No. 11

OPERATION ORDER NO. 13 BY LIEUT COLONEL J.H. CHADWICK COMMANDING 24TH BATTALION MANCHESTER REGIMENT.

REFERENCE, SHEET 57 D. N.E., Edition 4A, 1/20,000.

1.
- (a) The 7th Division will attack BUCQUOY.
- (b) The 46th Division will be attacking on the left of 7th Division.
- (c) No troops will be attacking on right flank of 7th Division nearer than an attack on LOUPART WOOD.

2. Zero date and hour will be notified later. All preparations will be completed for the attack to be made at dawn on 14th instant.

3. The 20th and 22nd Infantry Brigades will carry out this attack — the 22nd Infantry Brigade on right, 20th Infantry Brigade on left.

The dividing line between Infantry Brigades on the front of attack will be South along the main AYETTE — PUISIEUX Road as far as L. 3. d. 0.4. (inclusive to 20th Infantry Brigade) thence the Railway to L. 9. c. 2.7. — thence a straight line to Road Junction at L. 20. a. 5.0. (inclusive to 20th Infantry Brigade.

4. Attack by 22nd Infantry Brigade.
- (a) On capturing first objective parties will be detailed to work down BUCQUOY and ARNIN Trenches towards ACHIET-le-PETIT, to ascertain how far these trenches are unoccupied.
- (b) Strong points will be established at:-
  - (i) L. 10. a. 3.6.
  - (ii) L. 4. c. 7.8.
  - (iii) L. 4. a. 1.6.
  - (iv) F. 28. c. 8.5.

5. Attack by 20th Infantry Brigade.
- (a) The 20th Infantry Brigade will be entirely responsible for the capture of the New Trench in L. 2. b.
- (b) On reaching final objective, posts will be established in touch with right of 46th Division which is going to rest at F. 21. d. Central.
- (c) Strong Points will be established at:-
  - (i) L. 3. a. 0.6.
  - (ii) L. 3. a. 6.9.
  - (iii) F. 27. c. 1.2.
  - (iv) F. 27. b. 6.2.
  - (v) F. 22. c. 1.2.

6. The 24th (Pioneer) Battalion The Manchester Regiment will be in Divisional Reserve.

Sheet 2.

7. O. C. Companies and as many Company Officers as possible will reconnoitre the roads from PUISIEUX to BUCQUOY and the position of the R.E. Dump at PUISIEUX.
NOTE:- See Administrative Instructions (attached)

8. Headquarters will be established on Zero minus one day as follows:-
Divisional H.Q. at APPLE TREES.
20th Inf. Bde. H.Q. at L. 20. c. 3.9.
22nd Inf. Bde. H.Q. at L. 20. b. 8.9.
91st Inf. Bde. H.Q. at CAFE JOURDAIN

The two forward Infantry Bde. H.Q. will move forward to PUISIEUX as the attack progresses.

9. Issued at 6-30 p.m., 12-3-17.

Copy No. 1. Commanding Officer.
2. 2nd in Command.
3. O.C. "A" Coy.
4. O.C. "B" "
5. O.C. "C" "
6. O.C. "D" "
7. Quartermaster.
8. Medical Officer.
9. Transport Officer.
10. Lewis Gun Officer.
11 & 12. War Diary.

(Signed) A. St. G. WALSH, Lieut. and Adjutant.
24th (Pioneer) Battalion The Manchester Regiment.

SECRET

24th (Pioneer) Battalion The Manchester Regiment.

ADMINISTRATIVE INSTRUCTIONS FOR OPERATIONS IN
ACCORDANCE WITH OPERATIONS ORDER NO. 13, DATED 12-3-17.

1. **SUPPLY OF S.A.A., GRENADES, etc.**
   (a) The Divisional Dump has been established at J. 32. d. 5.3. on S. side of Road and on Tramline.
   (b) Brigade Dumps have been established at N. end of PUISIEUX.
   Left Brigade at L. 14. c. 4.6.
   Right Brigade at L. 14. d. 8.4.

2. **WATER**
   (a) Drinking Water. Water in captured territorkty is on no account to be used for drinking or cooking purposes until tested. A.D.M.S has arranged for samples to be collected at earliest opportunity when supplies will be marked.
   (b) Horse Watering. At present no good supply for horses exists further East than MAILLY MAILLET and P. 6. b. 8.2.

3. **R.E. MATERIAL**
   Forward dumps have been formed at Quarry L. 14. c. 0.0. -b L. 14. d. 8.4. and L. 20. c. 5.9.

4. **MEDICAL** Advanced Dressing Station has been established at ROSSIGNOL HOUSE, L. 14. c. 5.4. and relay posts of bearers for evacuation of wounded by road or tramway, at L. 20. a. 6.2. - L. 19. c. 6.1. SERRE. SKUNK POST and SUCRERIE.
   Main Dressing Station REDHOUSE, MAILLY MAILLET.

5. **PRISONERS** The Divl. Prisoners Cage will be at SKUNK POST K. 34. d. 6.9.

Copies as O.O. 13. (Signed) A. St. G. WALSH, Lieut. and Adjutant.

WAR DIARY or INTELLIGENCE SUMMARY

Army Form C. 2118.

24th (S) Bn. The Manchester Regt.
(7th Divisional Pioneers)

Vol LXVIII   Nov 1918

Place	Date	Hour	Summary of Events and Information	Remarks and references to Appendices
MOLAINZEVILLE F.28.b.68 Matr Shocks S-7 D.N.E. 57c N.W. HQ 4 Coy, 3 Coy S at COURCELLES MAIZE A.16.B.4.8	1.		Weather - Mild; showery. Wind light W-SW. Work: 1 Pl/A Coy making gaps in hedges & ramps etc for overland track. ½ B Coy, C Coy P.g; clearing & laying CERVILLERS - MORY road. D Coy & Bns repairing MOLAINZEVILLE - ACHIET-LE-GRAND, BUCQUOY - ACHIET-LE-PETIT + PUISIEUX - MIRAUMONT roads. Casualties - Nil. Reinforcements - Draft of 49 O.R. joined Bn.	
	2.		Weather cooler; showers. Wind fresh S-SE. Some snow at night. Work: 1 Pl B Coy + 1 Pl D Coy making gaps in wire, filling trenches, making ramps etc. on MEN road for overland track. ½ B Coy, ¼ C Coy P.g repairing CERVILLERS - MORY road. D Coy (less 1 Pl Pl) repairing (1) ADLAINZEVILLE - ACHIET-LE-PETIT road via (BUCQUOY) (2) BUCQUOY - ACHIET-LE-PETIT road. 1 Pl H.Q. 50 men C Coy acted as carrying party for S.28th Field Coy R.E. with wiring material for strong points in front of CROISSILLES - ECOUST-ST-MEIN. Casualties - Nil.	

WAR DIARY or INTELLIGENCE SUMMARY

Army Form C. 2118.

Place	Date	Hour	Summary of Events and Information	Remarks and references to Appendices
	3		Weather Cold; 3" snow yesterday, but today thaw during day. Wind S-SE. Work A Coy, 3/4 C Coy, & ½ B Coy worked 6 hrs repairing ZAVILLERS-MORY road, scraping off mud & putting down brick & stone. ½ Pltn C Coy worked 2½ hrs on COURCELLES-HAMELINCOURT road (2½ hrs) ½ Pltn B Coy & ½ Pltn D Coy worked on cavalry track. 3 Pltns D Coy & Coy worked 6 hrs on ABLAINZEVILLE-COURCELLES and Casualties – Nil	[signature]
	4		Weather Milder. Wind S-SW. fresh – light. Work A Coy, C Coy & ¾ B Coy worked 6 hrs repairing ZAVILLERS-MORY road with 59 wagon carrying track. ½ Pltn B Coy & 12 men (Inf'y) making out cavalry track near COURCELLES & HAMELINCOURT. D Coy & Coy worked 6 hrs on cavalry track filling trenches, making up & fixing roads. Casualties – Nil.	
	5		Weather Mild Overcast. Wind SW-W light. A & C Coys worked 6 hrs repairing ZAVILLERS-MORY road. ½ B Coy worked 6 hrs repairing COURCELLES – HAMELINCOURT road	[signature]

WAR DIARY
or
INTELLIGENCE SUMMARY.

(Erase heading not required.)

Army Form C. 2118.

Place	Date	Hour	Summary of Events and Information	Remarks and references to Appendices
	6		1/1st B Coy working on improving 3 ramps & constructing new one for cavalry track.	Stopp
			D Coy filling trenches cutting wire making ramps (7 hrs) for cavalry track near BUCQUOY.	
			Casualties — Nil	
			Weather as previous day	
			Training 1 PLT per Coy off working parties, infantry drill, inspections etc.	
			1 Officer per Coy & 1 Senior NCO receives instruction in use of Bangalore Torpedoes.	
			Work Day as previous day, 5½ hrs.	
			A.M. Coy cleaning & repairing ERVILLERS – MORY road, 6 hrs.	
			½ B Coy " COURCELLES – HAMELINCOURT "	
			1/1st B Coy on cavalry track as previous day	
			Casualties — Nil	Stopp

WAR DIARY
or
INTELLIGENCE SUMMARY

Army Form C. 2118.

Place	Date	Hour	Summary of Events and Information	Remarks and references to Appendices
	7		Weather Snow cooler. Wind from N.E. Training 1 Plt per Coy as previous day. Work As previous day. Casualties – Nil	Appx
	8		Weather Fine. Wind light N.E. No work done. Divine Services were held during day at both camps. Casualties – Nil.	Appx
	9		Weather Some rain. Wind light N.E. Training B Coy did infantry training, kit inspections etc. Work D Coy 1 Plt repairing road; 3 Plts filling in trenches for Cavalry track ST. LEGER – VRAUCOURT. Digging St Leger River A & C Coys 2 Plts worked on defensive line. 6 Plts working posts. 6 Plts unable to work as above by day owing to exposed position, worked by night. Casualties — Nil	Appx
	10		Weather as previous day. Training B Coy as B Coy above. Work B Coy road repairs. A & C Coys worked on defensive line – as above by night; moving back to camp in anticipation of possible move. Casualties – Nil	Appx

Army Form C. 2118.

WAR DIARY
or
INTELLIGENCE SUMMARY.
(Erase heading not required.)

Place	Date	Hour	Summary of Events and Information	Remarks and references to Appendices
	11.		Weather Fine sunny morning, some snow in the evening. Work Bn was standing by from 4.30 AM in anticipation of probable move out to successful attack of First-Third Army's. A & C Coys eventually worked on ERVILLERS - ST LEGER road, clearing & repairing, 4 hrs; 1 Plt. making track round CRATER at B10.d.59. Move Bn. HQ. D Coy moved up to the detachment camp COURCELLES HALTE. Casualties - Nil	9.50pm
COURCELLES HALTE. A.16.c.4.8 Sh. c46 57cN.W. & 51BS.W.	12.		Weather Cooler. Some rain Work A & C Coys worked as previous day, 6 hours. B Coy standing by. D Coy worked 3½ hrs night on Defensive line, digging wiring posts. Casualties - Nil	9.50pm
	13.		Weather Mild, tried to clear, wind fresh WSW Work A Coy & Bays A Coy worked on ST LEGER-ERVILLERS road, filling craters & draining & repairing ruts, holes with track. B Coy filling craters in and near ST LEGER 6-7 hrs. C Coy working on defensive line. 4½ hrs night on defensive line, digging & 1 Plt. D Coy worked wiring no 13 post. Casualties - Nil	9.50pm
	14.		Weather fine, wind light westerly	

WAR DIARY
or
INTELLIGENCE SUMMARY.

(Erase heading not required.)

Army Form C. 2118.

Place	Date	Hour	Summary of Events and Information	Remarks and references to Appendices
	15.		Work A Coy worked 6 hrs on ERVILLERS - ST LEGER road.	
			B Coy " " " " HAMELINCOURT - ERVILLERS road.	
			C & D Coy worked 4½ hrs on support posts for defensive line in ST LEGER wood. Sapping clearing underwood running.	Forge
			Casualties — Nil.	
			Weather Wet; wind trend northerly.	
			Work B Coy 18/1/142 O.R. repairing ERVILLERS - ST LEGER road. Laying woodpaving.	
			10 wagons and 1 truck.	
			C Coy works 8 hours night wiring posts of defensive line 3 wagons took out of pickets from camp; wire laid to collected for various places.	
			Remainder of B Coy rested in camp during day. Casualties — Nil.	Hoffen
	16.		Weather stormy.	
			Work ½ B Coy & Band worked on ERVILLERS - ST LEGER & ERVILLERS - HAMELINCOURT roads.	
			A & D Coys worked on defensive line, improving posts wire & clearing underwood in front for field of fire.	Hoffen
			Casualties — Nil.	

WAR DIARY
or
INTELLIGENCE SUMMARY.

Army Form C. 2118.

Place	Date	Hour	Summary of Events and Information	Remarks and references to Appendices
	17.		Weather Showery wind northerly. Wind A Coy Training; infantry drill, inspection, bombing & L.G. training etc. B Coy Wiring posts of Defensive line L'HOMME MORT - St LEGER the 8 Coy carrying. 88 mm C & D Coys road repairs IRVILLERS - St LEGER & IRVILLERS - MANIELNCOURT roads. Casualties - Nil.	Asgn M
	18.		Weather Showery; wind strong, northerly Work D Coy on Defensive line, improving trenches etc. C Coy training as A Coy above; programme modified by bad weather. A & B Coys Road repairs as C & D Coys above. Casualties - Nil	Asgn M
	19.		Weather slight Showers, warmer; wind changed towards South. Work D Coy Training A Coy Road repairs on IRVILLERS - DETELLES road B Coy Road repairs on MANIELNCOURT - ERVILLERS road. C Coy improving posts turns on Defensive Line Casualties - Nil	Asgn M

Army Form C. 2118.

WAR DIARY
or
INTELLIGENCE SUMMARY.
(Erase heading not required.)

Place	Date	Hour	Summary of Events and Information	Remarks and references to Appendices
	20.		Weather — Previous day raining.	
			Work — B Coy training.	
			A Coy Road Repairs; ERVILLERS – ST LEGER road.	
			C Coy " " CRVILLERS – HAMELINCOURT road	
			D Coy on Defensive line; improving support posts & joining 12 wagons carrying bricks	
			up wire of front line posts	
			Casualties — 1 O.R. wounded. north-north east	18.9.17
	21		Weather Fine & warm; wind north-north east	
			Work A Coy training	
			B & D Coy road repairs as A & C Coys above.	
			C Coy 1 Pltn on crater COURCELLES – AYETTE road, pumping out water, filling with earth etc & making brick	
			& sleeper divisions	
			3 Pltns on defensive line as D Coy above & digging 2 flank posts on left	
			Casualties — Nil	8.54.17

WAR DIARY or INTELLIGENCE SUMMARY

Army Form C. 2118.

Place	Date	Hour	Summary of Events and Information	Remarks and references to Appendices
	22		Weather Bright & clear; wind light N.E. Coys rested. Divine services held in camp during day. Casualties — Nil.	
	23		Weather Fine & warm. Wind light N-N.E. C Coy Training, close order drill, artillery formations, signalling, bomb throwing. Work D Coy Journey to wire in front of posts of Defensive Line. A & B Coys Road repairs. Casualties — Nil.	
	24		Weather Fine & warm. Wind strong. Northerly D Coy training as C Coy above. C Coy worked as D above. A & B Coys Road repairs. Casualties — Nil.	
	25		Weather Cooler. Wind strong. N B Coy Training	

Army Form C. 2118.

WAR DIARY
or
INTELLIGENCE SUMMARY.
(Erase heading not required.)

Place	Date	Hour	Summary of Events and Information	Remarks and references to Appendices
	26.		Work C Coy repairing ERVILLERS - ST LEGER & ERVILLERS - HAMELINCOURT roads. A Coy enlarging posts of defensive line. D Coy improving & working on road B.3.c.8.4 to B in road. Casualties - Nil	ASPM
			Weather Cool, wind dropped to light. Work A Coy training; PT & BF, class order drill etc B Coy out 8½ hrs improving wire, enlarging & deepening posts & camouflaging defensive line. C & D Coys repairing roads ERVILLERS - ST LEGER, filling craters B.3.c.8.4 & B.6.c.00.75 making brick tracks across; out 7-8½ hrs Casualties - Nil	ASPM
	27.		Weather fine. C Coy training B & D Coys out 7-8 hrs on roads & craters as above. A Coy out 6 D's (night) digging 5 intermediate posts in the defensive line; 4 days 3 Traverses average depth 3 ft. Casualties - Nil	ASPM

Army Form C. 2118.

WAR DIARY
or
INTELLIGENCE SUMMARY.
(Erase heading not required.)

Place	Date	Hour	Summary of Events and Information	Remarks and references to Appendices
	28.		Weather fine. Bright/clear. Wind N-NW light. B Coy training. B Coy & C Coy out 6-8 hrs on road craters. #'s C Coy out 8 hrs making overland track from railway at A.16.d.4.0. to VILLERS. A Coy out 2½ hrs in the evening continuing above; marking ramps, filling trenches & clearing wire; marking out with white pickets. Casualties - Nil.	Appx M
	29.		Weather as previous day. Coys rested. Divine Services held. Sunday Day. Casualties - Nil	Appx N
	30.		Weather fine. Wind light N-NE. Work A Coy & C Coy worked 6 hrs completing overland track above & sitting out with white posts & notice boards. B Coy training D Coy out 7-8½ hrs night. Digging communication trenches from ST LEGER - VRAUCOURT road to 2 posts of the Sapeurs line. 250' x 80' long; half finished. Casualties - Nil	Appx N

A. Chadwick LIEUT-COLONEL
COMMANDING 24TH BATTN MANCHESTER REGT.

Copy No. 12

OPERATION ORDER NO. 15 BY
LIEUT. COLONEL J. H. CHADWICK COMMANDING
24th BATTALION THE MANCHESTER REGIMENT.

Reference - SHEETS 57B.S.W. and 57C N.W.

14th April, 1917.

1. On a date and at an hour to be notified later, the V Corps will be attacking the HINDENBURG Line, in conjunction with the 1st ANZAC Corps attacking on the right, and the VII Corps on the left.

2. The attack of the V Corps will be carried out by the 62nd Division with objectives as shewn on the attached map, which also shews the hour of departure from each objective.
The 7th Division will be in Corps reserve.

3. Action by 7th Division.
(i) The 220th Machine Gun Company is placed at the disposal of the G.O.C., 62nd Division.
O.C. 220th Machine Gun Company has already received verbal instructions to report at 62nd Divisional Headquarters on evening of April 15th.
(ii) The 22nd Infantry Brigade will be concentrated in the valley North-west of MORY by Zero plus one hour.
The Brigade Commander will keep in close touch with the situation and from Zero will keep a Staff Officer at 62nd Division Advanced Headquarters on the ERVILLERS - ARRAS Road (B.10.b.1.5), also one at the headquarters of the centre attacking brigade.
Headquarters 22nd Infantry Brigade near MORY at B.28.a.1.6.
(iii) The 20th Infantry Brigade will be concentrated at COURCELLES by Zero plus three hours.
(iv) The 91st Infantry Brigade will concentrate two battalions at LOGEAST WOOD, two battalions ABLAINZEVILLE, by Zero plus three hours.
Brigade Headquarters ABLAINZEVILLE.
(v) Divisional Headquarters will remain at COURCELLES in the first instance, and will be prepared to move to MORY as the situation develops.

4. The role of the 7th Division must depend upon the way in which the action develops.
It may be required to assist the 62nd Division; or it may be required to follow up the enemy.
All units will be prepared to move at short notice and to take with them only the baggage, supplies, and stores laid down in War Establishments.
No extra transport will be available.

5. (a) Company Commanders will ensure that their companies are ready to move at short notice when Zero hour has been notified.
(b) Waterbottles must be filled, iron rations packed, blankets and greatcoats rolled in bundles of ten.
(c) The Quartermaster and Transport Officer will make the necessary arrangements for storing surplus stores and moving.

ISSUED AT 4-0 p.m.
Copy No. 1. C.O.   Copy No. 2. 2nd in Command.
        3. O.C. "A" Coy.   4. O.C. "B" Coy.
        5. O.C. "C" "   6. O.C. "D" "
        7. Quartermaster   8. Transport Officer
        9. Lewis Gun Officer   10. Medical Officer
       11. War Diary   12. War Diary.

(Signed) A. E. G. WALSH, Lieut. and Adjutant.
24th Battalion The Manchester Regiment.

WAR DIARY or INTELLIGENCE SUMMARY.

24th (S) Bn. The Manchester Regiment (7th Divisional Pioneers) Volume 19.

Vol 19

Place	Date 1917 May	Hour	Summary of Events and Information	Remarks and references to Appendices
A.16.d.8. COURCELLES HALTE.	1		Weather: Bright & warm. Wind slight N. Work: Coy Training; Pl's "A" & "B", Coy in attack etc. D Coy worked in afternoon on COURCELLES HALTE – ERVILLERS road. B Coy worked on tramway in afternoon C Coy completed 2 communication trenches from & LEGER–IRANCOURT road to Divisional boundary. Coys commenced H.D. Coy trenches night previous night 16 officers proceeded to join 17th B. Casualties – nil	A.A.P.M.
11op65TMW 3-1 BSW	2		Weather: as previous day. B's rested; inspections held. Casualties – nil	A.A.P.M.
	3		Weather: Warm; wind light N–NE Move: B moved to camp NE of MORY; transport lines W of MORY. Coys held in readiness to work on SCOUST–BULLECOURT road; attack on BULLECOURT was not however sufficiently successful to permit work Casualties – nil	A.A.P.M.
B.17.c.a3	4		Weather: Cooler, wind WS slight – nil Work: B went out 9.50 pm to dig communication trench from BULLECOURT to W Bly Railway Embankment, owing to obscurity of the situation in BULLECOURT & consequent delays, it was impossible to finish the job. In accordance with orders B returned without working	

WAR DIARY
or
INTELLIGENCE SUMMARY.
(Erase heading not required.)

Army Form C. 2118.

Place	Date	Hour	Summary of Events and Information	Remarks and references to Appendices
	5		Casualties — Lieut Col J.H. Chadwick commanding the Bn & his runner No 14322 Rfn R. Archer (Military Medal) were killed by a shell while out with above party in front of ECOUST-ST-MEIN. Weather fine and light variable. SW in morning, veering to NW in evening. Work B&D Coys worked on MENNE MORT-defensive line (night) joining posts. A&C Coys worked (night) strengthening defences of Railway & joining post. Short lengths of tied strands dug.	Appx
	6		Casualties — Nil. The bodies of Lieut Col J.H. Chadwick & LCpl Archer (above) which had been carried back to camp were buried at military cemetery opposite the L'ABBAYE MORT. The A&A QMG & CRE 7th Divn. were present. Officers of RE & B&D Coys as well as members of all sections of the Bn were present. Command Major E. Vivier assumed command of the Bn. Weather Fine, cooler WSWxE light — NW. Work B&C Coys dug 570x of Comm Trench from ECOUST onwards (night) Casualties — Nil.	Appx
	7		Weather Fine Wind E. light — NW. Heavy rain at night. Work Draining Services (including Memorial Survey) held in camp. A B, C & D Coys completing comm. trench (above) ECOUST-BULLECOURT (night) About 1400x. depth 3'-5'. Fire positions put on Woods at W end.	Appx

WAR DIARY
or
INTELLIGENCE SUMMARY.
(Erase heading not required.)

Army Form C. 2118.

Place	Date	Hour	Summary of Events and Information	Remarks and references to Appendices
	8.		Casualties O/Rs - Nil; O.R. 2 killed, 6 wounded	
			Weather Fine & warm later; rain in morning. Wind N.W. light	
			Work A Coy improving S end of above trench; widening & deepening & laying trench mats & making resting places (night)	
			D Coy on N. end of trench, as above & making fire positions (night)	
			Casualties 4 O.R. wounded	
	9.		Weather warm Wind N-N-E light	
			Work B&C Coys as A&D above. C Coy also erecting screen on ECOUST-BULLECOURT road & digging 15-0" C.T. from main trench towards Bn HQ on above road.	
			Casualties - 6 O.R. wounded, all remaining at duty	
			Gas Alarm was given at 1am except 9.4.114 h, eventually proved to be false	
			Weather fine & warm. Wind S.E - N.E very light	
	10.		Work A Coy widening & deepening 780× of trench at N.E end (night); BULLECOURT AVE.	
			D Coy " " " 100× " " " S.W " ; also laid	
			30 Trench boards; & 1 Platoon deepening & continuing the trench to Bn HQ	
			Casualties O.R. - 1 killed, 2 wounded & 2 remaining at duty	

Army Form C. 2118.

WAR DIARY
or
INTELLIGENCE SUMMARY.
(Erase heading not required.)

Place	Date	Hour	Summary of Events and Information	Remarks and references to Appendices
	11		Weather. Fine and warm. Wind: Very light. S.E. Work. "C" Coy. One section cleared places blown in on Bullecourt Avenue Trench. Remainder of Coy deepening and widening Top* of same trench from C.3.a.6-2 to railway embankment. (night) Casualties Nil.	B.T.J.
	12.		Weather. Fine and warm. Wind S E very light. "B" Coy. Dug a trench from U.27.d.6.3 to U.27.d.35.40, along the railway embankment, also a trench from U.27.a.60.25 to U.27.a.58.35. "D" Coy. Deepening and widening BULLECOURT-AVENUE from C.3.a.8.6 to U.27.d.4.2 (350 yds) Carried 100 trench boards from C.3.c.1-2, and 80 to same. 1 Section repairing trench when blown in from U.27.d.4.2 to point 31. Gas masks were put on as traces of gas were felt. (night) Casualties. G.R. 3 wounded.	B.T.J.
	13		Weather Fine and warm. Very heavy thunder storms later. Wind S E day, S.W. at night. "A" Coy. Deepening, widening and repairing Bullecourt Avenue, especially 8 or 9 places where same had been blown in by hostile Shelling. Laid down 45 Trench mats. Cleared and commenced to dig trench from Pt. 31 to Bn Hq at U.28.a.5.2. It was impossible to complete or continue the work on this latter trench as there was no cover and the men were subjected to heavy shelling and (night) Casualties Nil	B.T.J.

WAR DIARY or INTELLIGENCE SUMMARY

Army Form C. 2118.

Place	Date	Hour	Summary of Events and Information	Remarks and references to Appendices
	14		Weather Showery. Wind Fresh. S.W.	

Work. "B" Coy. Detailed for clearing Bullecourt - AVENUE. Detained 1 hour before entering trench owing to a Guard being placed on it by relieving Brigade. Coy had to be withdrawn in consequence of enemy Gas Shells. No work done. (Night)

"C" Coy. Work. Trench from POINT 31 to U.28.a.30.45 (about 200 yards) dug to an average depth of 2'-6", and an average width of 2'-9" on top. (Night) Hostile Bombardment delayed the relief for 2 hours.

"D" Coy. Work. Communication Trench from U.27.D.45.8 to U.27.a.8.5-4. Entered Gas shell Barrage at 9.30 p.m. Gas helmets worn & to be put on. 109 men suffered from Gas poisoning. 54 men sent to Aid Post. 6 sent to C.C.S. The Company returned to Camp having been unable to get to the job. (Night)

During the day a H.V. enemy gun shelled the vicinity of the Camp which necessitated the removal of the men for a little time.

Casualties

	Officers	O.R.
Reporting Sick (Gassed)		66
Wounded		3
Gassed admitted to 7A		6
		77

WAR DIARY or INTELLIGENCE SUMMARY

Army Form C. 2118.

Place	Date	Hour	Summary of Events and Information	Remarks and references to Appendices
MAPS.	May 15.		C + D Coys Weather Dull. Wind NW light	
			Work A + B Coys. Communication Trench from U.27.D.4.5-8 to U.27.9.8.5-4. The Coys were unable to get on to the work, or beyond the Railway embankment in consequence of the light night and hostile machine Gun Fire. Left the embankment for Camp at 1 a.m. (night.) Casualties NiL	
MAPS. 57CNW 57DNE	16.		Move C + D Coys moved to Camp LOGEAST WOOD. F.30.C.8-4. Weather Very wet. Wind NW daytime. SW night. Move A + B Coys Moved to Camp LOGEAST WOOD. F.30.C.8-4. Transport moved to Camp LOGEAST WOOD. F.30.C.8-4. Casualties NiL	
	17.		Weather - Fine - Dull. Wind - Light SW Wind The Companies rested and held company inspections Casualties Nil.	
	18.		Weather Sunny. Wind S-W. light. The Companies rested, except for company inspections Casualties NiL	

Place	Date	Hour	Summary of Events and Information	Remarks and references to Appendices
	19.		Weather. Fine and Cool. Wind. S.W. Light.	
			Work. C & Co. Overland Tracks ACHIET-LE-GRAND – ERVILLERS.	
			Making Ramps at G.4.d.3.8, A.29.d.6.8, A.24.c.6.3 & B.13.c.55.05. Cutting wire, clearing, moving fallen trees at B.13.c.5.1 and generally preparing a track running through points as above 30' wide.	
			D. Co. Placed pickets on Overland Track from point G.4.d.3-8 to B.18.c.5.1 and from B.19.a.1-4 to A.18.a.2.8. also placed in 4 to Signposts.	S.T.J.
			A & B Co's. Company inspections.	
			Casualties NIL	
	20.		Weather. Fine & Warm. Wind.	
			Divine Service in Camp. Battalion inspected at 11-30 A.M. on Camp Parade Ground by Maj: General Shoubridge. The Battalion was thanked for its good work especially at Bullecourt.	
			Casualties NIL.	
	21.		Weather. Fine with exception of one Thunderstorm. Wind. S.W. to N.W. later.	S.T.J.
			B & D Coy's working on Achiet-le-Grand – ERVILLIERS Track in morning. A, C Coys " " " " in afternoon	

WAR DIARY
INTELLIGENCE SUMMARY
(Erase heading not required.)

Army Form C. 2118.

Place	Date	Hour	Summary of Events and Information	Remarks and references to Appendices
	22.		A & C. Coy's Bathed at ABLAINZEVELLE in morning	
			B & D " " " in afternoon	
			Hq. Transport " " during the day.	
			A Battalion Concert was held in LOCAST WOOD in the evening. A Piano was borrowed from a Hospital close by. A temporary platform was also erected during the day.	KJ
			Casualties N.L.	
			Weather. Very wet. Wind Northerly.	
			Work. A. Coy. Two Platoons on range, completed wadding the strafe bank behind Targets. Completed digging out of nearly Sides Connected and laid back. Two Platoons Erection completed handing of posts on Fon Iveo Trench and ACHIET-LE-GRAND — ERVILLIERS track	
			1 Section on Manure Dump	
			B. Coy. Work on Track ACHIET-LE-GRAND — BIEFVILLERS. Work done between BIHUCOURT and BIEFVILLERS. Track completed except for NoitreBoards. Frames etc which have which hampered work to some extent.	
			C.D. Coy's Training.	KJ
			Casualties N.L.	

WAR DIARY
INTELLIGENCE SUMMARY

Army Form C. 2118.

Place	Date	Hour	Summary of Events and Information	Remarks and references to Appendices
	23.		Weather Fine Warm. Wind. S.W. to S.	
			A. Coy. Two Platoons on track ACHIET-LE-GRAND to BIEFVILLERS. Fixing fair weather track signs and anchor boards. Pulling stumps and clearing track. Two Platoons making ramp on track at G.17.c.9.5-70. and clearing road from Ramp to G.17.d.0.5-8.0.	G.T.J.
			B.C. & D. Coys training. Casualties Nil.	
	24.		Weather Fine warm and Sunny. Wind. Westerly Light.	
			A. Coy. 2 Platoons less two sections and B. Coy. cleaning and repairing road and opening up drains from G.4.d.2.4 to A.28.b.8.1. Six G.S. waggons carting bricks for repair of road.	
			A. Coy. 1 Platoon reported to John Major ABLAINZEVELLE for clearing refuse &c.	
			A. Coy. 2 sections. One on ACHIET-LE-GRAND — BIEFVILLERS track. The other on ACHIET-LE-GRAND — GOMIECOURT — ERVILLERS track mending wooden boards and	
			Fair weather track boards. Casualties Nil.	G.T.J.

Army Form C. 2118.

WAR DIARY
or
INTELLIGENCE SUMMARY.
(Erase heading not required.)

Place	Date	Hour	Summary of Events and Information	Remarks and references to Appendices
	25.		Weather. Fine warm and very Sunny. Wind Westerly light. C & D Coys worked on Achiette GRAND - ERVILLERS ROAD cleaning and filling in shell holes with bricks. A & B Coys training. Casualties Nil.	KTW
Map. 57 2 N.W. and EQUISTRT-MIEN (town)	26		Weather Fine warm and very Sunny. Wind Westerly high. The Battalion moved to Camp B.15.c.0.8. No work done owing to move. Casualties Nil. The Battalion attached to 58th Division for work as from this date.	KTW

Place	Date	Hour	Summary of Events and Information	Remarks and references to Appendices
	27		Weather. Fine & Warm. Sunny. Wind North Westerly.	
			"A" Co. 250x Trench (average depth 1'-6") deepened and widened to 5'-0" depth 3'-0" top 1'-9" at bottom. U.28.d.2.1.2. — U.28.d.2.5. Ecoust-St-Mien Map 1/10,000	
			"B" Co. Dug the part of the above communication trench from the support line towards the Railway Embankment, to depth of 5'-0", 3' at top - 1'-9 at bottom	
			"C" Co. Dug 250x of above communication trench avg to average depth of 4'-9" width of 3' at top and 1'-3" at bottom, from U.28.c.8.2. to U.22.a.6.0. on Ecoust-St-Mien Map 1/10,000	
			"D" Co. Dug 210x of Trench from U.28.B.2.2. to U.28.B.5.5. to average depth 4'-3" width at top 3'-5", 2'-3" at bottom. (Night).	
			Casualties. 1 O.R. Wounded.	
	28.		Weather. Fine warm and Sunny. Wind North Westerley. Thunder storms later.	
			A. Coy. Working on communication Trench from U.28.a.2.1.5 to U.28.c.9.6. (350x) digging and improving trench.	
			C. Coy working on communication trench from U.28.a.1.1. to U.28.B.9.5.9.5. 279x8 and improving Depth	
			D. Coy. Working on Communication trench from U.28.d.1.08 to U.28.d.0.2. (32 yds) and from U.28.c.9.6 to U.28.c.9.9. (350 yards) digging and improving trench The Communication Trench from U.28.D.2.1.5. to U.28.B.9.5-9.5 was completed	

WAR DIARY
or
INTELLIGENCE SUMMARY.
(Erase heading not required.)

Army Form C. 2118.

Place	Date	Hour	Summary of Events and Information	Remarks and references to Appendices
	29		On the three Companies. H.Q. ECOUST-ST-MEIN. TIPPED. B Coy. The Company worked on communication Trench along the Embankment from BULLECOURT AVENUE in an Easterly direction P.27D.5.3 to V.28C.2.3 (Night) Causalties 1 O.R wounded. Weather. Close and dull. Thunder storms in afternoon. Wind S.W. to W. light. A Coy. Deepened widened and cleaned 300ˣ of trench to 5'.0" deep. 3'-6" wide at top and 2'-0 at bottom from V.26.C.3.2 to V.28.C.73. Map ECOUST-ST-MEIN 1/10,000 B Coy. Deepened widened and cleaned communication trench as above from C.4b.6.8 Coy at V.28.C.73 to C.4b.8.8 D.Coy. Deepened widened and cleaned communication trench as above from V.28.C.03 to V.28.C.3.2. C.Coy. resting. (night) Casualties. NIL.	6.T.J.
	30		Weather. Close and dull. Thunder storms. Wind South West. A Coy. 1 Section clearing embankment Trench of tree trunks and roots The Company (less 1 section) dug communication trench (putting in 8 fire steps and 8 traverses from C.4b.5.8 to C.4b.5.5	6.T.J.

Army Form C. 2118.

WAR DIARY
or
INTELLIGENCE SUMMARY.
(Erase heading not required.)

Instructions regarding War Diaries and Intelligence Summaries are contained in F. S. Regs., Part II and the Staff Manual respectively. Title pages will be prepared in manuscript.

Place	Date	Hour	Summary of Events and Information	Remarks and references to Appendices
	31st		B.Coy. dug communication trench (putting in 13 fire bays and 12 traverses) from C.4.b.5.5 to C.4.b.3.3	
			C.Coy. dug communication trench from C.4.b.3.3 to C.4.b.0.0	
			D.Coy. resting. (night)	
			Casualties. 1 O.R wounded	b.T.J
			Weather. Warm and Sunny. Wind. South West.	
			A.Coy. rested.	
			B.Coy. worked on the embankment trench from BULLECOURT AVENUE junction U.27.d.6.3. 160 trench mats were carried up. Two platoons went out each for a second load. The remaining two platoons started to make the trench ready for trench mats. 280 yards completed.	
			C.Coy. One platoon digging through to connect trench from BULLECOURT AVENUE with trench from Battalion Headquarters. b's from C.4.b.5.8 to C.4.b.6.7. and laying trench mats. One platoon deepening and widening trench from C.4.b.6.7 to Battalion Hq. at C.4.b.5.4.5 and laying trench boards. Two platoons and two platoons of D.Coy widening and deepening trench from C.4.b.5.6 Westwards.	
			D.Coy. Loaded 160 trench mats at MORY DUMP.	

Army Form C. 2118.

WAR DIARY
or
INTELLIGENCE SUMMARY.
(Erase heading not required.)

Instructions regarding War Diaries and Intelligence Summaries are contained in F. S. Regs., Part II. and the Staff Manual respectively. Title pages will be prepared in manuscript.

Place	Date	Hour	Summary of Events and Information	Remarks and references to Appendices
			Two Platoons unloading & carrying 160 trench mats from near Battalion Hq to "C" Coy. Three two platoons been employed during and widening trench from C n.6.b.6 towards BULLECOURT AVENUE. Two Platoons with D Coy. Casualties 5 O.R. wounded (Night)	6.1.

E. Twist Major
comdg 2/4th(s) Bn. The Manchester Regt.
(7th Divisional Pioneers)

SECRET   Copy No. 12

24th Battalion The Manchester Regiment
PRELIMINARY INSTRUCTIONS FOR OPERATIONS No.1
                                                                11th May, 1917.

REFERENCE :- SHEETS 51.B S.W., 57 C N.W.

1.   On 12th May at an hour to be notified later, the 7th Division will continue its attack on BULLECOURT. This attack will be made in conjunction with an attack by the 5th Australian Division on our right, and with the co-operation of troops of the 62nd Division on our left.

The 91st Infantry Brigade will carry out the attack.

The protective barrage will lift from 0.2 at Zero plus four hours to enable patrols to be pushed forward to occupy this line from U. 22. c. 7.2. to U. 21. d. 5.6. if possible.

2. Royal Engineers.
(a) Strong points will be established at :-

    1. U.22.c.3.1.   2. U.21.d.8.1.
    3. U.21.d.5.1.   4. U.27.b.2.8.
    5. U.27.b.1.6.   6. U.27.b.5.6.
    7. U.27.b.5.3.

(b) On Zero night, a communication trench will be dug from the railway embankment to the village, along the line of the road running N.E. from U.27.d.2.5.

(c) The C.R.E. will arrange to construct this communication trench and for R.E. assistance to be given in the construction of the Strong points.

3. Headquarters.   Divl. Headquarters will remain at B.28.a.2.4.
       Advanced Bde. H.Q. will be in LONGATTE with a Brigade O.P. at C.2.d.9.9.

DISTRIBUTION:- As Operation Orders.

            (Signed) A. St. G. WALSH, Lieut. and Adjutant.

Vol XX

24th (S) Bn The Manchester Regiment
7th Divisional Pioneers

WAR DIARY
INTELLIGENCE SUMMARY.
(Erase heading not required.)

Army Form C. 2118.

Place	Date	Hour	Summary of Events and Information	Remarks and references to Appendices
Maps 57 C N.W. ECOUST-ST-MEIN YPRES (BULLECOURT)	1917 June 1st		Weather. Fine Warm and Sunny. Wind. Light North Westerly.	Vol 2
			A Coy. — Loaded 240 Trench Mats at MARY DUMP. Unloaded 240 Trench Mats at AVENUE CU68.U28.D.1.1 and carried 240 to EMBANKMENT trench and carried 240 to EMBANKMENT trench from H9 end towards BULLECOURT and laid 240 Trench Mats.	
			B Coy. — Rested	
			C Coy. — Widened and deepened communication Embankment trench from CU6.5.9 to U 28.D.3.4 and fully prepared such portion to receive trench mats.	
			D Coy. — Widened and deepened communication trench from U 28.A.3.4 to U 28.D.2.8 and fully prepared such portion to receive trench mats. Work in all jobs hindered by Infantry carrying parties. Ration parties etc. (Night).	6T1
			Casualties 1 O.R. wounded	
	2nd		Weather. Fine warm and sunny. Wind. Light North Westerly.	
			A Coy. — Widened and deepened embankment trench in several places carried and completed laying of trench mats	
			B Coy. —	
			D Coy. — Widened and deepened TOWER ALLEY U 28.b.3.3 to U 28.b.5.5 and	

WAR DIARY
or
INTELLIGENCE SUMMARY.

Army Form C. 2118.

Place	Date	Hour	Summary of Events and Information	Remarks and references to Appendices
	3rd		Infantry came ready to receive trench mats. Carried and laid 191 trench mats from EMBANKMENT TRENCH. & at C.4.b.4.5–9.0 to U.28.b.1.3. C.Coy. Rested. D. Coy. Widened and defence TOWER ALLEY. from U.28.D.05–90 to U.28.B.3.3. Carried and laid 191 Trench Mats from EMBANKMENT to U.28.D.1.3. Casualties 2 O.R's wounded. The vicinity of the Camp was heavily shelled by a 13 inch Naval Gun, which necessitated moving the Camp out of range for an hour. Weather. Fine during but colder. Wind. S.W. Fairly strong. A Coy. deepened and Widened 230 yards of trench to 5'6" × 3'6" × 2'6" from Support line down TOWER ALLEY towards EMBANKMENT. U.28.b 9.5–9.5 to U.28.b 6.6.5. B Coy. deepened and widened 170 yards of Trench to 5'-6" deep × 3'-6" at top × 2'.6 at bottom from U.28.b 6.6.5 to U.28.b.5.5. TOWER ALLEY. TOWER ALLEY we now take a shelter its whole way. C Coy. Carried 200 trench mats from C.4.d.2.4. to U.28.a.3.4 and laying in Tower R ALLEY from U.28.a.3.4 to U.28.b.3.3. To complete TOWER ALLEY needs Trench mats from U.28.b.3.3. to U.28.b.9.5–9.5 Widened and deepened 12 fire bays and made fire steps constructed barrier and levelled parapet also deepened 18 traverses to 5 feet in TANK ALLEY. C.4.b.3.b. C.4.b.5.8.	KJJ (Night)

Army Form C. 2118.

WAR DIARY
or
INTELLIGENCE SUMMARY.
(Erase heading not required.)

Place	Date	Hour	Summary of Events and Information	Remarks and references to Appendices
D. Coy rested. Casualties N.L.				677
	4.		Weather. Very hot. Brilliant sunshine. Wind S.E. light.	
A & C Coys			Work on EMBANKMENT TRENCH U.27.a.5.3 b.C.4.b.5.8. Prepared and completed 16 fire bays 18 feet long. 3 feet 6 inches wide 3 feet 6 inches deep with communications. to further fire bays started. Jotted small elephant shelters (7 ft x 7 ft) as under 2 completed. 4 nearly completed. 2 prepared for. 25 GRS under 2nd Lt Lace reported at ruins in a.a.16 BULLECOURT AV. for carrying. In addition two platoons were employed in carrying C.T. and Material from C.4.2.4 to 4.26.c.6.3	
B & D Coys			Cut communication trench for 420 yards 3 feet wide at top and an average depth of 3 feet back from POST 6A (U.19.b.9.5) though past A towards the Railway at U.19.a.5.7. The work was at layout (1) In consequence of having to wait for guides at L'HOMME MORT until 9.50 p.m. (2) The encountering most broken by the gradient w.3/4. The Ten Jean ST LEGER (3) The non existence of the old German trench shown of a new which notion 9 ~ 12 p.m. (4) In consequence of having to leave the job at 2 a.m. wide instructions from the C.B. in the line. As a result of (1) (2) the party did not arrive at the job until 11.45. (NqW)	677
			Casualties Nil.	

(Copy)

To Adjutant. 24th Bn. The Manchester Regiment 6/6/17

The Brigadier who came up during the night expressed great appreciation of our work which he described as very fine.

Will you particularly inform my commanding Officer of this.

H. L. Wilkins
Capt.
G.C. Coy 24th Manchesters.

Weather fine Warm. Wind. Southerly light.

A & C Coys worked on EMBANKMENT TRENCH U 27 a. 5.3 to C a 46. 5. 8.
Four unfinished fire bays completed, 18 feet long 3'-6" new, 3'-6" deep.
6 additional fire bays started. One completed.
Added Sunset elephant shelters as under.
Six unfinished shelters completed
Eight new shelters completed
Five new shelters nearly completed
Five new shelters prepared for.

L. Coy. Other ranks supplied by 2/10 & 2/12 London Regt. reported for carrying. In addition two platoons of Pioneers who employed in carrying C.S. and material.
The entire length of trench from BURGCOURT AVENUE to TOWER ALLEY in Puisieux-au-Mont at intervals of about 15 yards except for five fire steps which are yours completing.

WAR DIARY
or
INTELLIGENCE SUMMARY.

Army Form C. 2118.

Place	Date	Hour	Summary of Events and Information	Remarks and references to Appendices
	15/9		B.D. Coys Deepened and widened Communication Trench from U.19.b.9.5 to U.19.d.9.8 from Post 6A through Post 6 towards the Railway. Dug 200 yards of communication Trench from U.19.d.9.8 to Post 2 on road U.19.d.8.6. (Night) Casualties 1 O.R. wounded. Weather Dull & colder. Wind Westerly to N. Westerly. Strong at times. A Coy & C Coy worked on EMBANKMENT TRENCH U.27.d.5.3 to C.4.5.8. 9 unfinished shelters completed. 4 emplacements for New Shelters cut out ready to receive corrugated Shelters. No material available for Shelters at 170 R.D.0.17.P. 4 New fire bays cut out and completed. 3 unfinished fire bays completed. B.D. Coys dug 400 yds through U.19.b.8.7 to U.19.b.95.45. Posts 6C to Post 6A, width U.13.d.7.0.05 & depth 3-3" wide at top, 2'-6" at bottom from Boral Section of 30 X near point U.19.b.8.7 where it is only 3 feet deep. One Platoon completed to full depth the trench from Post 6 to Post 2. (Night) Casualties Nil.	

Place	Date	Hour	Summary of Events and Information	Remarks and references to Appendices
	7.		Weather. Fine & warm. Wind S E light.
A Coy rested.
C. Coy. Carried C1 and material for shelters from C 4.a.4.2 to EMBANKMENT TRENCH.
6 unfinished shelters completed.
6 new shelters dug out, roofed and completed by two platoons.
1 shelter head cover completed.
The remainder of the company were employed improving the bottom of the trench and relaying several trench mats.
B Coy. dug 280 x of communication trench 5 feet deep 3' wide at top 2' wide at bottom from U.19.a.75.70 to U.19.a.65.15. (night)
Casualties Nil.	G.T.J.
	8.		Ceased to be attached to 58th Division for Work after work in the night of the 7 – 8 inst. 6.C. 2/6th Manchester's Pioneers "General Fanshawe will ride over between 11 and 11.30 A.M. to say good bye to your officers and thank you for the good work you have done. He does not want any sort of parade ordered." (Signed) H. Stockdale Capt. G.S. 58 Div.
Battalion rested all day.	Affiliated M.B.C.

Army Form C. 2118.

WAR DIARY
or
INTELLIGENCE SUMMARY.
(Erase heading not required.)

Instructions regarding War Diaries and Intelligence Summaries are contained in F. S. Regs., Part II. and the Staff Manual respectively. Title pages will be prepared in manuscript.

Place	Date	Hour	Summary of Events and Information	Remarks and references to Appendices
	14.		Weather. Fine. Wind Easterly light. A. C. D. } Companies Training. B Coy working on Dugout S.1.d.7.2. Casualties Nil.	
	15.		Weather Fine. Wind N. westerly light. B. C. D. } Companies Training. A Coy on Dugout S.1.d.7.2. Casualties Nil.	G.T.J.
	16.		Weather Fine. Wind Southerly light. B. C. } Coy Training. A Company a mined dug out S.1.d.7.2. Constructing mined dug out under supervision of 254th R.E. Coy who are doing timbering. Working 10 hours 5 men. 2 hour shifts. Extra Pay of 1/5 per sapper & 2/- sapper.	
26.16.			Casualties Nil	B.T.J.

WAR DIARY
or
INTELLIGENCE SUMMARY.

Army Form C. 2118.

Place	Date	Hour	Summary of Events and Information	Remarks and references to Appendices
	17.		Weather. Fine. Wind Southerly Light.	
			Battalion rested. C of E & N.C. of E Church Service	
			Casualties Nil. D Coy moved to Camp B. 13. Central for work in ERVILLERS-ST LEGER ROAD.	A.T.
	18.		Weather. Dull and showery. Wind S. Westerly.	
			A. Coy. worked on Dug out. G.1.d.7.2.	
			Provided ABLAINZEVELLE Party 2 O/ypes and 1 N.C.O. for filling up subways in road with Earth	
			B. Coy. Carting away manure and cutting two openings in preparation for New Div. Hq. H.2.a.	
			D. Coy. Repairing and putting down broken Brick opening of Sumps ERVILLERS - ST LEGER ROAD	
			C Coy Rested	
			Battalion Sports at 2 P.M. at LOGEAST WOOD. Given 300 entries in the evening by Regimental Band. Prizes were distributed	6 T J
			Casualties Nil	
	19.		Weather. Very Wet. Heavy Showers. Wind S. Westerly Storms.	
			A Coy as yesterday.	
			B. Coy. moved to Camp H. 1.d, for to continue making new Div. Hq.	
			C Coy training	

Army Form C. 2118.

WAR DIARY
or
INTELLIGENCE SUMMARY.
(Erase heading not required.)

Instructions regarding War Diaries and Intelligence Summaries are contained in F. S. Regs., Part II. and the Staff Manual respectively. Title pages will be prepared in manuscript.

Place	Date	Hour	Summary of Events and Information	Remarks and references to Appendices
	20.		D Coy. Repairing ERVILLERS-ST.LEGER Road from B.13.b.12 to B.13.B.o.17. (complete) (& Sump holes opened up.) continued this afternoon	G.T.J
			Weather Fine 8.0am. Wind S. westerly	
			A Coy. in yards doing	
			B Coy. continued clearing & setting up new Divisional Hq at H.2.a.	
			C Coy. Training	
			D Coy. Repairing ERVILLERS - ST. LEGER ROAD from B.13.b.2.2 & B.8.b.3.0.	W.T.J
			Casualties Nil	
	21.		Weather Damp and much colder. Wind, S. Westerly Strong.	
			A Coy. Training	
			B Coy. continued clearing & setting for New Divisional Hq at H.2.a.	
			C Coy. Training	
			D Coy. Repairing ERVILLERS - ST. LEGER Road from B.8.b.30 to B.3.c.60 and clearing Sand.	G.T.J
			Casualties. Nil.	

Army Form C. 2118.

WAR DIARY
or
INTELLIGENCE SUMMARY.
(Erase heading not required.)

Place	Date	Hour	Summary of Events and Information	Remarks and references to Appendices
	22		Weather. Fine & warm. Cold at night. Wind. W. weekly.	
			A. Coy. Repairing Road when crane of Dnn Major & ABLAIZEVELLE. at. F.23.c.7.5. Work completed	
			B. Coy. Cleaning ground, cutting away manure. Digging and building latrines, cutting steps to road and making gaps in hedge for New Divisional Hq. Camp Behagnies. H.29.a.4.8.	
			C. Coy. Working on range at ERVILLERS	
			D. Coy. Repairing and Draining ERVILLERS - ST LEGER Road B.8 & 3.0. - B.3.c.6.0. Now completed	
			Casualties. Nil.	

WAR DIARY or INTELLIGENCE SUMMARY

Army Form C. 2118.

Place	Date	Hour	Summary of Events and Information	Remarks and references to Appendices
	23		Weather. Heavy Rain. Wind N.Westerly. Fresh. A} Coy's moved at 9 a.m. to Camp B.15.d.0.3. from LOCUST WOOD. C} B. Coy " " " Camp at B.15.c.0.3. from H.1.D. D Coy Repairing ERVILLERS-ST-LEGER ROAD D Coy moved to Camp at B.15.c.0.3. from B.13.c. Casualties Nil.	B.T.J
	24		Weather. Fine but dull. Wind South Westerly light. E. Coy deepening and widening front line trench LONDON TRENCH U.22.d.20.- U.22.d.50. A Coy " " " U.22.d.50.- U.26.b.90.95. D " " " U.26.b.90.95.- U.29.a.40.9. Only about an hour's work was done when hostile barrage was put down on the kind and a withdrawal compelled. B. Coy. Widening and deepening and preparing for Dumb Boards communication trench PELICAN AVENUE. U.27.a.39.- M.21.c.3.1. (night) Casualties. 1. O.R. Killed. 20 O.R's wounded.	B.T.J

WAR DIARY
or
INTELLIGENCE SUMMARY.
(Erase heading not required.)

Army Form C. 2118.

Place	Date	Hour	Summary of Events and Information	Remarks and references to Appendices
	25.		Weather fine during day. Wet at night. Cool. Wind Mostly Light.	
			B Coy Two Platoons on communication Trench PELICAN AVENUE U.27.a.3.9 – U.27.a.00.75. 90x of trench widened and deepened to 6'-0" and made ready for Duck Boards, and one firing place made.	
			A Coy Two Platoons on communication Trench KNUCKLE AVENUE deepening and widening to 5'-6" deep, 2' wide at bottom, 3'-6" at top. 70 yards completed. Trench boards were carried from ECOUST. RAILWAY. DUMP. 24 Trench boards laid.	
			The remainder of the Battalion rested in connection of Brigade Relief. (Night)	
			Casualties NIL.	
	26.		Weather Dull & cold. Wind Westerly Strong	
			½ A Coy Deepened and widened KNUCKLE AVENUE for box row 5'-6" deep 3'-6" wide at the top and 2' at it's bottom	65.1
			½ A Coy Rested	
			½ B Coy worked on PELICAN AVENUE communication trench widening and deepening 250 x of LONDON TRENCH working from junction of depth 5'-9". Raining place made and exit steps made.	
			C Coy Widening and deepening 250 x of LONDON TRENCH working from junction of GORDON SWITCH and LONDON TRENCH towards TANK ALLEY. A great amount of

Army Form C. 2118.

WAR DIARY
or
INTELLIGENCE SUMMARY.
(Erase heading not required.)

Instructions regarding War Diaries and Intelligence Summaries are contained in F.S. Regs., Part II. and the Staff Manual respectively. Title pages will be prepared in manuscript.

Place	Date	Hour	Summary of Events and Information	Remarks and references to Appendices
	Sept 26		cleaning when necessary, and on dead bodies equipment bombs &c. D Coy Rested. Casualties 1. O.R. wounded.	G.T.J
	27.		(Night) Weather Fine morning Rain afternoons. Wind South Easterly. Light. "A" Coy dug KNUCKLE AVENUE U.20 b.5.9 to U.14 c.75.05 (where it joins the front line trench) a distance of 162x to a depth of 5'-6", width at top 3'-6" width at bottom 2'. Dug KNUCKLE AVENUE U.20 a to 8.5 & U.20 a 3.8 a distance of 70x similarly. B Coy worked in communication trench PELICAN AVENUE dug 200x NE from TIGER TRENCH C Coy Dug 250x of front line LONDON TRENCH U.22 a 3.0 to U.22 d 7.0. D Coy Dug 250x of front line LONDON TRENCH U.22 d. 7.0 to U.29 a 4-9.7 (Night) Casualties NIL	G.T.J
	28.		Weather Fine until noon. Violent storm at night. WIND South Easterly light A Company working on KNUCKLE AVENUE. 160x yards dug to required dimensions U.19 b 9.6 towards front line. B. Company working on PELICAN AVENUE. U 26 b. 7.4 — front line. U 26.b.7.4 U 26 b 2.2	

Army Form C. 2118.

WAR DIARY
or
INTELLIGENCE SUMMARY.
(Erase heading not required.)

Instructions regarding War Diaries and Intelligence
Summaries are contained in F. S. Regs., Part II.
and the Staff Manual respectively. Title pages
will be prepared in manuscript.

Place	Date	Hour	Summary of Events and Information	Remarks and references to Appendices
	28th		C. Coy. rested. D. Coy. worked on LONDON TRENCH from U.28 b.9.95 to U.29 a.4.9.7 = 250ˣ. Work was much impeded by water from heavy storm. (Night) Casualties - Nil.	S.T.J
	June 29		Weather Showery & colder. Wind S Westerly to North Easterly. A) B) Coy's nothing. D) C Coy. widening and deepening 200ˣ of LONDON TRENCH from U.22 d.6.0 to TANK AVENUE. (Night) Casualties 1 O.R. wounded	
	June 30th		Weather Very wet and cold. Wind Easterly strong. "A" Coy. wiring in front of LONDON TRENCH Work done. 1st party. 200ˣ Pickets and wire. 2nd party. do do Dugouts for 160ˣ and all loose wire in the 160ˣ wire.	S.T.J

WAR DIARY or INTELLIGENCE SUMMARY

Army Form C. 2118.

Place	Date	Hour	Summary of Events and Information	Remarks and references to Appendices
			2nd Party 200' picketed and wired	
			2nd line too " " "	
			B. Coy. picketed and wired front line & posts from U.21.c.00.55 to U.21.d.05.15 in three parties. The centre party completed its stretch the other two parties nearly did so. There were 1 Officer, 1 Sergeant and 24 men to each party. The remainder of the Company were used as carrying parties for maintaining its supply of material for each carrying party. Length of wiring 600'.	App. D
			D. Coy. Carried 260 iron pickets and 36 bundles of wire and unloaded 4 G.S. waggons from RAILWAY EMBANKMENT to point U.29.b a 7.5. 200' 1st line complete. 3 rows 100' diagonal and 50' loose wire put in. 8 pickets up for this distance. 1st turned up for carrying and only 28 of the former party 50 infantry instead of 100 turned up for carrying work who unpaced through lack of material reached their destination consequently.	
			C. Coy. constructing Berm on each side of track BULLECOURT AVENUE between points U.27.d 51, and point U.28.c 27. distance being 450'. Deepening and widening trench in places between these two points.	
			Casualties Nil.	

J.S. Courtney
Major
O.C. 2/4 Bn Monmouth Rgt.

(C O P Y).

Headquarters,
    7th. Division.

For your information hereunder is set out copy of a message received from the G.O.C., 58th. Division:

"General FANSHAWE will ride over between 11-0 &.
" 11-30 a.m. to say good-bye to your Officers
" and thank you for the good work you have done.
            "(Signed) Hd. STACKPOOLE, Captain,
8/6/17.   "G. S., 58th. Division."

General FANSHAWE called at out Headquarters at 11-0 a.m. and after saying Good-bye to the Officers he requested them to express to alll ranks of this Battalion the grateful thanks of the G.O.C., Officers and all ranks of the 58th. Division for the work done by the Battalion whilst attached to the 58th. Division.

    (Signed)   W. TAYLOR-JONES, 2/Lieut. &. A/Adjutant,
8/6/17.   for Lieut. Colonel,
        Commanding 24th. Bn. The Manchester Regt. (Pioneers).

C O P Y   7th Div. No. G. 343.

24th Bn. Manchester Regt.
  (Div. Pioneers).
———————————

        The Divisional Commander has received your letter dated the 8th inst enclosing remarks made by the 58th Division on the work done by you whilst attached to that Division. He is very pleased indeed and asks me to inform you that it is only what he expected from your Battalion, and further that the greatest test of the efficiency of a Battalion is when it works well for a formation other than its own.

        I attach a letter that the Divisional Commander has received from the G.O.C., 58th Division.

       (Signed) E.C. GEPP,   Major.
9-6-17.   General Staff, 7th Division.

                         58th Div. No. G.S. 694.
                                 8-6-17.

G.O.C.,
  7th Division.
———

        I should like to bring to your notice the extremely good work that has been done by the 24th Battalion Manchester Regiment, during the time that the Battalion has been attached to the 58th Division.

        We are all very grateful to both Officers and men for the great assistance that they have so cheerfully given us.

       (Signed) H.D. FANSHAWE,   Major-General,
                Commanding 58th Division.

C O P Y.

O. C.
   24th Bn. Manchester Regt.

   I wish to express my appreciation of the good work you have done for my Division. The work carried out has been thorough and good: please let your officers and men know that I very much appreciate the work they have done for me.

   (Signed) E.M. NEWELL, Lieut-Colonel. R.E.
7th June, 17.   C.R.E., 58th Division.

The C. R. E.,
   58th Division.

   All ranks join me in thanking you for your kind message.

   It is very pleasing to know that our work is appreciated.

   (Signed) E. VINER, Lieut-Colonel,
8-6-17.   Commanding 24th Bn, Manchester Regt. (Pioneers).

7th. Division.
3124/60/A.

Officer Commanding

    24th. Manchesters.

        The G.O.C. wishes to inform all C.O's that he has received a letter from the G.O.C. 58th. Division, thanking him for the excellent condition in which the various camps and billets in the COURCELLES-ABLAINZEVELLE-LOGEAST WOOD area were handed over.

        He particularly drew attention to the fact that the many Recreation Rooms, tables, beds etc. which had been made were handed over in good condition instead of being removed as is too often the case, and he wished to inform all units of the 7th. Division how much this was appreciated by the relieving units of the 58th. Division.

        The G.O.C. has much pleasure in bringing this to the notice of all units, as it is a proof that such action largely contributes towards maintaining the reputation of the 7th. Division.

Divl. Headquarters.
June 30th. 1917.

(SD). W. WINGFIELD, Lieut. Colonel,
A.A. & Q.M.G., 7th. Division.

WAR DIARY

VOL XXI.

24th (S) Bn. The Manchester Regt. Army Form C.2118.
(7th Divisional Pioneers)

VOL 21

Place	Date	Hour	Summary of Events and Information	Remarks and references to Appendices
MORY. BISCO 3. MAPS 57cNW ECOUST-ST MEIN 1/10,000 (BULLECOURT MAP)	1917 July 1st		**Weather** Fine but very cold. Wind. North Easterly Strong. **Work.** A Coy. KNUCKLE AVENUE U.20.c.17 to U.20.a.4.8. Deepening and widening Dead from a point 100ˣ along KNUCKLE AVENUE for a distance of 220ˣ, also a berm of 2' but on two sketch and 105' trench boards laid. B. Coy. PELICAN AVENUE Berm was cleared for 1'-6" from the lip end of Pelican Avenue to within 200ˣ of TIGER TRENCH 45 trench boards laid, channels being dug in the floor of the trench. Other parts of the trench were deepened widened and cleared. D Coy. BULLECOURT AVENUE, 40 yards of Mats relaid. Deepening and widening trench continuation of BULLECOURT AVENUE for 450 yards. Completed nearly for trench boards from C.3.c.113 to C.8.b.77. C Coy. resting. Casualties Nil.	
	July 2nd		Weather Fine & warmer. Wind North Easterly. **Work.** A Coy. widened and deepened KNUCKLE AVENUE from point U.20.a.3 to 6. front line. Distance 450ˣ also laid trench mats on same. B. Coy. resting. C. Coy. Unloading 200 trench mats from train at ECOUST. Loading 200 trench mats from ECOUST and carting same to point U.27.a.5.1	KTN

A5834 Wt. W4975/M687 750,000 8/16 D.D. & L. Ltd. Forms/C.2118/13.

WAR DIARY
or
INTELLIGENCE SUMMARY.

(Erase heading not required.)

Army Form C. 2118.

Place	Date	Hour	Summary of Events and Information	Remarks and references to Appendices
	1917 July		Carrying 150 trench mats from point U 27a.5.1 and placing same in BULLECOURT AV: from the EMBANKMENT ready for firing Cutting out box & chance frames. 30 hurdle mats also in same. D Coy rested Casualties Nil.	5.T.J
	3		Weather. Fine Warm. A. Coy rested. B. Coy. continuation of work on PELICAN AVENUE. The whole of the trench as far as the junction with TIGER TRENCH was trench boards 200" was channelled in addition. Boom cleared for 200' SO×0 of TIGER TRENCH C. BULLECOURT AVENUE to POINT 31 from EMBANKMENT deepened widened and cleaned and trench mats laid. The Coy afterwards worked on that part of the trench from EMBANKMENT to U 27d.3.4 by taking up trench mats deepening and cleaning trench afterwards replacing trench mats in position. D. Deepening and cleaning LONDON TRENCH U 29a.40.97 & U 29a.77.250.* (Night) Wind North Easterly Light. (Night) Casualties 1.6R Killed. 2 O.R's wounded.	5.T.J

WAR DIARY
or
INTELLIGENCE SUMMARY.

(Erase heading not required.)

Army Form C. 2118.

Place	Date	Hour	Summary of Events and Information	Remarks and references to Appendices
	9.		The Battalion moved at 9 a.m. to Old Camp at LOG EAST WOOD. Weather fine & very warm. Wind Light N.W. Casualties Nil	65.T.I
	10.		Weather Very Wet. Wind. Rather Strong N.W. Baths at ABLAINZEVELLE whole Battalion. Casualties Nil	65.T.I
	11.		Weather fine. Wind. S. Westerly Light. Battalion Inspected by Companies. Training programme arranged. Casualties Nil	65.T.I
	12.		Weather fine - Very warm. Wind S Westerly Light. A } C } Companies Training. D } B Coy working on dug out G.10.7.2. Casualties Nil. Weather fine but colder. Wind. Strong N Easterly	
	13.		A } C } Training D Coy improving cross country track, new plank bridge constructed over drain on to the road. Watercart parks improved and wheel guards arranged along the side. B. 26 a.b.75. Casualties Nil.	65.T.I

Army Form C. 2118.

WAR DIARY
or
INTELLIGENCE SUMMARY.
(Erase heading not required.)

Place	Date	Hour	Summary of Events and Information	Remarks and references to Appendices
	July 1917 4.		Weather. Fine & Sunny. Wind. North North Easterly.	

A Coy. worked on KNUCKLE AVENUE from STRANGEWAYS - FRONTLINE.
(1) Deepening to dept of 5'-6" and where possible widening the trench to 5' at top & 2'-6" at base. (This was very difficult as the ground here is one mass of shell holes & loose earth) from U.20.a.55.95 to U.20.a.49.90 app. 80'.
(2) Deepening to 5'-6" widened to 5' at top and 2'-6" at base from U.20.a.25.82 to U.20.a.40.65 app. 180' x laid hurdle mats again.
app. 145 Sumps made under trench mats made 2 crossing places, 2 steps and burned.
(3) Deepened to 5'-6" widened to 5' at top & 2'-6" at base burned and laid hurdle mats from U.20.a.25.82 to U.20.a.06 with its exception of 33' from STRANGEWAYS which did not require it. Steps, 18 Sumps & Sumping place constructed.

B. Coy. worked on KNUCKLE AVENUE from STRANGEWAYS. S.W. deepening and widening and laying hurdle mats. and also main begins

C. Coy. (a) Deepening & widening 3 traverses in BULLECOURT AVENUE at LONGATTE. Carrying and laying 190 hurdle mats in BULLECOURT AVENUE working from point C.3.c.0.2. left, rear of LONGATTE.
(b) Deepening & widening BULLECOURT AVENUE at point C.3.b.1.8. to point C.3.b.3.9. about 140'

D. Coy. Deepening and laying 40 hurdle mats thus completing TANK AVENUE. Deepening and widening LONDON TRENCH from U.28.b.85.97 to U.29.a.89.70.
(Night).

Casualties. 1 O.R. wounded.

61.J.

WAR DIARY
or
INTELLIGENCE SUMMARY.

(Erase heading not required.)

Army Form C. 2118.

Place	Date	Hour	Summary of Events and Information	Remarks and references to Appendices
	1917 July 5th		Weather. Fine & Sunny. Wind Northerly & N.W. Slightly. A Coy. worked in KNUCKLE AVENUE deepening and widening (5'x 2'6") & making sump holes having N400 and slabs. B Coy. worked on PELICAN AVENUE. 47 Trench boards carried from Dump and Dropping and improving trench for 50' at junction with TIGER TRENCH and a further 240' defened and widened making sumps and relaying trench boards D Coy. Defened widened and cleaned BULLECOURT AVENUE for 150' Also completed trench to the road junct C.8.b.5.5. and layd trench boards. 125' BULLECOURT AVENUE from joint C.3.b.2.7 Defened widened and cleaned to U.27.A.4.0 (Night) C Coy Rested Casualties 2 O.R's killed , 6 O.R.'s wounded remaining at duty	6.T.J
	July 6		Weather. Fine Sunny & Warm Wind North Easterly light. A B & D. Coy's rested C. Coy. Two Platoons on KNUCKLE AV. from U.20.c.5.9 to U.26.c.7.1 cleaning and deepening & trench to a depth 2.7.p. relaying trench mats. Two Platoons on PELICAN AVENUE worked on 200 x of trench making it 6ft deep also making them a trench for 200' Casualties Nil. (Night)	6.T.J

A5834 Wt. W4973/M687 750,000 8/16 D. D. & L. Ltd. Form/C.2118/r3.

WAR DIARY
or
INTELLIGENCE SUMMARY.
(Erase heading not required.)

Army Form C. 2118.

Place	Date	Hour	Summary of Events and Information	Remarks and references to Appendices
	1917 July 7		Weather. Fine during day. Very heavy thunder Winds Easterly. Light. storms later.	
			A Coy worked on KNUCKLE AVENUE. dug new trench from U.19 d 8.7 towards EMBANKMENT 200ˣ completed to depth of 6′ 3″. 5′ wide at 15ᵖ	
			B. Coy. Deepening and widening trench and clearing berm, making sump holes and replacing trench boards for 300ˣ from Railway cutting. PELICAN AVENUE	
			C. Coy. Worked in BULLECOURT AVENUE. Cutting berm from EMBANKMENT to Sunken Road 250ˣ. Deepening and widening 175ᵖ ᵇ Trench to 6′ deep. 5′ wide at 6ᵖ 2-6′ wide at bottom. Rem completed.	
			D Coy. Worked on TANK AVENUE. Widening trench to 5′ at 15ᵖ and deepening to an average of 6'-6" from U.72 d.86.00 to 28 b.7.8. 150ˣ also been cleared (night) Casualties Nil.	B.J.
	July 8		Weather. Wet. Wind South Easterly.	
			A Coy. Carrying for Engineers from Dump at U.19 b.6.6 to U.14.c.4.5. 83 Coils of wire and 410 Pickets.	

Army Form C. 2118.

WAR DIARY
or
INTELLIGENCE SUMMARY.
(Erase heading not required.)

Place	Date	Hour	Summary of Events and Information	Remarks and references to Appendices
	1917 July 8.		B. Coy. deepening to average depth of 4'-9" QUEENS AVENUE from Post L1 towards front line. (This trench is very much worse than reported. It is very shallow, narrow and badly traversed.) (Night). Casualties N.I.	G.S.J.
	July 9.		Weather fine but dull. Wind Westerly	
			C. Coy. left Camp 3.0 A.M. worked on BULLECOURT AVENUE - C.3.c.1.3. - U.27.d.6.3 as follows:- (1) C.3.c.13 - C.3.a.9.4. drained sweet sumps dug under boards (2) C.3.a.9.4 - C.3.b.2.6. deepened to 5'. (3) U.27.a.4.0. - U.27.d.6.3. deepened and widened to 6'-6" deep. 4'-6" wide at top (day)	
			D Coy working left east 3.0 A.M. worked on TANK AVENUE from the RAILWAY. EMBANKMENT forwards deepening and widening. Good work done for 3 hours when the party though working in the trench were spotted and the trench was shelled with 77.4.7. and then with shrapnel. So the Coy was withdrawn. 150 77, 30 4.7, as an after math. (day) C. & D. Coys worked during the day as an after mark. (day)	
			A Coy Carried up wire and pickets by tram from ECOUST to from Tramway carried foot to front line. 2 dumps formed for wiring at U.20.a.9.7. & 20.b.25.50. (Night)	

Army Form C. 2118.

WAR DIARY
or
INTELLIGENCE SUMMARY.
(Erase heading not required.)

Instructions regarding War Diaries and Intelligence Summaries are contained in F.S. Regs., Part II. and the Staff Manual respectively. Title pages will be prepared in manuscript.

Place	Date	Hour	Summary of Events and Information	Remarks and references to Appendices
	1917 July 9.		B. Coy worked on QUEENS AVENUE widened and deepened to 6'0" in stretch worked on last night. New portion dug for 50' to depth 5'6". (Night)	
			Casualties NIL.	
			DETACHED PARTIES	
			Weather	
			BEHAGNIES-ERVILLERS road. Anti Aircraft defence. 2 L.G's. 7 Men	
			DOULLENS AREA " " 4 L.G's 1 Off 25 Men	
			MORY Permanent loading party on R.E. Yard 15 Men	
			ECOUST Divisional Tramway Officer.	K.T.J
	July 10.		Weather fine and bright. Wind North Strong.	
			A. Coy. used in front of THE KNUCKLE, 360'. Work nearly completed on Italian Com French	
			D. Coy continued work of narrow tine in BULLECOURT AVENUE worked backwards from it 180'. widened to 4'-6" at top 2'-6" at bottom dpt to 6'-6". 200' been cleared. (Night)	K.T.J
			Casualties NIL.	

WAR DIARY or INTELLIGENCE SUMMARY

Army Form C. 2118.

Place	Date	Hour	Summary of Events and Information	Remarks and references to Appendices
	1917 July 11		Weather Fine. Wind Northerly.	
			C. Coy. on BULLECOURT AVENUE widening and trimming sides from EMBANKMENT — C.30.9.7. (526*) laying and fixing on trestles 160* of trestleads.	
			C. Coy. on BULLECOURT AVENUE widening & deepening and digging berm in C.36. 40* mats laid on trestles. Parts repaired where blown in by shell fire. (a.m.) (p.m.)	
			D. Coy. on TANK AVENUE. 300* from RAILWAY forward widened and deepened and ready for trestles. Tape laid for continuation of TANK AVENUE had to the NOREUIL ROAD. The tape was not laid for the last 150* — 200* both road owing to insufficient outfits. (Night)	
			Detached parties as before.	
			In addition 1 Off + 30 O.R's. dismounting huts at AVELUY.	
			Casualties. 1 O.R. kicked by a horse buried in BULLECOURT AVENUE this morning but was returned to camp.	
			Wind S. Westerly.	B.T.S.
	July 12		Weather Fine. Warm.	
			A. Coy. completed wiring the KNUCKLE	

WAR DIARY
or
INTELLIGENCE SUMMARY.
(Erase heading not required.)

Army Form C. 2118.

Place	Date	Hour	Summary of Events and Information	Remarks and references to Appendices
	July 12		(b) cleaning bom. both sides QUEEN'S AVENUE for 250ˣ. (Night).	
			C. Coy. in BULLECOURT AVENUE cleaning berm on each side from Railway to U.27.a.40.25ˣ laying hurdle paths and firing on hostiles for 40ˣ. Deepening own weakening trench and cleaning berms C.3a.9.7 – C.3.a.6.2. 240ˣ. (Night)	
			D. Coy on TANK AVENUE from RAILWAY forward. 88 trestles carried up. 170ᴰ more trench deepened to 6'.6" deep. 4'.6" wide at the top. Berm cleared on itso. Still and a little worked on last night. (Night)	
			B. Coy Pushed up the tramway. ECOUST – End of TANK AVENUE and carried on to LONDON TRENCH work U.29.a.88. Evening Material. (Night) Casualties 5 Coy. – 1 OR Killed 6 OR's wounded 16 R. " remaining at duty. (Night)	
			Detailed parties at AVELUY. MARY. DOULLENS. VALHEUREUX. & BETHAGNIES.	
			Weather: Fine. Warm. Wind S. Easterly	[Sd.]
	July 13		A. Coy on QUEEN'S AVENUE. 220ˣ widened deepened and bermed. B. Coy 160 Coils wire and 600 Screw pickets called from ECOUST to TANK AVENUE	

WAR DIARY
or
INTELLIGENCE SUMMARY.

(Erase heading not required.)

Army Form C. 2118.

Place	Date	Hour	Summary of Events and Information	Remarks and references to Appendices
	1917			
	July 13		C Coy in BULLECOURT AVENUE deepening, widening & making berm in 220ᵈˢ of Trench	
			90ˣ Trench gats laid on trestles.	
			D Coy 150ˣ TANK AVENUE dug out to 6'-6" x 4'-0" (lagging completed to second Tank)	G.T.J
			Casualties 1 O.R. wounded (Night)	
			Weather Fine Wind S Easterly	
	July 14		The Battalion rested. C of E & R.C of E services in Camp	
			Casualties (N.L)	G.T.J
	July 15		Weather fine Wind S Westerly	
			C of E & N.C of E services held in Camp	
			A Coy less 1 Platoon 76ˣ of QUEEN'S AVENUE deepened to 6'-6" widened to 5'-0"	
			at top 2'-6" at base, from Post U.20.a.2.3 to U.20.a.10.25 Cleared and laid 150 lineal	
			yds from ECOUST to QUEEN'S AVENUE also 150 trestle.	
			64ˣ of KNUCKLE TRENCH dug to average depth of 5'-9" width 5' at top 2'6" at base	
			(extended from U.19.d.7.3 to U.19.a.6.25.	

WAR DIARY
or
INTELLIGENCE SUMMARY.
(Erase heading not required.)

Army Form C. 2118.

Place	Date 1917	Hour	Summary of Events and Information	Remarks and references to Appendices
	July 15		B Coy. 180* of TANK AVENUE in respects work left erecting B. Coy to carry)	
			B Coy. 95 long screw Pickets and 36 coils of wire carried from C to S.6 in LONDON	
			TRENCH. 70* high wire erected from DIVISIONAL BOUNDARY inclusive to left in	
			area of RYECROFT	
			C Coy Deepened and widened and making berm for 220* BULLECOURT AVENUE	65J
			Casualties Nil. (Night)	
	July 16		Weather Showery. Wind S. Westerly, moderate strong.	
			A Coy Laying 180* of KNUCKLE AVENUE to 2'-6" deep 3" wide at top. Ground very	
			hard but quarry in top. Work slow. (Night)	
			Coy 2 Platoons	
			B Coy / Carried 15 Coils wire and 45 screw pickets from DUMP. C at B. 67 to Company	
			Hq. LONDON TRENCH. Wired 85* length in front of LONDON TRENCH. (Night)	
			C Coy on BULLECOURT AVENUE cleaning up, repairing trench in Madden by day	
			when necessary laying 40 boards on trestles	
			(2) Clearing out wire each cleaning trench in 500*. 3 paying places started Trestles	
			(3) Cleared out when blown in in 5 places near Br Hq. Division G wire	

WAR DIARY
or
INTELLIGENCE SUMMARY.
(Erase heading not required.)

Army Form C. 2118.

Place	Date	Hour	Summary of Events and Information	Remarks and references to Appendices
			informed when completed. The portion of trench shelled all night. (Night).	
			D Coy. 150ˣ of TANK AVENUE commenced last night completed. 1 Platoon or term all day. 1 section laying boards by day.	
			A Coy by day. 1 Platoon on QUEEN'S AVENUE clearing up work done on night of 15-16. 9 laid 136 boards on trestles.	
			B Coy by Day. 1 Platoon dug out collecting 200ˣ M'strengthements 9 3 > knife rests from BETHUNES AREA, part dumped 400ˣ S. of waterpoint, part dumped at crossing of Railway road, part conveyed to MORY R.E. Yard. 3 Platoon at AVELUY.	
			Usual aliching parties at DOULLENS, MORY, AVELUY.	
			Casualties L/6.R wounded (shell shock)	
	July 17ᵗʰ		Weather Fine. Wind S. Westerly.	
			A Coy. 1 Platoon by day deepened KNUCKLE AVENUE fr 120ˣ from 3'6" 4'-6" also cut through from New trench into old one.	
			3 Platoons by night carried by trolley from ECOUST DUMP to U.19.d. (trestles Ryan) 500 Pickets 190 Coils of wire	

WAR DIARY
or
INTELLIGENCE SUMMARY.
(Erase heading not required.)

Army Form C. 2118.

Place	Date	Hour	Summary of Events and Information	Remarks and references to Appendices
			Making dumps at (1) U.20.a 40.7.0. 195 Pickets 60 Coils wire	
			(2) U.20.a 6.9. 300 " 76 " "	
			(3) U.19.a (Sunken Rd). 75 " 54 " "	
			B. Coy. 1 Platoon by day collecting wire at REMPLACLIFFE AREA	
			& AVELUY.	
			2 Platoons by night 16-17. 31 Coils wire. 30 long screw pickets carried from Coil 67	
			to forward dumps in LONDON TRENCH. 85ˣ of wire erected in front of LONDON	
			TRENCH in continuation of work previously done.	
			C. Coy. 1 Platoon by day on BULLECOURT AVENUE cleaning, repairing trench and repairing	
			trench mats from EMBANKMENT to SUNKEN ROAD.	
			3 Platoons by night, repairing & improving from GORDON SWITCH to TANK AVENUE. Wire	
			and pickets were conveyed from dump at ECOUST and dumps forward at	
			(1) U.28.a. 6.6. 25 Coils wire & 150 Pickets	
			(2) U.28.c 2.3. 25 " 150 "	
			D. Coy. conveyed 100 Coils wire and 250 Pickets from ECOUST DUMP to Dump at C.4.b.6.6.	
			80 Coils of wire 150 Pickets carried from C.4.b.6.6. to forward dumps. 150ˣ of	

WAR DIARY or INTELLIGENCE SUMMARY

Army Form C. 2118.

Place	Date	Hour	Summary of Events and Information	Remarks and references to Appendices
	1917			
			Fence wire erected in front of LONDON TRENCH.	
			Casualties NIL. Usual detached parties DOULLENS, MORY AVENUE	G.S.T.J.
	July 18th		Weather. Fine but cold. Wind S. Westerly. Strong.	
			A. Coy. 20 Men by day improving trench & fixing french boards. KNUCKLE AVENUE	
			B. Coy. 1 Platoon 20 Men Collecting M. Frames thumb nuts BEHAGNIES.	
			C. Coy. 20 Men cleaning trench and fixing wire boards. BULLECOURT AVENUE.	
			Digging 20 Officers & other ranks tonight getting up wire from DUMP at ECOUST to C.4.b.6.6.	
			Remainder of Battalion rested.	
			Usual detached parties. Casualties NIL.	G.S.T.J.
	July 19th		Weather. Fine and warm. Wind S. Westerly.	
			A. Coy. Carried 120 Coils of wire and 470 Sickets from ECOUST DUMP to fixed DUMP at KNUCKLE.	
			Wired 3 stakes wide wire in front of KNUCKLE AVENUE from SHANGWAYS to QUEENS AVENUE.	
			12 O.R.'s employed repairing KNUCKLE AVENUE was front line	
			B. C. Coy's carried pickets and wire from EMBANKMENT u6.156. Wind a rough fear	
			0.3 wire from aff. U.28.a.65 to TANK AVENUE.	

WARS DIARY
or
INTELLIGENCE SUMMARY.
(Erase heading not required.)

Army Form C. 2118.

Place	Date	Hour	Summary of Events and Information	Remarks and references to Appendices
	1917			
			B Coy 1 Platoon at AVELUY (ondykapment)	
			C Coy 2 Platoons by day repairing ERVILLERS-STEEGER ROAD from B.13.6.3.3. to B.20.1.6.	
			Unload 15 loads of metal and used 10 of them. Remaining 5 dumped at side of road.	
			D Coy carried 30 Coils wire and 80 long screw pickets from C.4b.6.6. to No.3 Machine Gun Post	
			in LONDON TRENCH. Wired 120 lengths front of LONDON TRENCH in continuation of	
			work previously done.	
			Casualties 1 Shell Shock returning to Camp.	W.T.J
	July 20.		Weather fine and warm. Wind S.W. Light	
			A Coy 200 of Apron and Fence wire completed from QUEENS AVENUE to offshoot U.19.a.95.80.	
			340 Coils wire, 250 Pickets carried up from ECOUST DUMP to QUEEN'S AVENUE.	
			Dumps on KNUCKLE AVENUE removed to U.19.d.95.80.	
			B Coy one Platoon on KNUCKLE AVENUE cleaning and improving forward end	
			one Platoon on PELICAN AVENUE cleaning and improving	
			one Platoon on Detachment at AVELUY (taking down Nissen Huts)	
			C Coy Wiring LONDON TRENCH. carrying material from RAILWAY EMBANKMENT to	

WAR DIARY
or
INTELLIGENCE SUMMARY.
(Erase heading not required.)

Army Form C. 2118.

Instructions regarding War Diaries and Intelligence Summaries are contained in F. S. Regs., Part II. and the Staff Manual respectively. Title pages will be prepared in manuscript.

Place	Date	Hour	Summary of Events and Information	Remarks and references to Appendices
	1917 July 20.		to dumps in LONDON TRENCH. One stretch of 100ˣ was completed & further 50ˣ was skilled one row of stakes up & 5 strands wire.	
			D Coy. Two Platoons on BULLECOURT AVENUE cleaning & revising 100ˣ finished. Two Platoons on TANK AVENUE cleaning and revising 200ˣ but of 100ˣ finished.	
			Casualties 2 O.R's wounded (Machine Gun Bursts)	6 J J
	July 21.		Weather Sunny and very warm. Wind S.W. (Calm)	
			A Coy KNUCKLE TANK AVENUE LINE 230ˣ of Apron and Fence were completed from U.19.a.95.90 to U.20.c.50.48. (Sunken Road) 380 Pickets and 80 Coils of wire conveyed from ECOUST Dump to Sunken Road U.20.c.	
			B Coy Deepening and widening of KNUCKLE AVENUE and PELICAN AVENUE.	
			C Coy Wiring LONDON TRENCH in U.22.d. Wind 130ˣ completed. Conveying 60 coils of barbed wire & 550 Pickets from ECOUST Dump to ETAPIVILLE	
			and one EMBANKMENT between dumps	
			D Coy. 8 Men and 1 N.C.O. leading mules at ECOUST & pushing same along	

WAR DIARY
or
INTELLIGENCE SUMMARY.
(Erase heading not required.)

Army Form C. 2118.

Place	Date	Hour	Summary of Events and Information	Remarks and references to Appendices
	July 22		railway to TANK AVENUE 250 Pickets. To destroy runnel from CAGE to TANK AVENUE. 20 men on Relief 30x of diagonal barb wire scarefence. also completed astride 100' of wire from U.23.c.1.6 to U.27.d.9.6. 36 gun defences widened & digging sump hole on TANK AVENUE U.26.b.53 — U.28.b.54. (Night)	GTJ
			Casualties 1 OR wounded remainder all at duty	
			Weather Sunny very hot. Wind N Easterly (light)	
			Voluntary C of E from Coy E services in Camp in afternoon	
			Casualties Nil	GTJ
	July 23		Weather Fine very hot Wind Nil.	
			A Coy. Revet'n hie from KNUCKLE AVENUE 250x dug 6' wide at top 2' to 4'6" deep according to hardness of ground 12'x 21'.	
			B Coy. One Platoon on KNUCKLE AVENUE maintenance One Platoon on PELICAN AVENUE maintenance One Platoon at AVELUY.	

WAR DIARY
or
INTELLIGENCE SUMMARY.
(Erase heading not required.)

Army Form C. 2118.

Place	Date	Hour	Summary of Events and Information	Remarks and references to Appendices
	1917			
	July 13		One Platoon providing small details for the B Coy. LONDON TRENCH. 1 Platoon wiring. 1 Platoon carrying from EMBANKMENT to jn. 1 Platoon making French mats & bottles from ECOUST DUMP to BULLECOURT AVENUE & then carrying wire from EMBANKMENT to jn.	
			D. 100x of wiring was completed. 70x commenced, both lines of pickets and three straight wires in centre pickets. 1 Platoon on BULLECOURT AVENUE cleaning trench and putting up broken trench boards.	
			D. Coy. Wired from TANK AVENUE to FOX TROT. U.22.d.9.1. to U.22.a 65.05. 200x of wire. 60x of trench boarding laid in TANK AVENUE. Carried were from ECOUST DUMP 40 Corks and Pickets 180.	
			During the afternoon D Coy moved their quarters from CAMP B 15.c.0.3 to near the Sucrerie at VRAUCOURT. (Night)	WTJ
			Casualties Nil	
	1917 July 24		Weather Thunder very close Wind - EASTERLY VERY LIGHT	

WAR DIARY or INTELLIGENCE SUMMARY

Army Form C. 2118.

A Coy. Reserve line from KNUCKLE AVENUE U.20.c.0.6 to U.19.d.9.7. 250x defended to an average depth of 4'6". 36 Coils of Wire carried up for wiring.

B Coy. divided into two parties one on maintenance of KNUCKLE AVENUE. One on maintenance of PELICAN AVENUE.

C Coy. 1 Platoon wiring 130x LONDON TRENCH working from R.6.b.
1 " camping wire Pickets from EMBANKMENT dump to job.
1 " picked up by tramway from ECOUST DUMP to EMBANKMENT. a Cable trench wire, 150 long Pickets, 150 short, 450 French wire.
1 Platoon on maintenance of TANK AVENUE, BULLECOURT AVENUE.

D Coy. Completed wiring from U.22.a.6.1 to U.22.a.21. approx 200x. 1 Platoon
1 Platoon picked up to EMBANKMENT by tramway wire & Pickets
1 Platoon carrying wiring defence from EMBANKMENT Jct.
1 Platoon on maintenance of TANK AVENUE. (N.7.W)

D Coy working from R.5.b. tramed up with E. Coy. thence private parties to AVELUY DUGOUTS. MORY -12. Remainder W.L.

WAR DIARY
or
INTELLIGENCE SUMMARY.
(Erase heading not required.)

Army Form C. 2118.

Place	Date	Hour	Summary of Events and Information	Remarks and references to Appendices
	1917 July 25th		Weather. Fine Warm. Wind. Westerley.	
			A Coy. New Queen Line Left Sector (KNUCKLE) Completed to C.C. finished trench and lowered parapet of trench 250ˣ from U.20.c.0.6. to U.19.a.9.7. Dug 50ˣ of new trench 6' from wire from U.19.d.80.75 to U.19.a.97. to an average depth of 3'.1".9". Carried 20 coils of barbed wire 1700 yards from KEUST DUMP to U.20.c.0.5.	
			B Coy. 1 Platoon improving and maintaining PELICAN AVENUE & KNUCKLE 1 " " " " 1 " at Avenue taking down hessian huts 1 " finding smoke parties attending wire.	
			C Coy. 2 Platoons wiring on new support line in R.9.W. Sector in U.28.b. aft. & Enteans carrying from EMBANKMENT to RR 1 Platoon making material from KEUST DUMP R.R. 1 Platoon on maintenance of RAVINE BOULECOURT AVENUE. 400ˣ of wiring was completed with exception of the outside apron. A further 100ˣ started. the 2nd rows of pickets were put up. Some dugouts were	

WAR DIARY
or
INTELLIGENCE SUMMARY.
(Erase heading not required.)

Army Form C. 2118.

Place	Date	Hour	Summary of Events and Information	Remarks and references to Appendices
	1917 July 25th		D. Coy. Erected single wire fence (3 Wilson Pickets 3" apart) from TANK AVENUE (U.28.b.55.40) to the Horseshoe (U.29.c.20.85) a distance of 520x. 3 Platoons carried wire one journey from EMBANKMENT to forward DUMP and afterwards in [erecting] TANK AVENUE. (Night) Casualties Nil.	ST.J
	July 26th		Weather fair indoor. Wind Westerly. The Battalion rested. In the evening the Battalion played the 1/10 Manchesters at Rugby Football (Northern Union rules) at COURCELLES S. Very large attendance. The Battalion won 11 points against 3.	ST.J
	July 27		Weather Heavy hot. Wind South Westerly (light) A Coy on MANCHESTER RESERVE. Enemy transport and parties heard and generally observed it occupied to 6' for stopped which got from KNUCKLE AVENUE U.19.a.80.70 to U.19.d.9.7. Working party to take trench mats from U.20.a.6.6 U.19.a.9.7.	

A6945 Wt. W11422/M1160 350,000 12/16 D.D.&L. Forms/C/2118/14.

WAR DIARY
or
INTELLIGENCE SUMMARY.

(Erase heading not required.)

Army Form C. 2118.

Place	Date	Hour	Summary of Events and Information	Remarks and references to Appendices
			and awaited for slips	
			A Coy. on maintenance KNUCKLE AVENUE. Carried up 50 duckbts and 11 trench mats.	
			Sent 20 trench mats on position. Work on 50ˣ deepening and widening	
			on maintenance PELICAN AVENUE carried 38 Knifes and 12 trench mats framed	
			Amp. ECOUST and laid same in trench. Widening and deepening 50ˣ of	
			Knuckle shelf by 25ˣ men punction TIGER TRENCH which had been blown in	
			was cleared.	
			C Coy. from GORDON SWITCH to TANK AVENUE. Pushing material from ECOUST to	
			EMBANKMENT (2) Carried material from EMBANKMENT on trolleys and using	
			Shelf completed with the exception of the outside Apron.	
			1 Platoon on maintenance and improvement of BULLECOURT AVENUE	
			D Coy from TANK AVENUE to HORSESHOE. Drenching 55 Coy. were sent 130 Pickets from	
			ECOUST Dump to EMBANKMENT. Carried material from EMBANKMENT on	
			to pits and wiring. Completed apron on wire from U.29.b.55.25 & U.29.c.17.	
			(Night)	
			Casualties Nil	6511

A6945   Wt. W14342/M1160 350,000 12/16 D. D. & L. Forms/C./2118/14.

Army Form C. 2118.

WAR DIARY
or
INTELLIGENCE SUMMARY.
(Erase heading not required.)

Place	Date	Hour	Summary of Events and Information	Remarks and references to Appendices
	1917 July 28		Weather. Fine + Very hot. Wind. Northerly. Light.	
			A Coy. Packed up from the ECOUST DUMP 259 Corks of wire and 170 Pickets and formed dumps as at U.14.a.3.5., U.20.a.2.9 and U.20.a.1.8. 1517ans endeavour deepened and revetted MANCHESTER RESERVE trench where required.	
			B Coy. on maintenance of PELICAN AVENUE	
			C Coy. 1 Platoon pushing up tramway material from ECOUST DUMP to EMBANKMENT 2 Platoons carrying from EMBANKMENT on to pit and wiring Gunfield. 350ˣ apron fence GORDON SWITCH – TANK AVENUE + further 100ˣ half completed.	
			D Coy. 1 Platoon on maintenance of BULLECOURT AVENUE. Completed wire belt from TANK AVENUE U.28.b.55.40 to the Horseshoe (U.29.c.2.0.8.5). 2 Gaps on left (1) 200ˣ from TANK AVENUE (2) 150ˣ from Horseshoe 1 Platoon on maintenance of TANK AVENUE	
			Casualties 1 Officer wounded seriously. (Night)	65 IJ
	July 29		Weather Very wet Thunderstorms Wind Northerly Light A Coy 225ˣ of wiring 3 stakes wide completed with apron and hope wire on it.	

WAR DIARY
or
INTELLIGENCE SUMMARY.
(Erase heading not required.)

Army Form C. 2118.

Place	Date	Hour	Summary of Events and Information	Remarks and references to Appendices
			the North side of KNUCKLE AVENUE between STRANGEWAYS and the front line. Also carried up 120 coils of wire and 400 Pickets	
			B. Coy. Wire trench M2/5 carried from DUMP near EMBANKMENT end of PELICAN AV. to end of PELICAN Avg. out ready for putting. 14 Nets laid and nailed on trestles.	
			C. Coy. Wiring 300 yds of apron fence GORDON SWITCH — TANK AVENUE and in front also rails of wiring. This job now finished. (2 Platoons) 1 Platoon putting up by Railway wire and pickets to D. Coy. 1 Platoon on maintenance of BULLECOURT AVENUE.	
			D. Coy. Pushed up by Railway 15 coils of wire 30 french boards 180 Pickets 230 Nettles.	
			Wiring along RAILWAY EMBANKMENT from U.27.c.9.7 to U.27.c.7.8 (about 1120x) in Peace and diagonal. This job was very difficult to find as grass was very long and no wire was to be found when started.	
			Band detached parties at Doullens, Villeneuve, Mory &c	

WAR DIARY
or
INTELLIGENCE SUMMARY.
(Erase heading not required.)

Army Form C. 2118.

Place	Date	Hour	Summary of Events and Information	Remarks and references to Appendices
	1917			
	July 29		Casualties 9 O.R's wounded	
			2. O.R's wounded remaining at duty	S.T.1
			Voluntary C of E Service in Camp at 5.30 p.m. (Night)	
	July 30		Weather fine but cool. Wind N. Westerly. Fresh.	
			The Battalion rested	
			In the evening the Officers played a team of Journalists at Association Football. Result Officers 2. Journalists 1.	
			Casualties Nil.	S.T.1
	July 31st		Weather Showery. Wind Northerly	
			A Coy. erected 130x. 3 stake wide wire entanglement with loose wire and Apron on the North side of KNUCKLE AVENUE. STRANGEWAYS END	
			90x of 3 stake wide wire completed with Apron and wire in continuation of MANCHESTER RESERVE.	
			Also carried up and dumped for further 14th Corps wire and 350 Pickets	

A6945 Wt. W11422/M1160 350,000 12/16 D. D. & L. Forms/C/2118/14

Army Form C. 2118.

WAR DIARY
or
INTELLIGENCE SUMMARY.
(Erase heading not required.)

Place	Date	Hour	Summary of Events and Information	Remarks and references to Appendices
	1917 July 31st		B. Coy. on maintenance of PELICAN AVENUE 40X at top was deepened and widened cleared been trafficed and boarded.	
			One Platoon on detachment at AVELUY.	
			C. Coy. Wiring the EMBANKMENT in U.26.d. Completed 130X with the exception of the Apron. 20X of Pickets were put up with no strand of wire on outside line.	
			1 Platoon pushing up by Tramway, wire and pickets from ECOUST DU17P	
			1 Platoon on maintenance of BULLECOURT AVENUE.	
			D. Coy. 300X of partly erected wire completed (U.27.9.5.6.5 – 4.27.45.80)	
			1 Platoon on maintenance of TANK AVENUE.	
			(Night).	
			Casualties Nil.	B.T.J

J.S. Humphrey
Lieut Colonel Commanding
24th Bn The Manchester Regiment
(attd Durnoval Pioneers)

Vol XXII
24.(S) Bn The Manchester Regiment
7th Divisional Pioneers
Army Form C. 2118.

WAR DIARY or INTELLIGENCE SUMMARY.
(Erase heading not required.)

Place	Date	Hour	Summary of Events and Information	Remarks and references to Appendices
MORY	19/7/17 August 8th		Wind - North Westerly. Rained all day.	
			A. Coy. 320' 3 sided wire was completed with apron and lose on its North side of KNUCKLE AV. This completes the wiring of the North side of KNUCKLE AVENUE between the front line and STRAWS X WAYS.	
			B. Coy on maintenance of PELICAN AVENUE. Platoon on detachment at AVELUY.	
			C. Coy Cutting away Boyohwood and overgrowth along the EMBANKMENT for 150' moving on C2 B 58 moving towards BULLECOURT.	
			BD. Coy. 1 Platoon wiring in U 26 d. completed 125' sawpit just apon. 1 Platoon pushing by tramway from ECOUST DUMP and carrying for the jt. U 22 corks wire 200 long & 156 short pickets 1 Platoon on maintenance of BULLECOURT AVENUE.	
			D. Coy Erected and completed wire for 150' from U 27 c. 45.80 to U 27 c. 25.60 line from ECOUST DUMP and finished to TANK AVENUE 9 coils of wire and 220 stakes. 1 Platoon on maintenance of TANK AVENUE, cut and one paring plan and out on fire late (Night) late	

Army Form C. 2118.

WAR DIARY
or
INTELLIGENCE SUMMARY.
(Erase heading not required.)

Place	Date	Hour	Summary of Events and Information	Remarks and references to Appendices
1st Army	1917 Aug 2nd		Weather. Very wet and cold. Wind. North westerly.	
			A.Coy. Bevered KNUCKLE AVENUE from STRANGEWAYS to U.19.a 40.25. off 900 yards battens.	
			B.Coy. 56" PELICAN AVENUE deepened and widened and 260" been cleaned to average depth. width of 1'-9"	
			C.Coy. Wiring along EMBANKMENT. 2 Platoons finished last night's work and started and completed westsite 270" and joined up to D Coy.	
			1 Platoon pushed up from ECOUST and carried on to job wire pickets	
			1 Platoon on maintenance of BULLECOURT AVENUE.	
			D.Coy. Wiring. Completed 220" wire and joined C.Coy at U 26.d.95.70. 200 long screw pickets 120. 3/4 pickets pushed from ECOUST to TANK AVENUE. 170 long. 80. 3/4 pickets and 25 coils of wire carried to HORSE SHOE.	
			1 Platoon on maintenance to of TANK AVENUE. 24" dug out, and 2 funk-bays completed	
			Casualties NIL	

Army Form C. 2118.

WAR DIARY
or
INTELLIGENCE SUMMARY.
(Erase heading not required.)

Place	Date	Hour	Summary of Events and Information	Remarks and references to Appendices
[illegible]	1917 [Jan?] 3		Weather very wet and cold. Wind Northwesterly. The Battalion rested. Casualties Nil.	6.1.J
	4		Weather Wet and cold. Wind Southwesterly. A Coy carried 250" 3 stake wire complete with Apron and large new screw pickets (continuation of 17 ANCHESTER RESERVE. also carried up 300 A.I pickets 600 screw pickets 183 Cab wire.	
			B. Coy. on improvement of PELICAN AVENUE. 2 Platoons 2 Platoons on detachment AVELUY.	
			C Coy wiring new screw line from point U.26.a.8.5 towards PELICAN AVE. 210 yds compltd. 1 Platoon putting up wire from ECOUST DUMP to EMBANKMENT. (By K.stry) 1 Platoon carrying from EMBANKMENT to 10L. 1 Platoon on maintenance of BULLECOURT AVENUE.	
			D. Coy. Completed 130" of wire from U.29.c.1.7 to U.29.c.4.6. also 1st fence from U.29.c.6.6 U.29.c.4.3 at 150°.	

Army Form C. 2118.

WAR DIARY
or
INTELLIGENCE SUMMARY.
(Erase heading not required.)

Place	Date	Hour	Summary of Events and Information	Remarks and references to Appendices
	1917.			
	August 5.		Pushed up 50 French Walk and 80 Trestles from ECOUST to TANK AVENUE. 38 gas watering and improving TANK AVENUE between points U.28.a.6.0 - U.28.a.6.2. 9 gas laying French rails in TANK AVENUE by day (NIGHT) Casualties Nil.	61.J
			Weather Showery & cold. Wind. NORTHERLY (light)	
			A Coy 200' 3 stake wide wire complete wiring apron and low from PELICAN AVE towards MANCHESTER RESERVE. (unmanoeuvring) 100' 3 stake wire complete with apron and loops in continuation of MANCHESTER RESERVE. Also carried up 120 A.1 Pickets. 260 screw. 280 Cobs wire.	
			B Coy 2 Platoons on maintenance of PELICAN AVENUE and KNUCKLE AVENUE 2 " " a detachment at AVELUY &c.	
			C Coy Wiring as yesterday. 300' completed. 2 Platoons wiring. 1 Platoon (less 1 section) pushing from ECOUST DUMP to EMBANKMENT & carrying up 6 jibs.	

WAR DIARY
or
INTELLIGENCE SUMMARY.

(Erase heading not required.)

Army Form C. 2118.

Place	Date	Hour	Summary of Events and Information	Remarks and references to Appendices
	1917. Aug 5.		1 Platoon laying track boards in BULLECOURT AVENUE.	
			1 Section pushing up track gale + holts to BULLECOURT AVE.	
			D Coy Loaded in lorries at ECOUST DUMP 200 slabs and 30 Coils wire and pushed same to TANK AVENUE.	
			Completing wire around HORSESHOE for distance of 170ˣ. TANK AVENUE wiring for distance of 80ˣ.	6.T.J
			(Night)	
			Casualties NIL	
	Aug 6.		Weather fine and warm. Wind Northeasterly.	
			A Coy 280ˣ 3 slabs was completed with Apron Fence and bose in continuation of Manchester RESERVE.	
			B Coy Thus complete the wiring from heart the remaining MANCHESTER RESERVE between (No Reserve line) + point of exit of C Coy —PELICAN AVENUE. (No Reserve line).	
			B Coy wiring and deepening 30ˣ PELICAN AVE. The trench had been badly worn in 3 places near SUNKEN ROAD. Wire was un-necessary.	
			C Coy continuing wire in New Reserve line from RAILWAY towards PELICAN AVENUE.	

WAR DIARY
or
INTELLIGENCE SUMMARY.
(Erase heading not required.)

Army Form C. 2118.

Place	Date	Hour	Summary of Events and Information	Remarks and references to Appendices
	1917 Aug 8	6ᵖ	105ˣ completed joined up with "A" Coy. Dump parties on new trench	
			B. POZIÈRES AVENUE & laying tram board.	
			D Coy wiring South Support. Completed wire from U.29.c.3.3 to C.5.a.5.8	
			9 joined up with 62ⁿᵈ Divᶰ wire	
			1 NCO & 10 men carrying material from TANK AVENUE 6/8.	
			54 men widening and improving TANK AVENUE between points U.28.a.52 to U.28.d.45.40.	
			(Night)	
			Casualties NIL	
			VALHEUREUX Detachment with machine Guns returned on 30 July 1917.	
			AVELUY	
			15 men from R.E. Dump MORY to return on the morning of the 9ᵗʰ August 1917.	
			Detachment on ANTI AIRCRAFT DEFENCE at DOULLENS to remain there for the present.	
			The above completed the work in the area prior to handing over	

WAR DIARY
or
INTELLIGENCE SUMMARY.

(Erase heading not required.)

Army Form C. 2118.

Place	Date	Hour	Summary of Events and Information	Remarks and references to Appendices
	1917			
	August 7th		Wind. N Easterly Light. Weather. Wet and Showery.	
			The Bn. in bed during the day. Football games in the evening	G.S.T.J
		8½	During the afternoon D Coy returned from Camp at VRAQUOURT to Hq Camp at B.15.c.0.3	
			Weather South Light Wet. Wind Southerly Light.	
			Company Parades for the purpose of getting equipment rifles &c clean. Casualties Nil	
			Football games in the evening	G.S.T.J
		9th	Weather. Heavy shower storms Wind S. Westerly Light.	
			Casualties Nil Battalion rested	
		Aug 10th	Weather fine & warm Wind S Westerly	G.S.T.J
			Reveille 6 a.m. Breakfast 6.45 A.M. Camp struck 7.15 a.m.	
			Camp material and packs loaded on light railway trucks in New Division	
			Sidings Indsing Camp	
			8.45 a.m. the Bn. Paraded and entrained in light railway trucks	
			9.0 a.m - 9.30 a.m. Three trains(left Old Camp at B.15.c.0.3 for new	
MAPS.			camp at PETERCOURT) 9.9. 9 ton bogey waggons each of 60 at intervals	
51 C and			of say 10 minutes each	
57 D.				
NEW CAMP				
51.E R27A 83.				

WAR DIARY
or
INTELLIGENCE SUMMARY.

Army Form C. 2118.

Place	Date	Hour	Summary of Events and Information	Remarks and references to Appendices
	1917 Aug 10		Bn Detrained at 11.45 a.m. and marched to new Camp at "BLAMONT MILL" BRETENCOURT R.27. d. 8.3. one mile from light Railway. Casualties Nil.	GTJ
	Aug 11th		Weather Showery. Companies completing erection of new Camp, making footway roads &c. Wind S. westerly. Strong. The Bn was inspected by the I.G.C. between 8th and 10th insts. The Lewis Gun detachment from DOULLENS returned Casualties Nil.	GTJ
	Aug 12th		Weather fair. C. of E. parade service in Camp at 9.30 a.m. Communion service at 10 a.m. Wind S. westerly light. Voluntary services C of E in the Cinema BRETENCOURT at 7 & 8 p.m. Non C of E Casualties Nil.	GTJ

WAR DIARY
or
INTELLIGENCE SUMMARY.

(Erase heading not required.)

Army Form C. 2118.

Place	Date	Hour	Summary of Events and Information	Remarks and references to Appendices
	1917			
August	13		Weather Showery. Wind S. Westerly. Light.	
			Battalion training. Close order drill. P.T. & Bayonet fighting and musketry.	
			Inter coron Games in the afternoon.	
			Casualties Nil.	G.T.J
"	14		Weather fair during day. Storming in the evening. Wind S. Westerly Light.	
			Work as yesterday.	
			Casualties Nil.	G.T.J
"	15		Weather Unsettled. Wind South Westerly.	
			Training as yesterday. Games in afternoon. Night Marching on compass.	
			Casualties Nil.	G.T.J
	16		Weather fair. Wind Westerly Strong.	
			Training during the morning. Games in the afternoon.	
			Regimental Officers service at Brouders. The G.R.E. Jameson and his Coy's attended.	
			Casualties Nil.	G.T.J
	17		Weather fine. Wind S Westerly Strong.	

WAR DIARY
or
INTELLIGENCE SUMMARY.

(Erase heading not required.)

Army Form C. 2118.

Place	Date	Hour	Summary of Events and Information	Remarks and references to Appendices
Argues	August 17th		Company training during the morning. Games in the afternoon. Lecture by Divisional Gas Officer to Senior Officers of the Battalion. Casualties NIL. Weather fair.	
"	18th		Wind Westerly Strong. Company training during the morning. Games in the afternoon. Casualties NIL. Weather fair.	
"	19th		Wind Westerly Strong. Wire Service in Camp. Games in the afternoon. 1 Company on Inspection of the ground for the Divisional Tour. Casualties NIL. Battalion dinner in Camp for NCO's men. Wind Westerly light. Weather fair.	
"	20th		Two Companies on Inspection of the ground for the Divisional Tour. A Coy on Technical training under the 528 R.E. Bridge Building. Remaining Coys on Platoon training. At night training and practice by Companies forming fire walling prior to neapic attack. Casualties NIL	

WAR DIARY
or
INTELLIGENCE SUMMARY.

(Erase heading not required.)

Army Form C. 2118.

Place	Date	Hour	Summary of Events and Information	Remarks and references to Appendices
	1917 August 21.		Weather fine. Wind. Westerly light. One Company on preparation of ground for Divisional fair. B Company on Technical training under R.E.'s (Bridge Building) Remainder of Battalion on Range practice. Casualties NIL	
	August 22		Weather fine. Wind. South Easterly to Southerly. Two Companies on preparation of ground for Divisional Fair. One Company on Technical training under 528 Coy R.E.'s (Bridge Building) One Company training. Casualties Nil	
	August 23		Weather Showery. Wind. S. Westerly light. One Company engaged on preparation of ground for Divisional Fair. Three Companies training. Than Coast was inspected by 16 G.O.C. 4th Division. Casualties NIL	

Army Form C. 2118.

WAR DIARY
or
INTELLIGENCE SUMMARY.
(Erase heading not required.)

Instructions regarding War Diaries and Intelligence Summaries are contained in F. S. Regs., Part II. and the Staff Manual respectively. Title pages will be prepared in manuscript.

Place	Date	Hour	Summary of Events and Information	Remarks and references to Appendices
August	1917 24th		Weather Showery. Wind Southerly, strong.	
			Two Companies on preparation of ground for Divisional Fair in morning	
			Two Companies in afternoon.	
			Casualties Nil.	G.T.J
"	25th		Weather Westerly Storm Fine. Wind Westerly Strong	
			Divisional Fair at MONCHECOURT	G.T.J
			No work. Casualties Nil.	
"	26th		Weather fine and warm throughout night. Wind Strong Southerly.	G.T.J
			C.O.E INC. O.E. service in Camp	
"	27th		Weather Southerly Storm	
			Battalion on taking down sections and clearing ground which forms	
			the site for Divisional Fair. Casualties Nil.	G.T.J
			Advance party for me to report at Douttens at 10 p.m.	
"	28.		Weather Wet and Stormy. Wind Southerly.	
			Two Coys on clearing Divisional Fair ground	G.T.J
			Casualties Nil.	

WAR DIARY
or
INTELLIGENCE SUMMARY.
(Erase heading not required.)

Army Form C. 2118.

Place	Date	Hour	Summary of Events and Information	Remarks and references to Appendices
1917 August	29th		The Battalion occupied in cleaning up and cleaning Camp and shirting. Casualties Nil.	G.T.J
August	30		The Battalion moved in accordance with attached Operation Order dated 28th August 1917. "Y" Party detrained at 4 P.M. at PROVEN and "X" Party detrained	
Map. BELGIUM & FRANCE SHEET 27.			at the same place at 10 P.M. and both respectively marched to Dallington Camp WIPPENHOEK AREA L.29.c.8.2 Map BELGIUM & FRANCE SHEET 27. troops The Battalion was reported present at 2 A.M. on the 31st inst. Casualties Nil.	G.T.J
Ypres. Edith 2.				
August.	31st.		The Battalion moved in Short Ulis by Motor Waggons from DALLINGTON CAMP and took up quarters J.13.B.28. in the tunnels there.	
MAP BELGIUM.			to ESPLANADE RAMPARTS YPRES ; in the tunnels there. J.13.B.28. The	
Sh.28.N.W. Edin. 6.A.			Transport proceeded to Camp at H.22.a.1.9. Map. BELGIUM 28 N.W. Edin.	G.T.J
to 5,000			6.A. 1,000. Casualties Nil.	

J.S. Oswald.
Lieut. Col.
c`mdg 24th Bn. The Manchester Regt.
& 7th Divisional Pioneers

SECRET   Copy No. **XII**

24th Battalion The Manchester Regt. (Pioneers).

OPERATION ORDER NO. 16.
28-8-17.

REFERENCE: 1/100,000., LENS and HAZEBROUCK.

1. The Battalion will move from the present area by rail entraining at SAULTY Station on the 30th August, as under:-
    "X" party:-   "A" Coy, Asst. T.O., "A" Coys Cooker and Tool waggons, 1 "B" Coy Tool waggon and 1 "C" Coy Tool waggon.
    "Y" party:-   The Battalion, less "X" party.
    March:- Via BRETENCOURT, GROSVILLE, BEAUMETZ and LARBRET.

2. (a) "Y" party will be entrained by 5-30 a.m., 30th instant. The Transport will leave camp at midnight, 29th/30th. "B" Coy., Band and Bn. Headquarters, "C" Coy, "D" Coy, (in above order) will be paraded ready to move off in column of route by 1-0 a.m., the head of "B" coy, being on the track and level with the ruins of the Mill.
    (b) "X" party will be entrained by 9-30 a.m., 30th instant, and will be under the command of Captain C.H. LEE from 1-0 a.m. 30th instant until they re-join the Battalion at its destination.
    (c) Transport of both parties will be loaded on their respective trains by a party of the 2nd Bn. Gordon Highlanders.
    (d) Lieut. H.E. BRAINE will proceed to the Station in advance of the Battalion to allot accommodation on the train for "Y" party.

3. (a) All tents, shelters and tarpaulins will be struck and stacked by Q.M. Stores by 7-0 p.m., 29th instant.
    (b) One Armstrong, One Nissen and two Summer Huts will be left standing: they will accommodate "X" party for the night 29th/30th. Any complete structure may also be left standing.
    (c) All bivouac material, etc., will be stacked by the Canteen Hut before Companies move.

4. "D" Coy., will be prepared to form the unloading party on arrival at destination.

5. (a) Breakfasts will be eaten at the Station prior to entraining.
    (b) Dry rations for consumption on the 30th will be carried on the man: meat, tea and sugar on the cookers.
    (c) Rations for consumption on 31st instant will be carried on the supply waggons which will be with "Y" party.

Issued at 4-0 p.m.

(Signed) A. St. G. WALSH, Captain and Adjutant.

Copy No.		Copy No.	
1.	Commdg. Off'r	2.	Captain C.H. LEE
3.	Quartermaster	4.	Medical Officer
5.	Transport Off'r	6.	O.C. "A" Coy.
7.	O.C. "B" Coy.	8.	O.C. "C" "
9.	O.C. "D" "	10.	Lieut. H.E. BRAINE
11.	Asst. Transport Off'r	12.	War Diary
13.	War Diary	14.	Office.

24(S)Bn The Manchester Regt
(7th Divisional Pioneers)
Vol 23

WAR DIARY
INTELLIGENCE SUMMARY

Vol XXIII

Place	Date	Hour	Summary of Events and Information	Remarks and references to Appendices
YPRES	1917 Sept 1st		Weather: Fine.	
MAPS: BELGIUM			The Battalion attached to C.R.E 47th Division for work.	
Sheet 28. N.W.			D. Company provided 250 men on 6 hour working shifts and worked under	
Edition 6a			177 Tunnelling Company in RAILWAY WOOD.	
1/20,000			C. Company provided 100 men for work on the laying of duck board track	
			towards BELLEWAARDE RIDGE	
			B. Company provided two shifts of 50 men, five hours each and carried	
			on with C Coy's job.	
			A. Company and the remainder of the men of B.C. and D. Companies	
			engaged on the improvement of the Battalion Billets, the tunnels in	
			ESPLANADE RAMPARTS YPRES.	
			A Wire was received from C.R.E. 47 Division instructing the Battalion that	
			it ceased to be under his orders from to-night and to report Evans	
			to rejoin the 7th Division immediately.	
			Casualties. 2 O.R's Killed 9 O.R's wounded	KE

WAR DIARY
or
INTELLIGENCE SUMMARY.
(Erase heading not required.)

Army Form C. 2118.

Place	Date	Hour	Summary of Events and Information	Remarks and references to Appendices
1917.	Sept. 2nd		Wma Westrly.	
			Weather Fine.	
			The Battalion employed in cleaning up the equipment & clothing and Company inspections held whilst awaiting Orders to move.	
1917.			A wire was received from the 7th Division at 5 p.m. stating that the Battalion will remain in present billets in Ypres for to-night and will be carried to HAZEBROUCK to-morrow. Corps Q is sending lorries at 8 a.m. to-morrow to YPRES ASYLUM to convey Battalion. Senior Officer with representative from each Coy on bicycles to HAZEBROUCK to-day to report to Town Major and arrange billets. Notify Town Major YPRES regarding detailed Transport to move by road to-morrow.	
1917.	Sept 3rd		Weather Fine Wind Southerly light A wire was received from 7th Division stating that the Battalion will Embus at H.12.a.3.4. and column will move off at 11 a.m. proceeding via	
MAP. BELGIUM HAZEBROUCK 5A. Can 2 '1/100,000			ABEELE and STEENVOORDE. Transport will move via RENINGHELST- GODWAERSVELDE and CAESTRE has in column to enter RENINGHELST at 10-15 a.m. The Battalion entered HAZEBROUCK about 4.30 p.m. and was billeted	

Army Form C. 2118.

WAR DIARY
or
INTELLIGENCE SUMMARY.

(Erase heading not required.)

Place	Date	Hour	Summary of Events and Information	Remarks and references to Appendices
			in the schools. Hq. and A Coy in School behind Town Hall	
			B and D Coys in School in Rue de l'ORPHELINAT	
			C Coy and Band in another School "	
			Transport in Farm in N. side of HAZEBROUCK	
1917	Sept. 4th		Casualties N.L.	
			Wind Southerly light Weather fine	G.T.J
			The Battalion rested and were allowed time to settle in their billets.	
			Casualties N.L.	G.T.J
1917	Sept 5th		Wind Southerly light Weather fine	
			Detailed cleaning of clothing Arms and equipment	
			Casualties Nil	G.T.J
	"	6th	Wind Westerly Light Weather fine generally overcast	
			As yesterday	
			Casualties N.L.	G.T.J
		7th	Wind S Easterly light Weather fair.	
			Putting together equipment properly and inspections by C.O.	
			Casualties N.L.	G.T.J

Army Form C. 2118.

WAR DIARY
or
INTELLIGENCE SUMMARY.
(Erase heading not required.)

Place	Date	Hour	Summary of Events and Information	Remarks and references to Appendices
1917	Sept 8		Wind Southerly, light. Weather fine. A note was sent to division stating that in view of the fact that the amount of ground available for training was extremely limited training would be carried on solely by Companies and advantage taken of any suitable ground in the vicinity of the town. Further fitting of equipment and inspections by O/C Companies and the Commanding Officer. In the afternoon an entertainment was given in C Coy's billet by the R.A.M.C. Casualties Nil.	65TJ
1917	Sept 9th		Wind S-Westerly, light. Weather Mild. C of E Parade service in the Town Hall at 10.15 a.m. N.C of E and R.C. services. Casualties Nil.	65TJ
1917	Sept 10th		Wind Easterly, Light. Weather fine. 100 Men of A Coy. on work at II ANZAC School MORBECQUE	

Place	Date	Hour	Summary of Events and Information	Remarks and references to Appendices
	1917 Sep.	11th	A Coy (remainder) ⎫ Preparation for detailed inspections of clothing, Arms and Equipment by the Commanding Officer. B Coy ⎬ C Coy ⎪ D Coy ⎭ Casualties Nil. Wind N Easterly Light. Weather Fine. 100 Men of B Coy on work at II ANZAC School MORBECQUE. Remainder of B Coy, A Coy, C Coy & D Coy also HQ. Reclim Coy the Commanding Officer on the progress of the War. Casualties Nil. The Officers held a Battalion Officers dinner at the HQ du NORD	65.T.J
	1917 Sept.	12.	Wind North Easterly fresh. Weather Fine. 100 Men of C Coy on work at II ANZAC School MORBECQUE. Remainder of C Coy A Coy, B Coy & D Coy training under Company arrangements.	65.T.J

WAR DIARY
or
INTELLIGENCE SUMMARY

Army Form C. 2118.

Place	Date	Hour	Summary of Events and Information	Remarks and references to Appendices
	1917 Sept	13	Casualties Nil.	WTJ
			Wind. Westerly Spring. Weather fine	
			Three Officers and 100 O.R's proceeded last night on detachment for work at the II Anzac Corps School HARBERQUE from to day until the 18th. to be accommodated and rationed by the School	
			The remainder of the Battalion moved to ARQUES by Man HAZEBROUCK - ST OMER road. Order of March Hq. B. C. D. A Coys and Transport	WTJ
			Breakfast 7.45 am. Move off 11.15 a.m. Haversack rations were carried and Tea issued on Harroyard. Casualties Nil.	
	1917 Sept	14	Wind Westerly Sun bright Weather fine	WTJ
			The Battalion rested in billets	
			Casualties Nil.	
	1917 Sep	15	Wind Westerly Weather fine warm.	WTJ
			The Battalion (less C Coys detached party) moved to WIZERNES via Wastin and thence ARQUES by 9 a.m. The Battalion took up Billets in WIZERNES at the MALTERIE FARM. 73.C.2.4	

MAP SHEET
36D N E
1/20,000

Army Form C. 2118.

WAR DIARY
or
INTELLIGENCE SUMMARY.
(Erase heading not required.)

Place	Date	Hour	Summary of Events and Information	Remarks and references to Appendices
1917	Sept 16th		Wind Westerly. Weather Fine & Sunny. The Battalion less C Coys detachment engaged in arranging and making comfortable and resting in Billets. Casualties Nil.	WTJ
"	17.		Wind S. Westerly. Weather Fine. A, B, D & C Coy other than detachment training with Company arrangement. In it evening a Battalion Assoc. Football match was held 24th Manchester -v- 2/3 Field Ambulance Manchesters winning 2-0. Casualties Nil.	WTJ
"	18.		Wind S.S.W. Weather Rain nuggle. A & B Coy's with tools reported at 54 Coy RE's Office AUSTRA (ESQUARPES) at 9a.m. They worked on digging shell holes & on Divisional Practice ground. Remainder of C Coy & D. Coy Training. Transport practising carrying loads by Pack Mule. Casualties Nil.	WTJ

WAR DIARY
or
INTELLIGENCE SUMMARY.

(Erase heading not required.)

Army Form C. 2118.

Place	Date	Hour	Summary of Events and Information	Remarks and references to Appendices
1917	Sep 19		Wind. Weather	
			A & B Coys on work digging shee holes on Divisional Practice Ground	
			ESQUERDES	
			C Coy (Lewis Gun Detachment) & D Coy on Company Training	
			D Coy on training.	
			The Detachment of C Coy returned by train from II ANZAC Corps School	
			MORBECQUE.	
			Transport on practice of carrying loads by Pack Mule.	
			Casualties Nil.	WTJ
1917 Sep 20			Wind Westerly light. Weather Damp.	
			A Company on training.	
			B Company on digging shell holes on Divisional Practice Ground	
			C Company on training and Rifle range	
			D Company on training and inspection by C.O.	
			Transport on practice of carrying loads by Pack Mules	
			Casualties Nil.	WTJ

Army Form C. 2118.

WAR DIARY
or
INTELLIGENCE SUMMARY.
(Erase heading not required.)

Instructions regarding War Diaries and Intelligence Summaries are contained in F.S. Regs., Part II. and the Staff Manual respectively. Title pages will be prepared in manuscript.

Place	Date	Hour	Summary of Events and Information	Remarks and references to Appendices
1917	Sept 21		Wind Westerly. Weather Fine & Warm.	
			A Company on Rifle Range and inspection by C.O.	
			B Coy in digging shell holes and Trenches on Divisional practice ground.	
			C Coy in Training.	
			D Coy less two platoons left on detachment by 175th Bde to	65TI
			Remaining two Platoons of D Coy Route March.	
			Transport carrying loads by Pack Mule were, preparts sandbags &	
			Casualties Nil.	
			The following wire order was received at 11.0 P.M.	
			To 24 Manchester Regiment.	
			2th Manchester Regiment will move to-morrow (Sept 22nd) to OUDERDOM by tactical train	Headquarters 2/785 VII Div
			Transport 1st + 2nd line by March Route.	
			Battalion will entrain at ARQUES marching so as to arrive there not later than 12-15 P.M.	
			Train scheduled to leave at 13 hrs. Arrive OUDERDOM 16 hours.	

Army Form C. 2118.

WAR DIARY
or
INTELLIGENCE SUMMARY.

(Erase heading not required.)

Instructions regarding War Diaries and Intelligence Summaries are contained in F. S. Regs., Part II. and the Staff Manual respectively. Title pages will be prepared in manuscript.

Place	Date	Hour	Summary of Events and Information	Remarks and references to Appendices
1917	Sep 21		The unoccupied portion of the current day's rations will be carried on the man.	
			Rations for consumption on the 23rd will be arranged by X Corps.	
			Transport 1st & 2nd lines complete will move by march route pending the night of 22-23rd in the Artillery portion of WALLON CAPELL area. Baggage & supply waggons will move report to O.C. 24 Manchester at WIZERNES by 10 a.m. on 22nd September.	
			Billetting representatives to report to Area Commandant WALLON CAPELL area at STAPLE who will arrange billets and will notify Officer i/c Transport the destination to which he will march on the 23rd. Transport will carry the unoccupied portion of the current day's ration and rations for consumption on the 23rd.	
			One lorrie will report to O.C. 2/4 Manchester Regiment at 9 a.m. to-morrow and will return to 50 Div Supply Column after delivering stores at OUDERDOM.	
			Arrangements are being made for the two platoons # now working at No 2 Casualty Clearing Station to rejoin the Battalion at OUDERDOM.	
			The Orders for the two platoons to proceed to 2nd ARMY GRENADE School are cancelled	
			Acknowledge.	
			Dist Hq 21.9.17.	
			Copy to C.R.E.	
			" " C.R.A	
			" " 50 Div Supply Column	
			" " X Corps	
			(Signed) N. Vyvyan Major	
			for Lieut Colonel.	
			AA & QMG. 7th Div	

WAR DIARY
or
INTELLIGENCE SUMMARY.

(Erase heading not required.)

Army Form C. 2118.

Place	Date	Hour	Summary of Events and Information	Remarks and references to Appendices
	1917 Sept.	22nd	Wind Westerly. Weather Fine. The Battalion moved off at 10.15 a.m. Grew of March HQ., C, D, Band, A & B Coys Transport and marched to ARQUES where they had dinner and entrained. Transport marching by road to Staple. The Battalion detrained at OUDERDOM and marched to Camp at RIDGEWOOD N.5.a.3.6. Sheet 28. The Battalion attached to X Corps; to work under C.R.E. 21st Div; and to 39th Div for rations and administration. Casualties: Nil	G.T.J.
Map BELGIUM and FRANCE Sheet 28. Edition 3.	1917 Sept.	23rd	Wind Westerly. Weather Fine. A,B & C Companies and the platoon of D Coy authorised for a Camp at C.T. went to work on the formation and laying of a plank road to be called Plumer's Drive in Sanctuary Wood. They were nominally taken up in Motor lorries but the shelling was so great however that the 17/14 lorries returned after going a short distance and the men had to walk. The Companies arrived back at Camp at 6 p.m. Casualties: 1 O.R wounded remaining at duty.	G.T.J.

WAR DIARY
or
INTELLIGENCE SUMMARY.

(Erase heading not required.)

Army Form C. 2118.

Place	Date	Hour	Summary of Events and Information	Remarks and references to Appendices
1917.	Sept 24		Wind Westerly light. Weather fine Warm	
			A & C companies left Camp at 6 a.m. to work on Plumer's Drive in Sanctuary Wood. They were conveyed part way by Motor Lorries	
			B & 2 Platoons of D. Coy left Camp at 12 noon and were conveyed part way to Sanctuary Wood by Motor Lorries to relieve A & C Companies on making of plank road in SANCTUARY Wood.	
			A & C Coys arrived back at Camp at 2 p.m.	
			B Coy & 2 Platoons of D Coy arrived back at Camp at 9 p.m.	
			Casualties 6 O R's wounded	
			3. O R's wounded remaining at duty.	6 T.J
1917	Sept 25		Wind Changeable S.& SE light Weather fine Warm.	
			A & C Companies left Camp at 6 a.m. to work on Plumer's Drive to SANCTUARY WOOD. They were conveyed part way in MOTOR LORRIES	
			B & 2 Platoons of D Coy left Camp at 12 noon and were conveyed part way by MOTOR LORRIES. They relieved A & C Coys.	
			Progress of work was slow in consequence of having to carry planks over	

WAR DIARY
or
INTELLIGENCE SUMMARY.
(Erase heading not required.)

Army Form C. 2118.

Place	Date	Hour	Summary of Events and Information	Remarks and references to Appendices
			a long way from the Dump to the jobs and also in consequence of hostile artillery barrages put up as a reply to practice barrages by our own troops.	
			Casualties Nil.	
	Sept 26		Wind Southerly light. Weather Fine & Warm (Dull)	65T.1
			In consequence of an impending attack on this front The Battalion did not leave Camp early. A.D.C. & 2 Platoon's J.D. Coy at 1/3rd strength left Camp at 10 a.m. for work on the plank road in SANCTUARY WOOD. They were conveyed part way in Motor lorries.	
			Casualties. 3.6 R's wounded	
			3.6 R's wounded returning at duty.	
			From to-night the Battalion ceases work under Orders of the C.R.E. 21st Divn and comes on to work under the C.R.E. 23rd Division	
	Sept 27		Wind. Westerly Light. Weather Fine	65T.1
			A & C left Camp at 6.30 a.m. and marched to PLUMER DRIVE and carried on with plating of plank road.	

WAR DIARY
or
INTELLIGENCE SUMMARY.
(Erase heading not required.)

Army Form C. 2118.

Place	Date	Hour	Summary of Events and Information	Remarks and references to Appendices
	1917 28th Sept		B & D Companies left Camp at 11-30 a.m. to relieve A & C Coy's on working of Plank road PLUMER DRIVE. Casualties Nil	65J
			Weather Westerly high W. Weather Fine	
			B Coy worked under C.R.E. 23rd Divn. 70ft of Plank Road completed in SANCTUARY WOOD leaving gap of 10ft between work finished 27th inst. 325 Planks carried from dump on Railway to Road.	
			A Coy & 1 Platoon of D Coy working under orders of CRE 5th Australian Division cleaning and repairing MENIN ROAD from the BIRR X Roads forwards for 600ft Eastwards. Work unfinished.	
			C Coy & 1 Platoon of D Coy working as record relief to A Coy.	
			D Coy less 2 Platoons still on detachment working on No 2 C.C. Station at OOSTERSTEENE.	
			Two Officers and 10 NCO's of A Coy still work Divisional HQ for purpose of tracing barrages at Divisional Drawing Ground WIZERNES	
			Casualties - 3 O.R's wounded	

WAR DIARY
or
INTELLIGENCE SUMMARY.

(Erase heading not required.)

Army Form C. 2118.

Place	Date	Hour	Summary of Events and Information	Remarks and references to Appendices
1917	Sept 29th		Wind Northerly light. Weather fine	
			A & C Companies working in two reliefs on repairing and making MENIN ROAD	
			HOOGE. 300x B formation made 100x of plank road laid.	
			B Coy & 2 Platoons of D Coy plus Hqr Pioneers and Joiners on clearing of	
			ground and erection of Nissen huts at H.30.a.5.0. Sheet 28.	
			11 Reinforcements from Base arrived late at night. 2 Platoons D Coy standing	
				W.T.J
			Casualties 1 O.R wounded remained at duty	
1917	Sept 30th		Wind Southerly light Weather fine	
			A Coy less one Platoon repairing plank road through CHATEAU WOOD from G.6.9	
			to J.13.a.9.0.9.B. 3 heavy plank constructed 1 bonneoa 1 partly bonneoa	
			Cleared the junction of the road with MENIN ROAD.	
			A Coy 1 Platoon constructed a gun track for No 25 Battery in J.7.c back	
			completed.	
			B. Coy worked on HOOGE DIVERSION. 100x of plank slabbing completed.	
			C. Coy work on 400x of Mule Track J.B. Central to P of POLYGONEVELD. They	
			worked for 35 minutes. The reason for the job not being worked on longer	

Army Form C. 2118.

WAR DIARY
or
INTELLIGENCE SUMMARY.
(Erase heading not required.)

Place	Date	Hour	Summary of Events and Information	Remarks and references to Appendices
1919	Sept 30		was in occupation of heavy shell fire. The Company worked the above Eng'rk of time under shell fire. When the Company had casualties the Company Commander withdrew the Company. He then decided to send back the Company less 20 men. He kept these men with him for 1½ hours. The shelling did not abate. He then decided to abandon the job for the day. Two Platoons of D. Coy in erection of barbed wire in front of Ground ? Sandbagging at Dw. Hq H.30.a.5.0. Casualties. 2 O.R'S Killed. 5 Wounded of which 2 remained at duty.	[illegible]

J Johnstone
Lieut Colonel
Commanding 24th Bn The Manchester Regiment
7th Divisional Pioneers

Army Form C. 2118.

24(S) Bn. The Manchester Regiment
(7th) Divisional Pioneers

Vol XXIV

WAR DIARY or INTELLIGENCE SUMMARY
(Erase heading not required.)

Place	Date	Hour	Summary of Events and Information	Remarks and references to Appendices
1917 BELGIUM & FRANCE SHEET 2B.	Oct 1st MAR. 60h 1st	1st	Weather Fine. Wind Southerly light. A Coy on repair of GLENCORSE TRACK. The Company commenced to repair track but was shelled off. Carried 130 Trench boards to N. end of PLUMER DRIVE. Run shelled off. B Coy on formation and slabbing of HOOGE DIVERSION. Worked on 50" of formation. Company had to be withdrawn in consequence of hostile shelling. Three attempts were made to get back to work. C Coy carrying Trench boards to make POLYGONEVELD TRACK. 100 Trench boards carried from H. in HOOGE to J.8.b.5.2 (near Bn Hq.) and 100 yards from X roads J.7.d.89.13. Enemy counter barrage prevented any more journeys. The Company was congratulated by the C.R.E. 7th Div. who saw them attempting to get through the barrage. D Coy Two Platoons on work at Divisional Hq. erecting Nissan Huts. D Coy less Two Platoons on detachment at OUTERSTEENE, evidence of remark wards at C.C.S. Casualties { 1 Officer wounded 1 Other wounded remaining at duty 5 O.R's wounded 6 O.R's wounded remaining at duty }	VA24 611

Place	Date	Hour	Summary of Events and Information	Remarks and references to Appendices
1917	2nd	6 p.m.	Weather Fine. Wind Southerly light	

A Coy on formation of a double track from J.13.a.35.35 to T.14.a.50.40 1200ˣ long
Carried up and laid on the track 400 Trench Boards = 800ˣ

B Coy on making track and placing and fixing Notice Boards. Carried 100 boards from HODGE to J.9.a.11. Trackéd out track from HODGE to J.9.99.15. just short of front line. The track is now through to the front. 6 C.B. Coy reported that the metalled road on the N. side of POLYGON WOOD is impassable for R.F.A.

C Coy making Infantry Track. Commenced and finished widening Infantry Track 6ft wide running from I.18.60.3 to and joining the CHATEAU WOOD at I.18.6.4.8

D Coy. Two platoons carrying up and erecting notice Boards WARRINGTON ROAD & "ZEBRA" TRACK. 9ʳˢ Bde, 20ᵗʰ BC, 7ᵗʰ Div.
Pioneers and Company Jones made 20 Notice boards "7 Div TRACK" 32 9ʳˢ Bde.
26. 20 Bde.

D Coy less two platoons arrived from detachment at OUTERSTEENE

WAR DIARY
or
INTELLIGENCE SUMMARY
(Erase heading not required.)

Army Form C. 2118.

Place	Date	Hour	Summary of Events and Information	Remarks and references to Appendices
1917	2nd	10b	Casualties 1 O.R. Killed	
			3 O.Rs wounded	
			3 O.Rs wounded remaining at duty	G.S.I.
1917.	3rd	Cold.	Weather. Some Rain. Wind. S. Westerly fresh	
			A & B Coys + 2 Platoons of C Coy waiting in view of pending Operations	
			C Coy on Platoon placing Notice & direction boards along Infantry Path	
			running from about I.13.b.29 and joining CHATEAU WOOD ROAD about I.13.b.5.8	
			D Coy in formation of 9th Suff Bn. Was between the points and covered	
			R.E's to place track boards in position.	
			1 NCO and party of 20 men as looking party at Divisional Hq. all day.	
			Casualties 1 O.R. missing (afward wounded)	
			7 O.R's wounded.	
			5 O.R's wounded remaining at duty.	G.S.I.

WAR DIARY
or
INTELLIGENCE SUMMARY.
(Erase heading not required.)

Army Form C. 2118.

Place	Date	Hour	Summary of Events and Information	Remarks and references to Appendices
1917	4th Oct.		Weather Damp some rain.	
			Nights of 3rd & 4th Cold Rain.	
			Wind S. Westerly. Breezy.	
			1. Platoon on maintenance of 91st Infy Bgds Track during the time the attacking troops	
			were going up to the position of assembly. (A Coy)	
			1. Platoon on maintenance of 20th Infy Bde Track during the time its attacking troops	
			were going up to the position of assembly. (B Coy)	
			After the last Battalion of each Bde had gone along the tracks respectively these two	
			platoons were withdrawn to the billets in the huts/tents on the East side of ZILLEBEKE	
			Lake which had been taken up by A Coy + 1 Platoon of C Coy and 1B Coy + 1 Platoon of	
			C Coy.	
			A + B Coys were not required for work by the Bdes during the morning of the 4th so	
			the two platoons of C. Coy were withdrawn leaving A + B Coy's intact. A Coy attached	
			to 91st Bde & B Coy attached to 20th Bde and . C + D Watch for Divisional Move.	
			After the Divisional troops had reached their objectives	
			C Coy on repair maintenance and improvement by reliefs of 4 hours 1 Platoon	
			to relief.	

WAR DIARY or INTELLIGENCE SUMMARY

Army Form C. 2118.

Place	Date	Hour	Summary of Events and Information	Remarks and references to Appendices
	1917 5th October		D Coy on repair maintenance and improvement by relief of 4 hours. 1 Platoon in relief.	
			B Company (under orders of 20th Infy Bde) on Forward Tracks. Carried out 20 Infy Bde Track from H+0.5.0 to J5 Central along the roads passing N.E. corner of POLYGON WOOD along utilizing road to J5.C.1.5 and thence to J5.a.6.2. This road was shown because (i) Off the road the ground is impassable (ii) 20th Bde side clipped 200xK N. un enquiring & being pushed by the 91st Bde who in turn had been pushed by 21st Divn. This road does not go to Battalion Hq. because they are closer at the Butt at POLYGON. Work was carried on under exceptionally severe circumstances. Ground very bad. Nearly knee deep in mud. Track passable for mules.	
			A Company (under orders of 91st Infy Bde) were not permitted to go out.	
			Casualties. 3 O.R's killed.	
			8 O.R's wounded	
			Weather. Rain Wind. Westerly. Fairly strong.	G.T.J.
			1 N.C.O and 20 O.R's of the 113 draft and an leading party to D.W. Wg	
			1 officer and 20 O.R.S of the 113 draft sent to LA CLYTTE loaded 1340 Mule Deck Mate	

Army Form C. 2118.

WAR DIARY
or
INTELLIGENCE SUMMARY.
(Erase heading not required.)

Instructions regarding War Diaries and Intelligence Summaries are contained in F. S. Regs., Part II. and the Staff Manual respectively. Title pages will be prepared in manuscript.

Place	Date	Hour	Summary of Events and Information	Remarks and references to Appendices
			On 1st Major Lewis guided to HOOGE DUMP and unloaded.	
			1 N.C.O. and 8 men of new draft of 113 reported to No 6. Supply Co. R.E. yesterday for duty being at POLYGON BUTT. The N.C.O. returned to camp and stated that the party were carried on to the job being Coy in every lorry. The R.E. Sergt. in charge was badly wounded during last night and that no other person knew the location of the job.	
			1 Platoon of C Coy. on maintenance and improvement of 20th Sept. Bde track to Jerichodway. Enemy position. 6A.D. to 10A.D. 100 Trench boards carried from CHATEAU WOOD to JARGON CORNER and laid. 500' half repaired.	
			C Coy on formation and laying fats on a rest gule track. The Company worked by Reliefs 1 Platoon at a time 4 hours each. Carried gule track mats from HOOGE DUMP to truck at J.B.C.C.A. formation of 109* of double track laid.	
			A Coy attached of 9th I.M. Bde to look to tracks.	
			D Coy on maintenance and improvement of 9th Sept Bde track. Worked by Reliefs. 356 Trench boards carried and laid along track. The track was passable and hand mats carried from the MENIN ROAD to beyond GLENCORSE WOOD.	
			Joined up to A Coy working in forward tracks.	

WAR DIARY
OR
INTELLIGENCE SUMMARY.
(Erase heading not required.)

Army Form C. 2118.

Place	Date	Hour	Summary of Events and Information	Remarks and references to Appendices
			A. Coy (under 91st Infy Bde) in maintenance and improvement by adding of 91st Infy Bde track forward for D Coy 3EB Dumps laid along track. These tracks carried from HOOGE DUMP. also through NONNE BOSSCHEN VALLEY.	
			B. Coy (under 20th Infy Bde) No work for them.	
			A & B Coys were relieved from attachment from the 91st and 20th Infy Bdes respectively. They return to the Battalion for work orders but are remaining in attachment at ZILLEBEKE LAKE.	
			Extract from Battalion Orders.	
			"MESSAGE OF" The G.O.C. 7th Division wishes it to be known how very greatly he	
			"APPRECIATES" appreciates the admirable manner in which all ranks in the Battalion have accomplished their arduous work in the section during the last	
			" fortnight.	
			" The above appreciation is to be made known to all ranks of the	
			" Battalion.	
			Casualties 1. O.R. killed 1. O.R. wounded 3. O.R's missing believed wounded	These casualties refer to those occurred yesterday in addition to those enumerated under date 15. 4/10/17

Army Form C. 2118.

WAR DIARY
or
INTELLIGENCE SUMMARY.

(Erase heading not required.)

Instructions regarding War Diaries and Intelligence Summaries are contained in F. S. Regs., Part II. and the Staff Manual respectively. Title pages will be prepared in manuscript.

Place	Date	Hour	Summary of Events and Information	Remarks and references to Appendices
1917.	Oct 6th		Weather. Damp and cold. Wind Variable Gusty	
			NEW GLENCORSE WOOD TRACK. Gun Company worked on formation, moved a dump and laid 40x-50x of Beams. (C.Coy)	
			MULE TRACK. Making mule track J.7.d.8.2 - J.8.c.2.3. Relaid 100x of track and continued track for another 250x. Carried up 250 Mule Track Beams. Track is now complete from about J.7.d.8.2. to J.8.c.2.3. Carrying party stopped for 30 mins owing to heavy barrage 10.45 - 11.15 a.m. (D.Coy)	
			Div. Hq: 1 N.C.O. 20 O.R's reported at Div: Hq: for loading.	
			Gl. Infy Bde Track. Carried up 34 Bundles of Facines and 230 Trench Mats and got the track ready up to POLYGONVELT B.C. (A.Coy).	
			Casualties 3 O. R's killed	6 S. I.
			5 O. R's wounded	
1917	Oct 7th		Weather Wet. Wind Westerly Strong.	
			NEW GLENCORSE PLANK ROAD.	
			Div. Hq: Loading Party 1 N.C.O. 20 O.R.S.	
			J.13.a.50.85. Gun Officer 26 O.R's and 4 Machine Guns Lewis. Protection of J.7."	

WAR DIARY
INTELLIGENCE SUMMARY

Army Form C. 2118.

Place	Date	Hour	Summary of Events and Information	Remarks and references to Appendices
1917	Oct. 7th		Divisional Artillery against hostile Aircraft since 3rd October 1917. 6A Clyde DUMP to I.12.c.WESTHOEK Road loading to G.S. Waggons with Fascines and Corded Rope. On waggons were unable to proceed further than WESTHOEK Road. 9th Duty Bde. Track. Maintenance and improvement of Track. 104 Trench boards carried up from HOOGE DUMP and laid in Track at about 200x from NONNE BOSSCHEN J.9.c.1.4. A few were laid in GLENCORSE WOOD. 25 Fascines were carried up from MENIN ROAD to J.8.c.5.1. Party delayed by Shell fire 11-11.30 a.m. MULETRACK Carried from HOOGE DUMP to J.8.c.8.6. Trench Track Boards. Laid their from that point for about 62x (date) & 89.1-7. 54 of the Party were unable to get any more loads up because of Hostile Shelling of CHATEAU WOOD TRACK from 9.50 a.m. to 10.5 a.m. & 10.15 a.m. until Party was withdrawn. 2 Relief carried 150 Track boards from HOOGE DUMP to J.8 at J.8.c.8.6. No boards were laid because of shelling until the party left at 4.15 P.M. Hours worked 4. Casualties 1.O.R. wounded	WJT

WAR DIARY or INTELLIGENCE SUMMARY

Army Form C. 2118.

Place	Date	Hour	Summary of Events and Information	Remarks and references to Appendices
197	8th	6 p	Wind Westerly. Weather wet.	
			Div. Hq. Loading Party 1 N.C.O. & 20 O.R's	
			LA CLYTTE DUMP to WESTHOEK RD. Loaded 4 G.S. Waggons with 100 Fascines and	
			Carried Same.	
			J.13.9.50.85 1 Officer 26 OR's and 4 Lewis Guns. Protection of 7th Div. Artillery	
			against Hostile Aircraft.	
			Mule Track Formation and Slabbing. Carried up 188 Mule Track Mats to	
			Track at J.8.b. also carried 54 Mats from MENIN ROAD to CHATEAU	
			WOOD and 21 Fascines from BIRR X ROADS to CHATEAU WOOD. Laid	
			140* of track to J.8.a.0.5.	
			GLENCORSE WAY TRACK Slabbing and Formation. 50x slabbing completed on	
			Track J.14.c.5.5. 2nd Party worked the whole line in the formation. Shelling	
			intermittent throughout the whole day. Party Shelled off 3 times	
			Casualties 1 OR wounded	OTJ

WAR DIARY
or
INTELLIGENCE SUMMARY.
(Erase heading not required.)

Army Form C. 2118.

Place	Date	Hour	Summary of Events and Information	Remarks and references to Appendices
1917	9th Octr		Wind S. Westerly Weather Wet	
			Divn Hqs. Loading Party. 1 N.C.O. + 20 O.R's.	
			LA CLYTTE DUMP Loaded 4.G.S. Waggons with Scrim?? The waggons were returned in	
			transport lines loaded ready to be up early on the 10th	
			J.13.a.50.85. 1 Officer 26 O.R's + 4 Lewis Guns positions of 7th D.W. Artillery	
			against Hostile Aircraft	
			CHATEAU ROAD – MENIN ROAD JUNCTION. 1st Relief. A big reference CHATEAU ROAD at	
			I.16.b.16. Birrga Road — cleared dump at confluence of CHATEAU ROAD	
			+ HOOGE Diversion at I.8c.9.6 and built piers to carry road across the	
			corner 20' Ft. (Slab) made on MENIN ROAD (I.18.a.9.6) between HOOGE	
			CRATER.	
			2nd Relief. Carried 200 Slabs from BIRR X Roads to it. jct. had 55' of plank	
			road from I.18.b.8.5 to about I.18.b.9.5 (C Coy)	
			HOOGE DEVIATION. B Coy. 1st Relief. 200 Slabs carried from various points	
			between HOOGE CRATER and BIRR X roads.	
			I.18.b.2.8 and turning point at I.18.a.9.5.8 Ben platelets - 40×	

Army Form C. 2118.

WAR DIARY
or
INTELLIGENCE SUMMARY.
(Erase heading not required.)

Instructions regarding War Diaries and Intelligence Summaries are contained in F. S. Regs., Part II and the Staff Manual respectively. Title pages will be prepared in manuscript.

Place	Date	Hour	Summary of Events and Information	Remarks and references to Appendices
1917	9th	10 AM	Slab Track completed along N. side MENIN ROAD from turning point to Ambulance Car Stand against HOOGECRATER. "B"	
			2nd RELIEF D Coy. Carried 200 road slabs from BIRR X ROADS to HOOGE	
			DIVERSION. (These slabs were laid by the 95th Coy R.E.)	
			Casualties Nil.	G.T.J.
1917	10th		Wind S.W. Light. Weather Sunshine	
			Div. Hq. Loading Party. 1. N.C.O and 20 O.R's.	
			4, CLYTTE DUMP to MULETRACK. Loaded 130 Mule Track Mats on 4 G.S. Waggons. Waggons were taken to transport lines and retained there until tomorrow	
			A Coy. Repaired track and laid 65ft new slab track at HOOGE (I.18.a.9.6.) also carried up the slabs from BIRR X ROADS (3 Platoons)	
			1 Platoon made a Gun track for 25th Battery R.F.A. 200ft long at J.7.a.05.35.	
			C Coy. on MULETRACK. 65ft to track. And using a large number of Fascines Road work Track which had been damaged by shell fire. Carried Fascines from WESTHOEK near BIRR X ROADS also Slab boards from HOOGE DUMP to track 7P.	
			D Coy. 49 slabs were carried up from HOOGE DUMP BIRR X ROADS to GLENCORSE	

WAR DIARY
or
INTELLIGENCE SUMMARY.

(Erase heading not required.)

Army Form C. 2118.

Place	Date	Hour	Summary of Events and Information	Remarks and references to Appendices
	1917.		WAY ROAD at J.14.a.9.7. 115 feet of roadway laid from the joint forward. Park also making formation.	
			B Coy in readiness providing Sunday loading parties etc.	
			B Coy late in the day taped 9½" duty Bn. track towards front line from the east of the Trench Boards to the BUTTE de POLYGON.	
			B Coy provided 1 Officer 6 NCO & 20 men loads under cover from A.P.M. 7th	G.T.J.
			Div. for Pioquits & guiding relieving Bagages.	
			Casualty Nil	
	11th October		Wind N. Westerly. Weather Some rain.	
			A Coy carried two loads 107 Hurdles from BIRR X ROADS to GLENCORSE WAY TRACK.	
			B Coy constructed Gun Track & extricating the 105 Batty R.F.A. (8 Guns) and a	
			4.5 How Batty. As its 20 men detailed were insufficient for itself & the	
			O.C. Company put all available men on the job and both teams of carrying	
			D Coy Carried 110 slats from BIRR X Roads to GLENCORSE WAY TRACK	
			C Coy resting in Camp as bivouacs were wet.	
			Casualty Nil	D.I.

WAR DIARY or INTELLIGENCE SUMMARY

Army Form C. 2118.

Place	Date	Hour	Summary of Events and Information	Remarks and references to Appendices
1917	Oct 11	11am	Moved The Battalion rec'd orders to move the whole on for Instructions from X Corps Commander. The present Camp now in IX Corps Area and the Latter adjusts to the Bn being in their area whilst working for X Corps. Old Camp Map Reference N 5 d.3.6. New Camp N 10 b.9.6.	G.T.J.
1917	Oct 12		Wind Westerly, high. Weather Rain. The Battalion given a Day off to get a camp as the place allotted yesterday was a Corn field. C Coy who rested yesterday 3 Platoons carrying slabs. 70 carried from HODGE DUMP to GLENCORSE WAY TRACK. C Coy Gun Platoon on fireston and stabling in two places a Track 150' at J.7.c.84. 1 Officer, 2 N.C.O.S. 30 O.R.S. Wheat R.F.A. Battery length of Track. DUMP from 70 A.M. until 1.30 P.M. Working Party Worked as Party from X Corps. Lorries did not turn up so party withdrawn. Cagnicourt N.L.	G.T.J.

WAR DIARY
or
INTELLIGENCE SUMMARY.
(Erase heading not required.)

Army Form C. 2118.

Place	Date	Hour	Summary of Events and Information	Remarks and references to Appendices
1917	Octr	13th	Wind Westerly light Weather rain	
			"A" Coy carried 104 slabs on to GLENCORSE WAY. 83.g.1. above slabs were taken away by the 106 Battery R.F.A.	
			1 Officer & 25 O.R's reported to 106 Battery R.F.A. Made a slab road from GLENCORSE way to the Battery	
			B. Coy carried 66 slabs from BIRR X Roads I.7.b.2.8. to roadhead GLENCORSE WAY. J.14.b.0.9.	
			C. Coy carried from BIRR X Roads to GLENCORSE WAY ROAD 72 Slabs. Provided Guides for 6th Bn Leicesters to take them to GLENCORSE WAY Road.	
			1 Officer, 3 N.C.O's and 40 O.R's loading party at LA CLYTTE DUMP, guiding lorries to BIRR X Roads and unloading.	GTJ
1917	Octr	14.	Wind Westerly light Weather fair	
			B. Coy on GLENCORSE WAY ROAD carried 85 Slabs from BIRR X ROADS Co. J.14.b.0.9.	
			C. Coy " " 82 HODGE DUMP	
			D " " 96 to GLENCORSE WAY ROAD	

Army Form C. 2118.

WAR DIARY
or
INTELLIGENCE SUMMARY.
(Erase heading not required.)

Instructions regarding War Diaries and Intelligence Summaries are contained in F. S. Regs., Part II. and the Staff Manual respectively. Title pages will be prepared in manuscript.

Place	Date	Hour	Summary of Events and Information	Remarks and references to Appendices
1917	Oct	14	LA CLYTTE LOADING Party. loaded 29 Waggons at LA CLYTTE as under	
			24 Waggons with Slabs 40 each 960 16 Officers	
			5 " half logs 40 " 200 2 NCOs	
			1160 40 Privates	
			Antoana at T.18.a.40.65.	
			No.6 SIEGE Co. R.M.R.E. 1 NCO + 10 men guarding and unloading waggons. 6 waggons	
			guard from Siege Co Camp to BIRR X Roads, thols unloaded. G.S. Waggons guard	
			to LA CLYTTE, reloaded and returned to Siege Co Camp ready for the morning	
			of the 15th.	
			Copy Correspondence	Headquarters 4657.A 7 Division
			Headquarters	
			Second Army	
			1136 Other ranks have this day been placed under orders of the 24th (Pioneer)	
			Battalion Manchester Regiment, 7th Division I. Corps.	
			These men are ex R.E. who have been specially transferred to Infantry	
			Pioneer Battalions.	
			On their arrival an equal number of men now serving with the	

WAR DIARY
or
INTELLIGENCE SUMMARY.

Army Form C. 2118.

Place	Date	Hour	Summary of Events and Information	Remarks and references to Appendices
	14/9/17		Battalion on to be posted and sent as follows :-	
			50 to 2/7 Manchester Regiment 66th Division 2nd ANZAC CORPS	
			63 to 2/5 " " " "	
			Nominal rolls of men dispatched under the order should accompany them.	
			Copies being sent to this office.	
			G.H.Q. 3rd Ech	
	26.9.17		(Sd) C Maxwell Jones Lt-Col A.A.G	
			for Major-General Deputy Adjt-Genl	
			(2)	
	Headquarters X Corps		For information.	
			(Sd) C Maxwell Jones Lt-Col A.A.G.	
	26.9.17		for Major General Deputy Adjt Genl	
			X Corps No 28/91A	
	7th Division		For information and necessary action	
			(Sd) J Squires Major	
	28.9.17		DAAG X Corps	

WAR DIARY
or
INTELLIGENCE SUMMARY.
(Erase heading not required.)

Army Form C. 2118.

Place	Date	Hour	Summary of Events and Information	Remarks and references to Appendices
1917 Oct	14		24th Manchester Regt.	
			In preparation	
			Their army despatch of the 113 men to 66 Division Railway, and	
			under copy of nominal roll through this office	
	29.9.17		A.C.W.Chichester Major DAAG. 7th Division	
			Headquarters 4657A 7th Division	
			Headquarters Second ARMY.	
			265 StaffClerks have this day been placed under orders for 14.24	
			(Pioneer) Battalion Manchester Regiment 7th Division X Corps.	
			These men are R.E. who have been specially transferred to Infantry Pioneer Battalions	
			On their arrival an equal number of men was carrying with the	
			Battalion are to be posted and sent as follows:—	
			50.6.14.20 13th Manchester Regt. 7th Division X Corps	

WAR DIARY
or
INTELLIGENCE SUMMARY
(Erase heading not required.)

Army Form C. 2118.

Place	Date	Hour	Summary of Events and Information	Remarks and references to Appendices
			50 to the 21st Br Manchester Regiment 7th Divn X Corps	
			60 " " 22nd " " " " " "	
			60 " " 18th " " " " " VIII "	
			65 " " 19th " " " " 30 " VIII "	
			Nominal Rolls of men despatches under this cover should accompany	
			them copies being sent to this office.	
	2/10/17			
			Headquarters 7th Division	
			For information	
	3rd Ech. 2/10/17		(Sd) C Manuel Smith	
			Lt Col	
			for Major General	
			Deputy Adjutant General	
	2/4th Manchesters		In information since action.	
			Copy of Nominal rolls to be forwarded to this office asap	
			A.F.W. Chichester Major	
			D.A.A.G 7th Division	

WAR DIARY
or
INTELLIGENCE SUMMARY

Army Form C. 2118.

Place	Date	Hour	Summary of Events and Information	Remarks and references to Appendices

Headquarters
7th Division

Reference your 465/A of 29.9.17 and 465/A of 4.10.17 and copies of D.A.G's instructions contained thereon.

I desire to point out that the carrying out of the instructions will mean the complete evisceration of the Battalion under my command for the following reasons:-

The instructions are to send away to seven different units belonging to three different Divisions 37 B of the men at present serving with my battalion.

The units together with the 80 casualties which have occurred over the last course, include the line here would extract the whole of the working strength of the Battalion, leaving only a number of Senior N.C.O's, the Transport section and the Specialists.

The 37 B men I am instructed to take on are wholly untrained and undisciplined and their physical standard is too low. None have been across before & apparently low category men who have been kept at home to do work of various sorts in the Army. They do not possess the rudiments of a military training.

WAR DIARY
or
INTELLIGENCE SUMMARY

Army Form C. 2118.

training, have had no musketry training instruction, and scarcely know how to salute. They are called "Sappers" but certainly have no right to the name. I state this of my own knowledge, having personally examined 113 men of the draft who have been sent on to me. The behaviour of these men has been solid and was found to be very unsatisfactory.

I need scarcely say that, on the very difficult nature of its work which the Pioneers of the 7th Division are being called upon to do at the present time. It is work that demands the very highest form of intelligence and of physical fitness. This qualities the Battalion was, 79 Company have always itself to possess, but if the 7th were all drafted out and the new ones taken in, the standard of the work would be reduced to that of a training Battalion at home. To put it quite bluntly I could not guarantee to do the work we are doing with such a battalion.

I would draw attention to the fact that the excellent esprit de corps at present existing in the battalion, and the satisfactory way in which it has hitherto answered all its calls made upon it, are mainly due to the constitution

Army Form C. 2118.

WAR DIARY
or
INTELLIGENCE SUMMARY.
(Erase heading not required.)

Place	Date	Hour	Summary of Events and Information	Remarks and references to Appendices
			of the Unit which was originally recruited from a single town and has since largely drawn its reinforcements from the same quarter. At present there is perfect confidence and understanding between all ranks but this would entirely cease if the drafting instructions of the D.A.G. assumed not I want to wipe the force in the strongest point it names the contributors may be imited with a view to the recognition's being not drawn. (sg) J.S. Loveling Lieut Colonel Commanding 24th Bn. The Manchester Regiment (7th Divisional Troops)	
	10/10/17			
			A.568. 13th Reference my no 4657/A of 29th ult and Divnl number of the inst a.a.a Transfer of the numbers detailed for 20, 21, and 22. Manchesters should proceed forthwith by earmarkment with C.o.S. concerned a.a.a. Unless already despatched please delay despatch of numbers 6, 2/5, 2/7, 18, 9, 19, 17 pendulating till further orders a.a.a. Report of the 265 mentioned in my above number 6/4 wish have not been received and if not when you would like have send. J.Rose T.	

WAR DIARY or INTELLIGENCE SUMMARY

Army Form C. 2118.

To. 7th Division "A"

W.428. 13th. A.568

Numbers detailed for 20, 21, and 22 Manchesters will proceed to-morrow a.m.

Numbers for other Bns will be detailed the further notice. Shall each be warned?

100 to R.E. men now at Reinforcement Camp - also any of our men that are

Kept remaining 165 to R.E.'s at Reinforcement Camp

24th Manchesters.

A.J.G. Webb
2.35 P.M. Capt. A/

22nd Infantry Brigade
9th Infantry Brigade
7th Division "A" (for information)

Reference 7th Division 4657/A dated 29/9/17

140 Other Ranks of this Unit posted as under by orders of D.A.G.

to 20 Bn. 22nd Inf. Bde. 50.O.R.
to 21 " 9 " " 50.O.R.
to 22 " 9 " " 40.O.R.

WAR DIARY
or
INTELLIGENCE SUMMARY.
(Erase heading not required.)

Army Form C. 2118.

Place	Date	Hour	Summary of Events and Information	Remarks and references to Appendices
			normal rolls and conduct sheets known it	
			(2) This gun proceeded to join other Battalions this day adjutant is 16th Division.	
			(3) Please acknowledge receipt of men and Conduct Sheets.	
			(sd) F.S. Fanling Lieut Colonel Commanding 24 Bn Queensland Regiment	S.I.
	14/10/1917			
	1917 Oct		Wind Westerly light. Weather Fair.	
	15		A Coy worked in formation of GLENCORSE WAYTRACK. Worked on 100ˣ of track formation (R Hand Side) of which 20ˣ was completed to half width 15'.	
			C Coy carried 90 slabs from The CULVERT TENIN ROAD to roadhead GLENCORSE WAYTRACK.	
			D Coy carried 91 slabs from BIRR X Roads to roadhead GLENCORSE WAY-TRACK.	
			20 Men D Coy made Gun Trench position and got guns into position for 105 Bty at T.14.c.85.40.	
			One Officer 3 NCO's and 40 men board 30 lorries at LA CLYTTE with 40 slabs each	

WAR DIARY
or
INTELLIGENCE SUMMARY.
(Erase heading not required.)

Army Form C. 2118.

Place	Date	Hour	Summary of Events and Information	Remarks and references to Appendices
	1917 Oct. 16th	12:00	Unloaded the order HOOGE CRATER.	
			1 NCO and 10 men guided 6 G.S. Waggons from No 6 C RMRE Camp to BIRR X Roads with Slabs. Unloaded slabs and guided waggons back to Lt CLYTTE. Received waggons ready for to-morrow	
			4 G.S. Waggons an run transport took slabs to junction of CHATEAU WOOD ROAD and JABBER DRIVE. Waggons reloaded and returned in transport lines.	
			2 NCO's and 6 men in two relief on guard at BIRR X ROADS SLAB DUMP	
			2 " " " " " " WESTHOEK	ATJ
			Casualties Nil	
			Wind: Westerly Weather Fair	
			A Coy worked on 130° of GLENCORSE WAY TRACK formation (R hand side) about J8a.30.20 to J8a.60.30. Now complete	
			6 Coy carried up 70 slabs from BIRR X Roads to roadhead GLENCORSE WAYTRACK	
			D " " 75 " " " " " " "	
			Gui Offer 3 NCO's & 40 men with slab lorries as yesterday	
			RMRE waggons and an transport waggons & Guards as yesterday	

WAR DIARY
or
INTELLIGENCE SUMMARY.
(Erase heading not required.)

Army Form C. 2118.

Place	Date	Hour	Summary of Events and Information	Remarks and references to Appendices
	1917 Oct	16	Casualties 1 OR wounded	651
	1917 Oct	17th	Wind Westerly Weather Showery	
			A Coy worked on 150x of track from GLENCORSE WAY TRACK (R'Side) 110x completed	
			TBM 30.20 to 18a.60.30.	
			B Coy carried 80 slats from HOOGE DUMP to T'06.	
			C Coy " " 80 " " "	
			Gun track 12 men of B Coy under Sun Smith and returned team from trucks	
			for 106 Batty 7A at 17.a.0.0.	
			1.GH 3 NCOs & OR's loaded & lorries as usual.	
			R T R E waggons Transport waggons and Guards as previously	
			Casualties 1 OR Missing	
			1. OR wounded remaining at duty	651
	1917 Oct	18	Wind Westerly light Weather fair	
			The Battalion rested. Parades Inspection parades by Company	
			Casualties N.L	651

WAR DIARY
or
INTELLIGENCE SUMMARY.

Army Form C. 2118.

Place	Date	Hour	Summary of Events and Information	Remarks and references to Appendices
	1917 Oct	19	Wind S. Westerly light. Weather - Showery. The Battalion rested. Inspection Parades by Companies. Casualties Nil.	
	1917 Oct	20th	Wind S. Westerly light. Weather Fine. A Coy made permutation on the night of "E" track STIRLING CASTLE to make it into a double track 500ˣ between points T.13.d.80.30. and T.14.c.55.45. B Coy made permutation on the night of E track STIRLING CASTLE to make it into a double track 500ˣ from T.13.A.7.1 towards PLUMER'S DRIVE. C Coy made permutation on night of CLEMSON'S LANE to make it into a double track 400ˣ between points T.30.c.1.9 and T.30.c.8.7. D Coy made permutation for track continuation of CLEMSON'S LANE 400ˣ between points T.25.a.0.3 and T.25.a.5.8. 1 Officer and 146 O.R's put together 150 Trench Boards and laid 450 Trench boards at BRASSERIE DUMP leaving 210 Trench Boards in G.S. waggons. Waggons parked in the Coy. line for the night. Casualties 1.8.R. Killed 1.O.R. dangerously wounded 2 O.R's wounded 5 O.R's wounded remaining at duty.	

Army Form C. 2118.

WAR DIARY
or
INTELLIGENCE SUMMARY.
(Erase heading not required.)

Place	Date	Hour	Summary of Events and Information	Remarks and references to Appendices
			Wind S westerly light. Weather Fine	
1917	6th	21st	A Coy working on 20th Bde Track STIRLING CASTLE to MENIN ROAD. Carried up 97 Trench Mats (wired) and laid 102 in leavers (naked)	
			B Coy working on 20th Bde Track. Formation made 300' long x 5' wide x 1½' high in Marsh at J.19.a.00.00. 275 boards were carried up and laid by the side of the track. 100 x 1am permanently. All boards (wires) were clear from the dump.	
			C Coy. 3 Platoons starting by on the MONMOUTH ROAD which reconnaissance was made at various dumps for track mats. As none could be found, these 3 Platoons returned to Camp.	
			One Platoon making foundation from point I.30.a.5.1 to point I.30.a.5.3 (distance 50') and joining up to NORLAND AVENUE. Completed ready for track mats. Repairing CLEMSON's LANE from I.30.a.5.1 to I.25.a.3 where blown in since last working party.	
			D Coy. 3 Platoons on CLEMSON's LANE. 1 Platoon repairing formation which was made yesterday. Two Platoons returned to Camp as there were no track mats in the vicinity.	

WAR DIARY or INTELLIGENCE SUMMARY

Army Form C. 2118.

Place	Date	Hour	Summary of Events and Information	Remarks and references to Appendices
1917	Oct 21		Loaded 3 lorries with Grating Trench Mats 240 and guided and unloaded them at Track E.1/80.	
			1 Officer and 36 O.R's constructed 45 Gratings Trench mats of all available timber at BRASSERIE DUMP wind calm.	
			Casualties Nil.	
			Wind Westerly light. Weather fair.	65.T.J
1917	Oct 22		A Coy carried up 140 Trench Mats from MORLAND AVENUE to J.20.d.20.6.9. and laid a track from Track "A" about J.20.b.18.20 to Bn Hq about J.20.d.20.69. continued it to "Tens Bn" Hq at about J.20.d.22.60. Laid 120 Mats Tap & a dump of 20 mats.	
			B Coy carried up a load of Trench Boards to A Coy's post from 1th. bottom of MORLAND AVENUE after which B Coy carried on to STIRLING CASTLE "E" Track and laid 167 Trench Mats also carried up to this pt a further 25 Mats from PLUMERS DRIVE	
			D Coy loaded 6 G.S Waggons with 45 wired trench boards and 165 other mats at BRASSERIE DUMP. Conducted waggons and unloaded same on 1/2.	
			1 Serg & 30 O.R's leaving party at LA CLYTTE DUMP.	
			Refs 465/7/A. a wire A 679.g. 21st inst. from 7th Div in accordance herewith.	

Wt. W14422/M1160 359,000 12/16 D. D. & L. Forms/C./2118/14.

WAR DIARY
or
INTELLIGENCE SUMMARY.

Army Form C. 2118.

Place	Date	Hour	Summary of Events and Information	Remarks and references to Appendices
	1917 23rd Oct		125 men of this Battalion were sent to the 20th, 21st, 22nd Battalions of the Manchester Regiment	
			Casualties 2 O.R's severely wounded	
			2 O.R's wounded	
			Wind N.W. Visibility light. Weather Rain	
			A Coy carried 58 Trench boards from MANOR DUMP to "A" Track J19a1.5 via 2 loads (87) yds to junction of A & B tracks at J25a.10.95 where a dump was formed to the 227th Field Coy R.E. who were laying the track. A Coy continued its attention to carrying.	
			B Coy laid 200" of Track. The track is now close to within 200" of STIRLING CASTLE. Marked 20th Bn Track with Whiteboards the track crossing through MANOR - VERBRANDEN Rd junc: past MANOR FM: ZILLEBEKE: OBSERVATORY R'd & PLUMERS DRIVE.	
			C Coy carried 66 boards from T28a.2.9 to J19c.6.6. Laid down along Track. Second Carried 66 Track boards from I.30a.0.2 to J19c.3.2. & formed dump.	
			D Coy completed duckboard track from NORLAND AVENUE to "B" Track 254 track boards were carried up and laid also notice boards 9"x10" size Track	

WAR DIARY
or
INTELLIGENCE SUMMARY.

Army Form C. 2118.

Place	Date	Hour	Summary of Events and Information	Remarks and references to Appendices
			carried up and these carried up yesterday were put up along the above	
1917	23rd Oct.		track & also continued for about 400 yards along "B" track	
			6 GS waggons with 175 French boards and 30 cork tracks were conducted from Camp to and unloaded at I.30.a.1.2. The waggons were reloaded with 220 French boards at I.28.a.4.7 & conducted & unloaded at I.30.a.1.2. (The trail was laid up a few yards beyond I.30.a.1.2. The waggon could not proceed further).	
			BRASSERIE DUMP. Loading Party. 3 NCO's 30 OR's.	
			In accordance with 7th Div. wire AQ17 dated 21.10.17 the following men from the Bn were sent to as follows	
			30 to 20th Bn Manchester Regt	
			30 to 21st Bn Manchester Regt	
			23 to 22nd Bn Manchester Regt	
			Casualties. 1 OR Missing	65-1

WAR DIARY
or
INTELLIGENCE SUMMARY.
(Erase heading not required.)

Army Form C. 2118.

Place	Date	Hour	Summary of Events and Information	Remarks and references to Appendices
	1917		Wind N Westerly Weather Rain	
	24th		A Coy carried 196 Duckboards from MANOR RD DUMP to "A" TRACK and laid same along "A" Track (running a double track). Carried 60 of above boards to J.20.d.22.60 & continued track J.20.d.58.40 where the Coy came under direct Rifle and Machine Gun fire and had to stop work. 5. being hit. Boards placed at junction of MIDDLESEX & VERBRANDEN ROADS; MX & KNOLL Roads; KINDERP - MORLAND AVE- junction of A MS Tracks. ½ C Coy attached to A Coy. B Coy carried up and laid 8 Duckboards from VERBRANDEN ROAD to a point just beyond STIRLING CASTLE "E" track and laid in addition about 40 boards taken up yesterday were laid on the track in the rear side of STIRLING CASTLE. 6 Gunto on the track repaired. Two large rubber boards fires at I.28.a.2.9, I.23.c.7.0.55. D. Coy. No work done as immediately the Coy got on the job 18"Jack directed machine gun fire was opened on them. ½ C Coy attached to D Coy.	

WAR DIARY
or
INTELLIGENCE SUMMARY.
(Erase heading not required.)

Army Form C. 2118.

Place	Date	Hour	Summary of Events and Information	Remarks and references to Appendices
	1917 24	6 p.m.	6 G.S. Waggon loads of Trench boards taken up and unloaded at Head of MORLAND AVENUE.	
			3 N.C.O's & 30 O.R's reported at BRASSERIE DUMP at 7.30 p.m. as burying party.	
			Casualties 1 O.R killed	
			2 O.R's wounded	
			1 O.R wounded remaining at duty.	65 T.I
	1917 25th	6 p.m.	Mud wet & light Weather wet	
			2nd Lt MANSFIELD took on duty as Divisional Tramway Officer. 34 O.R's detailed with him for the work as tramway party.	
			4 Officers & 88 O.R's "D" Coy proceeded this evening to CANADA ST dug outs making the forward tracks during the following manner.	
			1 Officer, r10 O.R's + 2 Lewis machine Guns guarding 7" Div Artillery against Hostile Aircraft at J.14.A.87 + J.8.C.61 respectively	
			1 N.C.O and 8 men + 2 Lewis machine Guns guarding Divisional HQ in SCOTTISHWOOD against Hostile Aircraft.	
			D Coy proceeded to CANADA ST Dugout to be prepared	

WAR DIARY
or
INTELLIGENCE SUMMARY.
(Erase heading not required.)

Army Form C. 2118.

Place	Date	Hour	Summary of Events and Information	Remarks and references to Appendices
			BRASSERIE DUMP. 3 NCOs, 30 O.R.'s on loading party	
			A Coy carried up 66 Trench Mats from MANOR ROAD DUMP to Bn Hq at	
			I20d.2.8. 20 Trench Mats laid on track from Bn Hq to Coy Hq at I20d.8.1	
			Owing to barrage nothing else was done	
			B Coy carried 74 Trench Mats from MANOR DUMP to Bn Hq at I21 a 1.9. Heavy	
			hostile shelling interfered with work	
			C Coy carried 77 Trench Mats from I28 a 2.9 to I.B at I20d.5.1 and angle pieces	
			& panel track from I20d.5.1 to I.20d. 8.1 (200")	
			Casualties 3 O.R's wounded.	
			3 O.R's wounded remaining	
			at duty	GSJ
	26th GSJ		Wind Mostly light Weather Very wet	
			D Coy at Canada St Dugouts on repairing tracks	
			B & C Coys in reserve	
			A Coy resting in Camp	

WAR DIARY
or
INTELLIGENCE SUMMARY.
(Erase heading not required.)

Army Form C. 2118.

Place	Date	Hour	Summary of Events and Information	Remarks and references to Appendices
1917	Oct 26		BRASSERIE DUMP. LOADING PARTY 3 N.C.O's. 30 men	
	"		Drainage Party 3 N.C.O's & 50 men.	
	VOORMEZEELE		Divisional Tramways maintenance. 1 Offr. 34 O.R's.	
	SCOTTISHWOOD		Protection of Div Hq. against Hostile Aircraft 1 NCO 8 men and two Lewis Guns	
	T.14.a.8.7 } T.8.c.6.1 }		Protection of 7th Divisional Artillery against Hostile Aircraft. 1 Officer, 100 O.R's and two Lewis Guns.	G.S.I.
			Casualties Nil.	
1917	Oct 27		Wind Southerly Light. Weather Fair.	
	BRASSERIE DUMP.		Loading Party 3 N.C.O, 30 men.	
	BRASSERIE DUMP.		DRAINAGE Party 2 N.C.O's 20 men.	
	VOORMEZEELE.		Divisional Tramways Officer & maintenance party 1 Off & 34 O.R's	
	VOORMEZEELE.		Divisional Tramways. Evacuating wounded in Trolleys 1 NCO & 30 men	
	SCOTTISH WOOD		Protection of Divisional Hq: against Hostile Aircraft 1 NCO 8 men + 2 Lewis Guns	
	T.14.a.8.7 } T.8.c.6.1 }		Protection of 7th Div: Artillery against Hostile Aircraft 1 Off. 100 O.R's + 2 Lewis Guns.	

WAR DIARY or INTELLIGENCE SUMMARY

Army Form C. 2118.

Place	Date	Hour	Summary of Events and Information	Remarks and references to Appendices
1917	Oct 24		B Company "E" Track maintinance party. One load Trench Boards carried from MANOR DUMP to STIRLING CASTLE. 'E' Track 100x of track repaired and Trench Boards laid where track had been blown in. D Coy livin in Canada St Dugouts work as follows	
	25/10/17		Small parts repair to A Track & B Track during the afternoon. All night carried on. from J.20.a.20.90 to within 40x of J.20.d.60.20. Carried up Trench Boards from MORLAND AVENUE to 100 of A gardine Gun situated "B" track so the work had to be done from A track. Bn. Hq towards B. track.	
	26/10/17	16ff	1300 Rs repair A track from J.20.a.60.10 to J.20.b.10.10. (Canad) up 40 Trench boards from MORLAND AVENUE (Track gets blown up every few minutes. 12 D.R's filling in shell holes and repairing road to 91st Bde Hq.	
	27/10/17		One officer & 15 O.R's repaired AID POST in CANADA ST. from J.30.a.50.20 to J.30.a.75.30. Repairs Jump at Bn Hq J.20.d.20.90. One officer and 10 Men repaired A Track from J.20.d.20.90 to J.30.a.75.30. 25 men carried up 50 Trench boards to Bn from MORLAND AVENUE.	

WAR DIARY
or
INTELLIGENCE SUMMARY.
(Erase heading not required.)

Army Form C. 2118.

Place	Date	Hour	Summary of Events and Information	Remarks and references to Appendices
1917	Oct 27		A & C Coy's (right) carried up 64 Trench Boards from Manor Road Dug a mile 3ft deep & 3 ft wide from T.25.a.4.5.7.b to T.25.a.9.5.9.2 about 330ˣ long and laid 78 Trench Boards in above Trench	
			Casualties. 1 O.R. Wounded	
			1 O.R. Wounded remaining at duty	AT1.
1917	Oct 28		Wind. S.W. Light. Weather Fair	
			BRASSERIE DUMP. Loading party. 1 N.C.O. & 30 men.	
			BRASSERIE DUMP. Storeman & Cook relieved to day	
			VOORMEZEELE. Divisional Tramways maintenance 1 Off. & 34 O.R's. This party was relieved today by 39ᵗʰ D.L.I. & has returned to Camp	
			SCOTTISHWOOD. Protection of D.W. Hq. against Hostile Aircraft. 1 N.C.O. 8 men & 2 Lewis Guns.	
			J.14.q.a.8.7 } J.8.c.6.1.5 } Protection of Artillery against hostile Aircraft. 1 Off. 10 O.R's + 2 Lewis Guns	
			D Coy at GONBRAST DUGOUTS 27/10/17 Carried up 65 Trench Mats from MORLAND AVE	

WAR DIARY
or
INTELLIGENCE SUMMARY.

(Erase heading not required.)

Army Form C. 2118.

Place	Date	Hour	Summary of Events and Information	Remarks and references to Appendices
1917	28 Oct		Repaired loop on A Track from J.20a.50.10 to J.20b.10.10.350. Also repaired track between J.30b.10.60 & J.25.a.10.90.	
	28/10/17		16ft 170 ORs repaired "E" Track between J.24c.40.70 and J.14c.45.50	
			16ft 20 ORs repaired A Track between J.20a.50.10 & J.20b.10.10 also loop.	
			16ft 10 men repair to Track from J.25a.10.95 to J.20a.50.00. Surface very heavy firing at the latter point.	
			Casualties Nil.	GTJ
			Wind N.W. fresh. Weather Fair. Sunny.	
1917	Oct 29		"Copy Correspondence	
			"To OC FWD BR. The C.R.E. has not pleasure in forwarding the attached copy of a	
			letter required his swinging from the Division al Commander.	
			J.M.Cliff(?) Capt. R.E.	
			by for Lew-Eng	
			7th Division	
	28.10.17			N.C.883
				28th October 1917
			C.R.E.	
			7th Division	

WAR DIARY
or
INTELLIGENCE SUMMARY.
(Erase heading not required.)

Army Form C. 2118.

Place	Date	Hour	Summary of Events and Information	Remarks and references to Appendices
1917.	Oct. 29th		As I shall have no immediate opportunity of seeing the Field Coys RE & Pioneer Bataln Coy gn to bid them from me how much I appreciate the gallant and good work they have performed during our recent battles. Their work has been unceasing and under the most trying conditions as regards fire and weather, yet they have never once failed to carry out every task allotted to them. I should also like them to know that the Infantry speak in the highest terms of the Excellent roads and tracks which they made. They fully bring up also the great service which the Divisional Royal Engineers and Pioneers the difficult attack and marches we have had to carry out would have been impossible. Sd. H. Shubridge Major General. Commanding 1st D.V.	
1917.	Oct. 30		Wind. SW light Weather Fair The Battalion moved by MARCH ROUTE to ASCOT CAMP WESTOUTRE M.24.6.4	

A6945   Wt. W11422/M1160 350,000 12/16 D. D. & L. Forms/C/2118/14.

Army Form C. 2118.

WAR DIARY
or
INTELLIGENCE SUMMARY.
(Erase heading not required.)

Place	Date	Hour	Summary of Events and Information	Remarks and references to Appendices
	1917		Sheet 27. Canaples N.L.	
	Oct 31st		Wind. S.W. Weather Fair	
			The Battalion rested and were engaged in making arrangements for	OTJ
			Camp	
			Canaples N.L.	

J. Forster
Lieut Colonel
Commanding 24th Battalion The Manchester Regiment
7th Divisional Reserve.

REFERENCE ZILLEBEKE.
1-10,000.

Copy No 6.

3-10-17

SECRET

24th Bn. The Manchester Regt. (7th Divl. Pioneers)
OPERATION ORDERS NO. 1

vide 7th Division Operation Orders. The following will be details of the Battalion.

"A" Coy. will detail one platoon under an Officer for the purpose of keeping in repair the track taken by the 91st Bde., in moving up to its position of assembly. This platoon will be spread out from the beginning of the overland track at I. 13. a. 50.30 to the end of the track about J. 10. a. Central. Care must be taken to place the men where they are most likely to be needed, i.e., at the wettest points in the track. Their duties will be immediately to repair any portion of the track that may become damaged. They will remain at their posts until the last Battalion has moved up, and until the Officer in charge of the platoon gives the order to reform and march away. When reformed the platoon will be brought back to a point in the W. EMBANKMENT of ZILLEBEKE LAKE where the Company to which it belongs will have its Headquarters.

"B" Coy. will furnish a platoon to work as detailed above on the track which will be used by the 20th Bde., between I. 18. b. 0.3. and the POLYGON BUTT at J. 10. a. 60.80. The instructions above given will apply equally to this platoon.

Both platoons when moving up will take with them as many trench boards as they can carry for use in the marshy ground in NONNE BOSSCHEN WOOD and GLENCORSE WOOD i.e.q at any other bad points on the tracks. These platoons will pass Half Way House on their way up not later than 7-0 p.m. Arrangements have been made for "B" Coys., platoon to pick up a party of 9th DEVONS which is to picquet the 20th Bde., track at Half Way House at 6-45 p.m. The men of this party will be placed along the route at the same time as the men of the repair party by the Officer in charge of "B" Coy., platoon. Care should be taken adequately to picquet the track between I. 18. b. 0.3. and the point where it turns into the plank track through CHATEAU WOOD.

These repair platoons will take spades with them and a certain number of wire cutters.

"A" Coy., less one platoon, and plus one platoon to be detailed from "C" Coy., will be attached to the 91st Inf. Bde., for making forward tracks after the objectives of the Bde. has been gained.

"B" Coy., less one platoon, and plus one platoon to be detailed by "C" Coy., will be attached to the 20th Bde., for the same purpose.

"A" Coy., will send an Officer to H.Q., 91st Bde., at HOOGE CRATER at the time arranged to act as liason Officer.

Both "A" and "B" Coys., will arrange to detail two runners who know the way between HOOGE CRATER and ZILLEBEKE LAKE to report two hours before the Zero hour to H.Q. of the Bdes., to which the Coys., are attached at HOOGE CRATER.

"A" and "B" Coys., as constituted above will be quartered temporarily in the vicinity of the Western EMBANKMENT of ZILLEBEKE LAKE. The precise spot will be indicated later. These two Companies will leave camp for their quarters at ZILLEBEKE LAKE at 2-0 a.m. to-morrow.

Tools to be carried. Shovels with a small proportion of picks and some wire cutters, also tapes for marking track. A number of Pickets and Notice Boards have been prepared for marking the tracks and these will be equally divided between the two Coys. A G.S. waggon will be available for taking up tools and pickets to

Sheet 2.

ZILLEBEKE LAKE, also a limbered waggon for taking up rations and sufficient dixies for cooking breakfast and dinner to-morrow. Sufficient cooks for the purpose to be taken.

Dress for these Coys and also for the platoons detailed for repair work will be "Fighting Order" without packs and greatcoats. The cardigan will be carried rolled in the mackintosh sheet. 120 rounds of ammunition per man will be carried.

Five Officers per Coy., will go up, i.e., the O.C. Coy., and one Officer per platoon.

"C" Coy., less two platoons, and "D" Coy., will remain in camp prepared to move at a moment's notice after ZERO HOUR. Dress: as detailed above.

Captain R.V. DAVIDSON is detailed to be attached to A.P.M's Department for traffic control during the operations.

Issued at 4-0 p.m., 3-10-17.

(Signed) W. TAYLOR-JONES, 2/Lieut. and a/Adjutant.

Copy No. 1. Headquarters.
2. O.C. "A" Coy.
3. O.C. "B" "
4. O.C. "C" "
5. O.C. "D" "
6. War Diary.
7. War Diary.

Vol LXXV

WAR DIARY 2/4th (S) Bn The Manchester [Army] Form C. 2118.
or Regiment
INTELLIGENCE SUMMARY. (7th) Divisional Pioneers

Instructions regarding War Diaries and Intelligence
Summaries are contained in F. S. Regs., Part II.
and the Staff Manual respectively. Title pages
will be prepared in manuscript.

(Erase heading not required.)

Place	Date	Hour	Summary of Events and Information	Remarks and references to Appendices
			MAPS. BELGIUM/FRANCE SHEET 28	Vol 25
			LENS 11	
1917	Nov 1st		Wind. S.W. Weather Rain	
			ASCOT CAMP. WESTOUTRE Reorganisation and inspection of Companies	W.T.J
			Casualties Nil.	
1917	Nov 2nd		Wind S. Weather Dull Fine	
			Training by Companies	
			Casualties Nil.	W.T.J
1917	Nov 3rd		Wind S.E light Weather Dull Fine	W.T.J
			Training by Companies	
			Casualties Nil.	
	Nov 4th		Wind E. Weather Duel	6 S.T.J
			Non C.o.E parade service at 9.30 A.M.	
			C.of E Parade service in Camp at 11-45 A.M.	
			C Coy and half of A Coy Struck WOODCAMP NORTH M54.7.9 and loaded	
			Picks Rail boards latrine palisade and duck boards on wagons. Holloways form	
			Wagons and loads in horses Go Lub	
			Cloud West Camp Sept M52.3.6. I half the Coy in same in same as	

A6945. Wt. W14422/M1160 350,000 12/16 D. D. & L. Forms/C/2118/14

WAR DIARY
or
INTELLIGENCE SUMMARY.

Army Form C. 2118.

(Erase heading not required.)

Place	Date	Hour	Summary of Events and Information	Remarks and references to Appendices
			Wind Camp North. There were 80 tents in this Camp. In both cases the material had to be carried a considerable distance to the nearest point to which the transport could get. Erected 20 tents at ZOUCOTE CAMP M.5.a.3-8. Struck 96 tents of CARNARVON CAMP and stacked them ready for transport. Casualties Nil.	QTM
1917 Nov	5th		Wind: S.W. Weather Dull. C Coy. Tents 7 A Coy 6 Off. + 180 O.Rs. (a) Completed the striking of CARNARVON CAMP (M.11.a.1-5) including all latrines and ablution material and loading lorries. There were 60 tents to strike it to be sent. (b) Unloaded the above material and tents at new camp at M.11.a.5.4.9. M.17.a-5.3 also unloaded 50 incinerators from stores at WESTOUTRE. Erected 100 tents at M.17.a.5.4 + 9 100 tents at M.17.a.5.3 Plans all their material in their tents. (c) Erected 106 tents at VICTORIA CAMP (C.34.c.3.3) also latrines.	

WAR DIARY
or
INTELLIGENCE SUMMARY.

(Erase heading not required.)

Army Form C. 2118.

Place	Date	Hour	Summary of Events and Information	Remarks and references to Appendices
1917	Nov 6th		A & C Coy's and Carnotin N.d	
			Wind S.W. Weather Dull.	
			L/Off, 1125 O Rs C Coy's, 3 Offs, 132 O.R's A Coy struck 100 tents at CARNARVON CAMP and had them in lorries also lat loose and a	LSTJ
BELGIUM & FRANCE SHEET 28			aviation material. Unloaded them at ZEVECOTEN CAMP G35A z.u.	
			The British moved from ASCOT CAMP WESTOUTRE to ZEVECOTEN and	
1917	Nov 7th		Jutland Camp at G.35 d 2.4. Carnotin N.d	LSTJ
			Wind S.W. Weather Showery	
			A Coy filled 1000 Sandbags with Sandners from IX Corps dump, loaned 1500 Sandbags at IX & SDT Sandbags at X Corps dump. also loaded 18	
			lorries to carts from our I trench Gds 13 Entrance from X Cy dump	
			6 Coy dug in G.3 acup store under paper from G36.d.10 & G36.d.37	
			also from H.7 b. 6.28, 6 H.31. a.7.B a last length of 100' Sewer future covered with 3' earth over dug in.	
			D Coy. Corrected paper work Sand bags, and lewid cables all the following	

Army Form C. 2118.

WAR DIARY
or
INTELLIGENCE SUMMARY.
(Erase heading not required.)

Instructions regarding War Diaries and Intelligence Summaries are contained in F. S. Regs., Part II. and the Staff Manual respectively. Title pages will be prepared in manuscript.

Place	Date	Hour	Summary of Events and Information	Remarks and references to Appendices
	1917 Nov 7th	Micro	RENINGHELST. Tank No 8 also 50* of pipe in village	
			LACLYTTE-RENINGHELST Road TANKS No's 58,59. Reservoir pipes at N7a 2.4.	GTJ
			No 2 RESERVOIR PIPES above M 16 d 8 4. Casualties Nil.	
			Wind Westerly Weather Rain	
	1917 Nov 8th		A Coy. Completed the Westoutre RENINGHELST — WESTOUTRE — CANADA CORNER	
			pipe. Wrapped pipe at 11 places and covered 800* for a depth of 2'-6".	
			B Coy wrapped and laid the Interior portions of piping on which they worked	
			yesterday & also wrapped and laid pipe at two waterpoints H 31. c 8.7	
			Party to ABEELE X CORPS DUMP loaded lorry with Tar, brushes and fuels	
			and loaded Sandbags with Sawdust for the various Pts	
			Casualties Nil	GTJ
			Wind Westerly Weather Rain	
	1917 Nov 9		A Coy 1 Tank on Pipe running from RENINGHELST — VLAMERTINGE Rd to LA CLYTTE	
			BAILLEUL Rd every changing down	
			1 Party on ABEELE — RENINGHELST Rd (TANK ENo 55) to WESTOUTRE	

WAR DIARY
or
INTELLIGENCE SUMMARY.
(Erase heading not required.)

Army Form C. 2118.

Place	Date	Hour	Summary of Events and Information	Remarks and references to Appendices
	1917 Nov. 10		RENINGHELST RD (MAP NK N°5) Water to CANADA CORNER covered 3 (one) pipe.	
			1 party covered over pipe cross swamp M4b central - M9b central b	
			depth of 2'-6"	
			B Coy 150 x of piping covered around water point at M 28a 3-4.	
			wrapped and laired.	
			C Coy Tanks 57, 24 + 36 completed also pipe reservoir at 16 a 21. 200d piping dug into ground	
			50 men under 1 Officer field sandbags revt. sandcent at LA CLYTTE.	
			Casualties. Nil.	(S.T.J)
			Weather. Weather.	
			Horse troughs near 9th Corps Dump Piping wrather re-covered + tarred	
			Piping - 40 yds - covered at trough in Mobile V.F. Sec covered and water	
			lagged and tarred.	
			MURUMBIDGEE HUTMENTS near LA CLYTTE corner All latrine piping	
			lagged + tarred	
			N.B. q.1.5. No work done at this map reference.	

Army Form C. 2118.

WAR DIARY
or
INTELLIGENCE SUMMARY.
(Erase heading not required.)

Instructions regarding War Diaries and Intelligence Summaries are contained in F. S. Regs., Part II. and the Staff Manual respectively. Title pages will be prepared in manuscript.

Place	Date	Hour	Summary of Events and Information	Remarks and references to Appendices
			B Coy Completed erection of 2 Nissen Huts	
			1 80% of completion	
			1 40% "	
			65' of Horse line hutmts laid	
			C Coy Completed lining and completely roofed one hut in No 1 line & completely roofed one hut in No 1 line. All 3 huts in this line are complete.	
			Set foundation to one hut in No 2 line & roofed hut as far as ribs &c " " " 2 "	
			The one hut which was here to be put up was incomplete thro' not being up to its work back until its lorries with the other two huts arrived. These did not arrive till 2 P.M.	
			Completed its drains in No 4 line and laid 45 split logs. There were all that were available.	
			D Coy Completed one hut at H 32 d 0 3 & laid foundations for another eleven feet and dry ramming trenches for huts & standings	

A6945 Wt. W11422/M1160 350,000 12/16 D. D. & L. Forms/C/2118/14

WAR DIARY
or
INTELLIGENCE SUMMARY.
(Erase heading not required.)

Army Form C. 2118.

Place	Date	Hour	Summary of Events and Information	Remarks and references to Appendices
1917	Thos	11th	at same place. The Punts burned up until 2-30 P.M. Casualties NIL.	
		12th	The Battalion moved by Train from OUDERDOM to NEILLES by BLEQUIN and then marched to THIEMBRONNE. Transport by road	
			In Battalion watch	
		12	The Battalion marched to GOURNAY.	
		13	The Battalion replied to CAVRON ST MARTIN. Transport expenses	
		14/15		
		16	The Battalion stayed at CAVRON ST MARTIN and respected	
		17		
		18		
		19th	The Battalion entrained in accordance with the attached Movement orders dated 17/11/17. Train No 1.	
		20		
		21	Train journey via LONGEAU, DIJON, AVIGNON, MARSEILLES, NICE, VINTIMILLE	
		22		
		23	GENOA, MANTOVA to LEGNAGO. On the 25th the Battalion detrained	
		24/25		

WAR DIARY
or
INTELLIGENCE SUMMARY.
(Erase heading not required.)

Army Form C. 2118.

Place	Date	Hour	Summary of Events and Information	Remarks and references to Appendices
	26/11/17		and marched to BEVILACQUA.	
	27/11/17		The Battalion rested.	
			The Battalion closed up to ZIMELLA	
	28/11/17		The Battalion moved from ZIMELLA to RAMPEZZANO as per order no 2 attached dated 27/11/17	
	29/11/17		The Battalion rested.	
	30/11/17		The Battalion moved from RAMPEZZANO to ARLESEGA as per order No 3 attached dated 29/11/17	

J B Bunbury
Lieut Colonel.
Commanding
24th (5th Jullundur) Regiment
(Indian Pioneers)

24th. Battalion The Manchester Regiment. (Pioneers)

SECRET. **MOVE ORDER.** Copy No. 11.

Reference HAZEBROUCK 5A. 1/100,000

10/11/1917.

1. The Battalion will move to rejoin the Division in the THIEMBRONNE Area to-morrow, 11th. inst.

2. (a). The Battalion (less Transport) will move:
   (1). By march route to OUDERDOM.
   (2). By train from OUDERDOM to WIZERNES. NEILLES LEQLEQUIN
   (3). By march route from WIZERNES to destination. (NEILLES LEQLEQUIN)

   Times for above will be issued later.
   Route for (1), along RENINGHELST Road to cross roads immediately above "Z" in ZEVECOTEN: along the road running N.E. from this point and turn along MILLEKRUIS Road before entering OUDERDOM village.

   (b) The Transport will move by march route throughout, starting at 8-0 a.m. 11th. inst. and staging in WALLON CAPPEL Area for night 11th/12th.

3. Detailed administrative instructions are being issued separately.

ISSUED AT 7-0 p.m. (SD). A. ST. G. WALSH, Captain & Adjutant.

COPIES TO:- Commanding Officer, O.C. "A" Coy., O.C. "B" Coy., O.C. "C" Coy., O.C. "D" Coy. Quartermaster. Transport Officer, Medical Officer, Office & War Diary.

SECRET. 24th. Battalion The Manchester Regt. (Pioneers).

ORDER NO. 1.   COPY No. 11.

Reference: 1/100,000 LENS 11.   ~~16~~/11/1917.

1. The Battalion will move from this area by train as under.

2 (a). Bn. H.Q., (less details), "A" Coy., "B" Coy., and part of the Transport Section will entrain at ANVIN ("X" Train).

(b). "C" and "D" Companies, the Band, part of Bn. H.Q., and part of the Transport Section will entrain at WAVRANS ("Y" Train)

(c). Part of the Transport (under 2/Lieut. V.W. STANLEY) together with any details returning from leave, hospital etc., will entrain at ANVIN ("Z" train).

3. The part of the Battalion moving on "Y" Train is under the command of Major E. VINER by whom separate orders have been and will be issued.

4. Detailed administrative instructions have been issued under this office Nos. S.T./130/(1, 2, 3, 4, 5.)

ISSUED AT : 2 p.m   (Signed). A. ST. G. WALSH, Capt. & Adjt.

Copy No. 1.   Commanding Officer.
        2.   Second in Command.
        3.   O.C. "A" Company.
        4.   O.C. "B"   "
        5.   O.C. "C"   "
        6.   O.C. "D"   "
        7.   Quartermaster.
     8 & 9.   Transport Officer.
    10 & 11. War Diary.

SECRET   Copy No. 11.

24th. Battalion The Manchester Regiment.

(Pioneers).

27/11/1917.

ORDER No. 2.

Reference Sheet PADOVA, 1/100,000

1.   The Battalion will move to-morrow, 28th. November, to
        RAMPEZZANA (3 kilometres N. of ALBETTONE).
        Route.   ORGIANO - SOSSANO - BELNEDERE.

2.   Time Table.   REVEILLE -   6-30 a.m.
                        BREAKFAST -   7-30 a.m.
                        Blankets rolled and
                        stacked at Q.M. Stores 8-45 a.m.
                        MOVE OFF -   9-30 a.m.

3.   Order of March. - H.Q., "B" Coy., "C" Coy., Band, "D" Coy.,
        "A" Coy. & Transport.

4.   Dinners will be eaten en route.

                        (Signed). A. ST. G. WALSH, Captain & Adjutant.

Issued at :- 6-30 p.m.

Copies to: Commanding Officer.
            2nd. in Command.
            O.C. A. Coy.
            O.C. B. Coy.
            O.C. C. Coy.
            O.C. D. Coy.
            Quartermaster.
            Transport Officer.
            Medical Officer.
            War Diary.

SECRET　　　　　　　　　　　　　　　　　　　　　Copy No. 1

24th Battalion The Manchester Regiment (Pioneers),

ORDER NO. 3

Reference, PADOVA, 1/100,000.　　　　　　　　　　　29-11-17.

1.　　　The Battalion will move to-morrow, 30th instant, to ~~CARTURA CASELANO~~ ARLESEGA.

2.　Route:　Main Road to PONTE di NANTO - MONTEGALDELLA - ~~GRISIGNANO~~

　　Order of March:　H.Q., "D" Coy, "C" Coy, Band, "B" Coy, "A" Coy.

3.　Time Table:　Reveille　　　　　　　　　　　7-0 a.m.
　　　　　　　　Breakfast　　　　　　　　　　　7-45 a.m.
　　　　　　　　Blankets rolled & stacked
　　　　　　　　　at Q.M. Stores　　　　　　　 8-45 a.m.
　　　　　　　　Officers valises at Q.M. Store 9-0 a.m.
　　　　　　　　Move off　　　　　　　　　　　　9-30 a.m.

4.　　　Dinners will be cooked and eaten en route.

　　　　ISSUED AT 11-30 p.m.

　　　　　　　　　(Signed) A. St. G. WALSH, Capt. and Adjt.,
　　　　　　　　　　　24th Bn. The Manchester Regiment.

Copies to:-　　Commanding Officer.
　　　　　　　2nd in Command
　　　　　　　O.C. "A" Coy.
　　　　　　　　　 "B" "
　　　　　　　　　 "C" "
　　　　　　　　　 "D" "
　　　　　　　Quartermaster.
　　　　　　　Transport Officer.
　　　　　　　Medical Officer.
　　　　　　　War Diary.

www.ingramcontent.com/pod-product-compliance
Lightning Source LLC
Chambersburg PA
CBHW082357010526
44113CB00039B/2328